Searching for the WAY

A MARTIAL ARTS ODYSSEY

Nigel Sutton

This book is dedicated to my children,
Guo Lian and Hui Min, and my wife, Miao Feng.

❖

I also extend heartfelt thanks to all of my students
for their help in keeping me on the path, and to
my teachers for leading the way.

First published in 1999 by **Multi-Media Books**

Copyright © 1998 by Nigel Sutton

All rights reserved. No part of this publication may be reproduced or utilized in any form or by any means, electronic or mechanical, including photocopying, recording, or by any information storage and retrieval system, without prior written permission from Unique Publications.

LCC: 99-70222
ISBN: 1-892515-05-9

Distributed by:
Unique Publications
4201 Vanowen Place
Burbank, CA 91505
(800) 332–3330

First edition
05 04 03 02 01 00 99 98 97 1 3 5 7 9 10 8 6 4 2
Printed in the United States of America

Designed by George Foon • Edited by Mark V. Wiley

Table of Contents

Chapter One

First Steps

The author,
Nigel Sutton.

or the past two decades I have spent much of my spare time studying the martial arts of the Orient. It is hard to say just why these arts have held their fascination in me, although it is still quite clear to me why I started.

At the age of 13 my best friend started judo and used me as his hapless training partner. Although initially not as interested as he was, my enthusiasm was soon kindled by the promise of invincibility and the development of superhuman powers. I bought a copy of *Teach Yourself Karate,* and was very soon threatening structural damage to the house as I stamped up and down my room trying to perfect the various techniques described in the book.

Then along came the "kung fu" boom in the wake of the demise of Bruce Lee, and the market was flooded with gongfu books, magazines, and memorabilia. Having progressed from a book to attending karate classes, my interest deepened not so much because of the actual techniques that I was learning but because of the whole mystique surrounding the world of the martial arts.

At that time, however, I had little inkling that I would go on to live in China, visit the famed Shaolin Temple, train with many of the masters who were direct descendants of ones I had read about, and represent Britain in international competition in China.

Throughout my martial arts career there has been a logical and consistent progress, whereby I have met each particular teacher when the time was right. In this way I have traveled from art to art, finding those aspects which best suited me and which have served as the most appropriate vehicle for my continued development.

That such steady progress should have occurred, the Chinese would attribute to *yuan fen,* which translates simply as "fate." Indeed, they say that when the student is ready, the teacher will appear.

The twist of fate that launched me on my career in Chinese martial arts at first sight appeared to be a combination of bad luck and obstinacy on my part, but without those circumstances it is unlikely that I would have chosen the Chinese arts in preference to the Japanese, or those of another country.

Shortly after having acquired my brown belt in karate and training fanatically to gain a black belt in 1979, I tore a muscle in my thigh. Instead of resting I continued to attempt to train and the injury worsened.

At that point in my life karate not only provided me with a goal, it served as the focus of my social life and gave me a moral code to follow. The result of not being able

"Indeed, they say that when the student is ready, the teacher will appear."

to train was psychological devastation. My instructor quite rightly suggested that I should only train the uninjured side, but to me this did not seem right.

Finally, in desperation, I started to look around for some other art that I could study while my leg healed. At first I tried aikido, but it proved all too frustrating and, in favoring my injured leg, I broke my big toe. Being a prodigious reader and already having a growing library of martial arts books, I had come across references to taijiquan, which was commonly translated as "supreme ultimate boxing," which, in turn, led many authors to write that it was the most advanced form of martial art. Of course, as any experienced martial artist knows, there is no such thing as the ultimate style, only different systems to suit different preferences and capabilities.

I was, however, heavily influenced by a fine book called *Moving Zen,* in which author Chris Nicol described his encounter with a taijiquan master in terms that left no doubt that it was an art worthy of respect.

So I looked around for a teacher and found a class offered at a local natural health center. Located as it was in the center of the area's substantial "alternative" community, coupled with taijiquan's somewhat "hippy" image at that time, the class attracted more than its fair share of the lunatic fringe. The taijiquan being taught, however, was an authentic system and the teacher was both diligent and skilled. Later, by a strange twist of fate, he became a student in a class at which I was an assistant instructor. He subsequently became my friend.

I initially found taiji very hard to swallow. Indeed, there seemed to be nothing for me to really sink my teeth into.

Used as I was to karate, where with continued practice you could see yourself getting faster and more powerful, I found the slow-motion form practice of taiji very frustrating. I could see little or no connection between the slow movements of the solo form which we were being taught and the development of fighting skills. In fact, it was to be another eight years before my questions about this were to be finally answered.

At the same time I had just moved into lodgings with a Chinese couple. The husband was from Malaysia and the wife from Singapore and both being of immigrant background and now living and working in a foreign country, they wholeheartedly embraced things Chinese. Francis, the husband, was learning to read and write Mandarin Chinese, which he could not do as he had been educated in an English-medium school. He was also learning taijiquan from his language tutor. This was not only in my eyes at the time much more authentic—as the teacher was Chinese from China—but also far more convenient as the teacher came to the house.

So it was that I had my first exposure to the 24-step simplified Yang style form. This routine was devised in 1955 by a state-sponsored committee of experts. What was ironic was that the form taught in the classes I had previously attended was far more "traditional." Regardless, I stopped attending class and instead enjoyed private tuition. Then, in 1984, I got a job teaching English in China. This was my chance to study martial arts in the land of their origin. Karate and dreams of Japan left behind, in the intervening years I had trained briefly in Thai boxing, escrima, and wing chun, but all the time I had practiced the 24-step routine. I was not definite that I wanted to continue my study of taiji, all I knew was that I wanted to learn as much as I could in the time available.

Once again fate intervened, but not before I had been relieved of varying sums of money by assorted "teachers." One of my English language students, himself a martial arts enthusiast, took me to meet his master, Gao Zi Ying, a leading authority on baguazhang. Under the tutelage of the Gao family I learnt enough of their art that two years later I was able to represent Britain in bagua at an international competition in Tianjin, China. This event was significant for my subsequent martial arts career as it opened several doors for me in later years, enabling me to meet and practice with many leading teachers, in both Malaysia and Singapore.

At the same time that I was learning bagua I also continued my taiji studies. From a coach at Beijing Normal University I learnt the 48-step combined routine, simplified straightsword, and rudimentary pushing hands patterns. With other teachers I learnt mei-huaquan, xingyiquan, and Shaolin lohanquan. All in all, I managed to keep fairly busy!

Fate played a role again in the next step in my training career when, on my return to England, I met a Malaysian Chinese teacher of taiji who broadened my vision of Chinese martial arts, enabled me to enter the selections for the Great Britain Wushu team, and most importantly opened the door for me to the world of Chinese martial arts in Malaysia and Singapore.

The author with Masters Gan Oh Hai and Tan Swoh Theng and students.

Thus it was that in 1987, visiting Malaysia for the first time, I met many of the teachers who were to completely change my view of taiji and Chinese martial arts in general, enriching my understanding of the arts and teaching me how to train toward the goal of attaining the many skills which martial arts offer.

In Malaysia I found teachers who not only believed in their art but who had also put it to the test: Master Tan Ching Ngee, who was not averse to challenging those who disputed the martial nature of taiji; Master Lau Kim Hong, who entered a no-holds-barred fighting contest in order to prove the efficacy of his art; Master Wu Chiang Hsing, whose devout Buddhist beliefs flavored his practice so that taiji for him became a means for spiritual development; Master Lee Bei Lai, who in his youth was famous for closing down rival schools by defeating their teachers in personal combat; Master Koh Ah Tee, who in his search for the highest levels of the art challenged all the leading masters, but in such a spirit of earnest inquiry that they were not offended, yet in most cases, had no particular desire to face the challenge—such was his quiet intensity; Master Tan Swoh Theng, who on his master's death set off on a year long journey around Malaysia, making a living by selling medicine and treating the injured; and Master Liang He Qing, whose love for the arts has led him to study many different systems and whose daily training schedule involves rising at 3:00 A.M., to practice. Of course there were others, but these are the main protagonists whose words and actions will feature highly on the pages of this book.

The author with Master Liang He Qing.

In order to provide some structure for this book I have loosely organized it around the major components of Chinese martial art systems. Based on the numerous battered notebooks I have filled up and which have accompanied me on my journeys around the world of Chinese martial arts, I hope these observations prove as interesting and useful to the reader as they have to me.

Chapter Two

FORM: The Heart of Chinese Martial Arts

t the heart of all Chinese martial art systems lies the practice of sequences of defensive and offensive movements, usually referred to as forms. For the novice student of taijiquan, form practice is the usual starting point and in the Cheng Man Ching style is regarded as being central to the student's development, regardless of which level they have reached.

The form I first learnt was being practiced in the early years of this century before the major styles—as we now know them—had really crystallized into separate entities. This routine contained elements of both the Yang and the Wu style and consisted of over 100 sets of movements, taking an average of half an hour to perform. The classes were conducted in quite a traditional manner, with one or two new moves being taught each lesson, and most of the time being devoted to students following the teacher through the form.

In Chinese classes this is the normal method of instruction, although Westerners generally need more verbal explanation in order to make reasonable progress. Later on I was to regret never having completed this form, if only for the insight it could have provided into the historical development of the art. But instead I learnt the 24-step routine with Xu Laoshi.

Teacher Xu was a computer scientist on an exchange visit to a British company, and in common with all those of his generation he had learnt the simplified routine at university, where it was compulsory for all students. The fact that so many students have had to learn the art and that many have come to the West where they have passed on their often limited knowledge, has resulted in a considerable watering-down of the art.

Xu Laoshi tried his best, but he knew little of the theory or philosophy underpinning the art and what we were left with was little more than slow-motion calisthenics.

The 24-step routine is perfectly adequate for the purpose for which it was created: to popularize taiji and allow people who need its health benefits to practice without the level of commitment required to master the complete traditional curriculum. If, however, you wish to progress to the highest levels of the art, then something more is needed. This I attempted to look for in China.

Due to the recent history of the People's Republic of China, martial arts in that country have a unique flavor based on the utilitarian role they are seen as fulfilling. With the aesthetic aspects of the art being stressed, and also due to the persecution of martial artists during the 10 years of the Cultural Revolution (1966–76), the practical aspects are often played down and it is arguable that the overall level of skill in the combative elements of the arts has greatly declined.

At that time, however, although I was vaguely aware of criticisms made of the state of martial arts in the People's Republic, I felt that there would still be many valuable things to learn there. Indeed, this proved to be right, if nothing else in terms of the experience I was to gain.

My taijiquan teacher, Coach Peng, was a young teacher at the Beijing Normal University, a teacher training institution where he taught taiji, taiji straightsword, and sanda, the unarmed combat system taught to the police and the army.

He himself had little faith in the efficacy of taijiquan as a fighting art, seeing it instead as a series of beautiful movements. The form he taught me was the 48-step routine, which is based on movements from the five major styles of taiji. It was originally devised both as a more challenging routine for those who had completed the 24-step form, and also as a competition routine. In the latter respect, however, it was later to be superseded by the 42-step form.

Practiced as a piece of performing art, this routine is extremely satisfying with its graceful low postures, high kicks, and explosive emissions of power, alternated with smooth, flowing motions. But still there seemed no clues as to how the art could actually be used.

Certainly Coach Peng could demonstrate exactly what each move was for, but he had never been taught to systematically practice their applications. Our training only consisted of endless repetition of the form, with particular emphasis placed on those aspects that judges in competition would be interested in, including eye focus, waist movement, height of kicks, and smoothness of transition between movements.

To find traditional taijiquan I had to return to England where, under the tutelage of Huang Jifu Laoshi, I learnt the 108-step Yang family form. Huang Laoshi had trained in his youth at a branch school of the renowned Jing Wu Association, whose branches throughout Asia have done so much to spread Chinese martial arts.

Having come himself, originally, from a background in the external martial arts, Huang Laoshi was also at a loss to explain exactly how taiji worked. He was, however, fond of telling the tale of how he had tasted its effects first hand when, as a youth in the 1950s, he had gone on stage at the invitation of a visiting taiji master to test his gongfu. This master was none other than Cheng Man Ching, and Huang Laoshi recounts how he and a martial arts classmate had gone up together and, working as a team, launched a frenzied attack on the middle-aged teacher. But they had been far from successful, both ending up on the floor. Huang Laoshi continues the story, saying that afterward he approached Cheng and asked him if he had really been using taijiquan, as it had been fast and he had always thought of taiji as being slow!

At the time that I first heard this story I had no idea that in only a few years time I would

The tomb of Professor Cheng Man Ching, Taiwan.

"Almost as soon as I started this form the "classics" came alive."

be an initiated student in the tradition handed down by Master Cheng himself.

My first introduction to Cheng style taijiquan in Malaysia came when I met Master Wu Chiang Hsing. Master Wu teaches the art in a town in the southern Malaysian state of Johor. Eager to introduce me to what he saw as being the real taijiquan, and none-too-impressed with my high-kicking rendition of the 48-step routine, Wu took me to Singapore to meet the master from whom he had learnt his pushing hands: Master Tan Ching Ngee.

Having always regarded Cheng style as being too floppy to be of any real use—from what I had seen of practitioners of the style in England—I was not eager to rush out and learn this form. I was, however, impressed by Master Tan's pushing hands ability, and it was only after he repeatedly assured me that this was entirely due to his practice of Cheng's 37-posture form that the message finally sunk in and I consented to learn it.

The change was startling. Almost as soon as I started this form the "classics" (those written documents left by masters of the past) came alive. It seemed as if this was the taijiquan that I had read about for so long, these were the feelings and experiences referred to by the masters of old. The relaxation required of the exponent of this form seemed far more profound than I had encountered before. What was more, Master Tan and the other teachers, in the pragmatic climate of the martial arts circle in this part of the world, actually used their art and were prepared both to explain and to demonstrate exactly how fighting skills could be developed.

After I had undergone the initiation necessary for me to become a formal disciple of Master Tan, he proceeded to completely restructure my form and in so doing changed my whole attitude toward the art.

The first and most vital thing that Tan stressed was the importance of relaxation, particularly of the waist and hips area and the underparts of the buttocks. This would provide a relaxed and solid base, for the body weight around this area, aided by gravity, serves to "glue" the supporting leg to the floor.

Just looking at the way I stood in the opening move of the form, Master Tan noted that I allowed my weight to fall through my heels instead of the *yongquan* points—toward the front and in the center of the feet—where the weight naturally falls when the body is correctly physiologically aligned. When the weight is falling through these points the exponent has the feeling that he is leaning slightly forward, but in fact an observer can reassure him that his spine is perfectly erect.

Looking at my feet, Master Tan observed that I was gripping the ground with my toes, and assured me that this would only fight against the very force of gravity which I should be using to develop a root. Indeed, he noted that Cheng himself had trained so hard that his feet were completely flat.

All of this before I had even started to move! When I did, the first thing Master Tan picked up on was the way in which, during transitional movements, I pulled the unweighted leg into the other leg before stepping out. This was definitely not

Master Tan Ching Ngee
performs taijiquan.

> **"First train for health, then for self-defense. If you are not healthy then you cannot train for other things."**

allowed as far as he was concerned, as the moving leg had to be as relaxed as possible so as to facilitate speedy kicks. In other words, using only those muscles necessary to move the leg and particularly keeping the hips loose and relaxed. This relaxation would also aid in rooting the load-bearing leg.

Next, Master Tan shifted his attention to my shoulders. He shook his head and muttered that there was too much tension. Pulling me into a normal standing position and grasping my wrist, he raised my right arm straight up into the air, straightening it out in the process. Then he let go. My arm remained pointing up in the sky and Master Tan burst out laughing, throwing his head back in a paroxysm of hilarity. When, as directed, I lifted his arm up in the air and let go, it dropped straight down to his side.

"It's all in the shoulders," he explained. When I tried it again, but this time paying attention to relaxing my shoulders, my arm also dropped down. This level of relaxation should also be achieved during form practice so that the arm at the elbow always feels heavy and weighted down. This heaviness in turn serves to make your striking techniques more powerful and effective.

By the time Master Tan had finished correcting just the first few movements, my head was spinning and I thought that I would never cope with all this input. The lesson was not over, though, for when we had adjourned to a nearby coffee shop and were thirstily lapping up pint mugs of hot soy bean milk, Master Tan started to lecture the assembled students on the reasons for form practice.

"First train for health, then for self-defense. If you are not healthy then you cannot train for other things. With the skill of pushing hands your form can improve. As you practice these things you will become more clear about relaxation and, from this, clarity about the more advanced sensitivity skills. This, in turn, will lead to the development of taijiquan's fighting skills."

We listened and sipped and I desperately hoped that I would be able to remember all he was saying.

For the next few years every time I returned to Singapore Master Tan cast his professional eye over my form. Even when I was ostensibly studying pushing hands or weapons, somehow we always returned to the subject of the form.

One of his classes was conducted twice weekly at an old and ramshackle Buddhist temple run by one of his long-time disciples. This building stands on about half an acre of land surrounded by jungle and wasteland. It is a favored area for development but, because of its use as a place of worship, it has thus far avoided compulsory purchase. The single-story wooden building is crammed almost to bursting with statues of the Buddha, prayer wheels, and other items used in ceremonies. At the front is a concrete area with a roof supported on posts at a height of about 15 feet and open at the sides and front.

14

Because of its uniquely Oriental flavor, this was a place I especially enjoyed training at, and it was great for photos. The classes here always followed the same pattern. Master Tan would lead the students through a series of warm-up exercises, then standing post positions were adopted, usually the posture known as "lift hands," while Master Tan went off to make a pot of Chinese tea. So it was that the poor, hapless students were left desperately waiting for the welcome whistle of the kettle, at which point the posture would be abandoned and there would be a rush for steaming glasses of tea. Only after several of these glasses had been consumed by each student and much discussion had been enjoyed, would form practice commence.

On one such occasion, after my first glass of tea, I asked Master Tan why it was that so much emphasis was placed on form practice.

The question was greeted with some laughter from the other students, younger brother Nigel, the strange Englishman with his constant questions! But a scowl from Master Tan silenced them.

"You should follow his example and ask more questions," Tan rebuked them. Then he settled back into his chair, lifting one leg and placing the ankle so that it rested on his other knee and supported his hands.

"If you ask me what is the most important aspect of form practice I must answer you that it is the training and development of *jing* (applied whole body power), *hua* (neutralization), and *qi* (internal energy). Now how do we emphasize these three aspects in our practice? All of these are related to the key role of raising the energy to the top of the head, moving the waist, and swing and movement. When you understand swing and movement you will understand *fa jing* (emitting power). The waist's importance lies in the role it plays in attacking the opponent. Thus, by lining up the waist and head, you train the three elements of *jing, hua,* and *qi.* Indeed, this lining up corresponds in Western medicine to the parasympathetic nervous system.

"If your form movements embody this correct alignment, then when you apply them in push hands they will be effective. If your form is not correct then your applications will fail.

"Only when the body is correctly aligned can you neutralize an opponent's attack, and only when there is the proper structure can your *qi* be developed. For all of these reasons form practice is essential."

I looked around at the rest of the students who seemed to be equally divided in their reaction between nodding sagely and trying to cover-up their boredom—they had heard all this before. I also nodded in what I hoped was a wise manner and grunted a couple of times before saying thank you. Master Tan stood up and the tea session was over. Time for the practice break!

Later on when the class was over, and we were back in Master Tan's 21st floor apartment, I sought clarification about this process of raising the energy to the top of the head which he had mentioned earlier.

"Good question, good question," he muttered as he disappeared into the kitchen, emerging shortly afterwards with two glasses and a six-pack of beer. I opened my notebook on the glass-topped table in anticipation as he opened the sliding windows to let

"Borrow the strength of the earth and the qi of the heavens."

in the salt-scented sea breeze that at that height perpetually blew. The large scrolls pinned to the wall clanked uneasily in the draft as Master Tan sat down.

"Like many other pieces of advice that sound complicated, the answer is very simple and lies in correct posture. As long as you keep the head raised the *qi* will sink and the spirit will rise up. Keep the feeling that you are hanging, suspended from the top of your head."

This was all very well but I had heard a lot of talk about *qi* and still didn't really grasp what was meant, so I asked for clarification.

Master Tan thought for a moment and then replied, "While *qi* is important in taijiquan the most important thing, as I said earlier this evening, is to make sure that the postures are correct. When that is the case you can start to consider *qi*. In so doing, however, it is the *yi* (intention) that you must actually pay attention to; for when you use *yi* your *qi* automatically follows it. If this is not the case then you will simply be using brute force *(li)*. *Li* and *qi* are vastly different. If you are using *li* in pushing hands, for example, then you will find that your ability to use *ting jing* (sensitivity) will be virtually nil. When you are using *yi* and *qi* your sensitivity is enhanced so that your responses are much faster.

"Beginners in taijiquan should pay attention to placing the mind in the *dantian;* when this becomes habitual then the *qi* is naturally sunk to that area. After this has happened it becomes natural for the qi to gather and accumulate in that region. At this point in time you no longer need to pay attention to the *dantian* for the *qi* will move as it should. If at this time you continue to pay attention to the accumulation of *qi* in this area then your gongfu will stop at the level you have reached. You will no longer improve. That is because once the *qi* is gathered in the *dantian* it must be allowed to spread throughout the body and enter the bones."

This was fine but how would I know just when the *qi* was sunk? I asked Master Tan. "The upper half of your body feels empty and comfortable while the lower half feels full and is doing the work. This is what Cheng Man Ching meant when he said 'borrow the strength of the earth and the *qi* of the heavens.' Practice your form slowly and precisely so that you can be aware of all these sensations and to give you time to check that everything is correct."

He smiled at me, "I think you should sleep now because we have to be up early for training tomorrow!"

In the years that I have been practicing taijiquan, whenever I have had a problem and seemed to have reached a plateau in my training I have learned that the best course of action is to return to form practice.

• • •

When I first arrived in Malaysia in 1987, Master Wu Chiang Hsing was the first teacher of Cheng style that I met. A short, stocky Hakka, born and raised in Malaysia, in his youth Wu had studied li style boxing with a famous teacher who had been a friend of his father's back in China. This master, Chen Yi Shan, was brought over to Malaysia to teach his boxing style to fellow Hakkas as at that time there was a lot of trouble between the different dialect groups. As Master Chen's great gongfu became more widely recognized, like many masters of his generation, he fell prey to the wine, women, and song with which his wealthier students plied him in order to learn his secrets. Attracted by these same students to go to Singapore to teach, he did so, leaving Chiang Hsing, who then abandoned his training.

Several years later, however, Wu Chiang Hsing was invited by a friend to accompany him to a taijiquan class run by Master Lim Suo Wei. Reluctantly, Chiang Hsing went along but slowly became hooked. The clinching factor was when Master Lim invited him to spar and trounced him.

Later on, having become more interested in learning about the origins of the Cheng style he was learning, Master Wu became a disciple of Tan Ching Ngee, for Master Tan had not only met the great Cheng Man Ching but had also trained with many of his leading students.

The author with Master Wu Chiang Hsing.

What lends a unique flavor to Master Wu's interpretation of Cheng style taijiquan is his devotion to Buddhism. There is something of the austerity of Chan (Zen) meditation in his form practice and I have found his advice always to be both profound and useful.

Time after time Master Wu has reminded me that continual practice of the basics guarantees progress. In solo form training he advises that the student should hold each posture for as long as possible. This enables the exponent to check that every movement accords with the art's principles. Of course, practicing like this involves a great deal of pain in the legs. But, as Master Wu points out, if there is no pain, gongfu is not being trained.

Drawing parallels with meditation, Master Wu is fond of reminding me that sitting practice is also extremely painful. He urges his students to augment their form training with seated meditation for, as he notes, it is all about quietness and taijiquan is quietness and stillness in motion.

It is about a two hour drive from Singapore to Batu Pahat, the small town that is my wife's birthplace and also Master Wu's hometown. Whenever I visited Malaysia, since the flight usually arrived in the early evening, it was about midnight before I would reach my in-laws' house, but always there to greet me was Master Wu. A businessman,

"If there is no pain, gongfu is not being trained."

Wu runs a small clothing shop and during my visits I often spent hours in his cramped little office discussing the theory and philosophy of the art we both love.

In those early days, when I came to Malaysia once or at most twice a year. In Batu Pahat there was little opportunity for excessive amounts of sleep, for every morning at 5:00 Master Wu's Honda Accord would roll up, horn blowing. Bleary-eyed and very often bad-tempered, I stumble out of the house and into the freezing air-conditioned atmosphere of his car.

At 5:30 on the dot, on a large recreation park in front of the police station, scores of Master Wu's students gather to practice *qigong*. As it does not become light until about 7:45 it is quite an eerie sight, the files of students only able to see the people directly around them, being directed by Master Wu at the front, shouting instructions through a loud-hailer.

The following description of a typical training session will give the reader a flavor of what training with Master Wu is like.

First was *qigong*. I wouldn't have minded puffing, panting, and contorting my body before dawn if it were only a little cooler than in daylight. But the fact was that it still felt like exercising inside a sauna. By the time first light streaked the sky with red, the first session was over and only the real die-hards were left. Now was the time for form practice and one-by-one people began to run through either the 37-posture form or one or other of the solo *san shou* routines, which are comprised of sets of taijiquan movements performed at fast speed so that their martial applications are obvious. Master Wu meanwhile went from student to student, offering a word of advice here and correcting a posture there.

At about half past eight the session formally ended, but not for Master Wu and I; for now it was time to adjourn to his training hall which is unfortunately situated on the sixth and top floor of an office building. By the time we had climbed the final flight of stairs there was no part of my body that was not completely soaked with sweat.

In the hall which is shared with a Chinese music school, we first of all ran through the form three times then raced through *san shou* A and B, followed by the straightsword form and, at last, pushing hands.

The usual end to such a session would be breakfast.

Unless you have had chapattis and curry after four hours of exercise when the temperature is 90 degrees Fahrenheit in the shade, you cannot appreciate what an experience this is. For me, however, this time often proved extremely valuable, for it was now that we would discuss the art in all its many and varied aspects.

When I asked Master Wu what he felt the importance of form practice to be, he first of all reminded me that the form must be practiced over and over until you are so familiar with it that you don't have to think about the movements. When you get to this stage then you are training the real taijiquan. In practicing form the exponent is aiming to return to the natural state so beloved of Daoists, and so, in line with the principles underlying the art, the body must move naturally. The breathing, too, must be natural. Indeed, as you progress in your practice you should become less and less aware of your breathing so that ultimately it becomes just as natural as when you go out for a walk. Additionally, all the movements must be completed. That is to say, you must not be so concerned with flowing from one movement to another that you do not fulfill the intention of each posture.

• • •

Whenever he is free, Master Wu likes to drive down to Singapore to visit Master Tan Ching Ngee for more training. Traditionally, the most auspicious time for such visits is the Chinese New Year and thus it was, one steamy February morning, that I found myself stuck in a traffic jam with Master Wu waiting to go through immigration in Johor Baru. This, the largest and most expensive town in Malaysia because of its proximity to Singapore, has several well-known taiji masters. But on this occasion we were just passing through, albeit slowly.

Two and a half sticky hours later we were in the new town of Bukit Batok. As usual, we were not exactly sure which of the towering cream and brown painted blocks of flats was the one housing Master Tan's flat. Finally I saw a landmark I thought I recognized and then we were there.

Master Tan was waiting for us at the door, a smile on his face, and of course his first words were an invitation to eat. After this serious business was finished and the social niceties were over it was time to get down to taijiquan.

I had been having trouble putting into practice the classic advice to "differentiate substantial and insubstantial." Indeed, I was not exactly sure what this meant. Master Tan started off by explaining that in Cheng's taijiquan, when differentiating between substantial and insubstantial, the leg on which the weight rests is the substantial one but the other leg must remain completely relaxed so that it is almost impossible to lift it off the ground, in this way the leg is truly insubstantial. This does not mean that it can be lifted high in the air at will because it is "empty," for to do so would mean having too much tension in the muscles around the hip joint.

Standing up and enlisting our aid to move the furniture back against the immaculate white tiling of the walls, Master Tan proceeded to demonstrate how taijiquan's kicks are different from those of the external arts.

Starting from *lou xi ao bu* ("brush knee twist step") Master Tan moved into *jing bu ban lan chui* ("step forward, move, parry, and punch").

"Now watch carefully," he remonstrated. "My left leg is forward and bearing my weight. If as I step forward I bring my right foot up to my left and then out as a low cutting kick, the only force of the technique is from the power of my leg. If, on the other hand, I keep my right hip relaxed and allow the turning of my waist to overcome the resistance between my loosely hanging leg and the ground, the kick will have the same kind of power that you get from releasing a tightly-compressed spring. This is substantial and insubstantial in action."

He sat down again and then continued, "As you move through the form it is not that every posture should have a 90/10 weight distribution, but rather this distribution depends on the function of the posture. So, for example, in *jing ji du li* ('golden cock stands on one leg') the supporting leg is 90 percent substantial but the raised leg must also have 10 percent substantiality holding it up. Then, when you put the leg down, it is placed lightly on the toes—at that point you put down the weight, making it relaxed and sunk.

"Taijiquan in application is based on the principle of speed x weight = power."

"If you wish to examine this matter in detail, then look at the changes in substantial and insubstantial that occur as you move from 'squatting single whip' to 'golden cock stands on one leg'."

One of the great influences on Master Tan's life and art was the late Master Ong Zi Chuan. In his native Shandong, Ong had been a renowned Chinese wrestler and it was only repeated defeat at the hands of Cheng Man Ching that convinced him of taijiquan's efficacy and turned him from a critic into a fervent devotee. It was Master Ong who convinced Tan Ching Ngee that taijiquan was a viable and effective martial art and it was he who introduced the young Tan to Grandmaster Cheng.

Despite being twice Cheng's weight, Ong had failed to subdue Cheng. Thus, Ong had complete faith in the principles and application of the art and this he transmitted to Master Tan. Taijiquan's great value lay not only in the external techniques but more importantly in its internal functioning. This was a lesson that Master Tan continually sought to impress upon me.

One of Master Tan's classes is held at a community center in one of Singapore's numerous new towns. The lessons take place on a basketball court outside the main hall. After several years of my visits the students were used to me and generally ignore my presence in the shadows at the back of the class.

After the warm-up and form practice the class generally breaks up into small groups as people work on specific techniques or particular elements of the curriculum. On this occasion I was going through the form trying to incorporate all the corrections I had received over the last few weeks.

Master Tan came over and gestured some of the senior students to join him. Motioning me to carry on practicing, he started to explain to them:

"The form is the basic exercise of the art and contains all that you need to know about taijiquan, but it is not just the external aspect that is important. The higher your level of ability the more you think about *qi* and relaxation. An emphasis on these aspects must then be fully developed by training in pushing hands, which inevitably will lead to the development of fighting skills. So you can see that everything comes from the form. We have a well-known axiom, that states: 'One moves all moves.' This not only means that all parts of the body move together, but also that the *yi* and the *qi* move together.

"Taijiquan is a form of *qigong*, but it is also wushu (martial art) and is trained from the inside to the outside. We therefore call it *neigong* (internal skill). When your *qi* permeates throughout the body it makes it agile and relaxed, also you feel that your hands and arms become very heavy. This heaviness is not just perceived but actual, as a result of the *qi* condensing within the bones to form extra-heavy bone marrow.

"Taijiquan in application is based on the principle of speed x weight = power, just as much as are external martial arts. The more you relax the quicker you are, also the more you relax the heavier you are. These are the principles upon which taijiquan's effectiveness are based."

By this time I had finished the form and was standing uneasily, wondering at my part in this lesson. I didn't have long to wait as Master Tan indicated that I should start again.

"Nigel has copied the external aspects of the art quite well but still he has not internalized it."

To me he said, "Now just keep your attention on the *dantian*. After you have practiced for a long time you will become aware of the *qi* moving through the *xiao zhou tian* (small heavenly circulation) and then the *da zhou tian* (large heavenly circulation). This happens naturally, but to get it working throughout the time you are practicing the form, from start to finish, is the work of a lifetime. But remember, there is no need to think of the *qi* moving in any particular direction, just pay attention to the *dantian*."

• • •

One thing I have noticed since first training in Southeast Asia is how much more comfortable form practice is in that part of the world. Because of the temperature and the humidity it is quite easy to feel as if, in the words of Grandmaster Cheng, you are "swimming on dry land." It is not just the physical climate; it is also a matter of the mental climate. By this I mean that practitioners of Cheng style in this part of the world have a total commitment to not only the practical aspects of the art but also the theory and the philosophy that underlie it. Imbued with something of their enthusiasm and belief, I find it easier to approach the art in a taiji manner.

The peoples of Asia, generally, have a more laid-back attitude to life. It is hard to rush around when the temperature outside is 90 degrees Fahrenheit and there is 90 percent humidity. Instead, you have to learn to go with the flow.

When I arrived in Malaysia for the first time, for a two month visit, I ran around from place to place, desperately intent on taking in as much as I could. As a result, I spent a good deal of time in bed with various complaints, ranging from food-poisoning to flu to heat exhaustion. It was only when I changed gears and started to live like the locals that things settled down.

Training in taijiquan requires a similar attitude. It cannot be rushed. When the time is right then the skills you have been striving to develop will manifest themselves. Of course you have to work hard—that is what gongfu is all about—but you also have to allow your skills to ripen and mature.

Teachers in the Cheng tradition are fond of quoting the founder's comparison of the development of the art's skills to the laying down of sheets of tissue paper. You do not notice the pile getting thicker, but it does.

Another thing that contributes to make training in the East more pleasant is the way in which students accept that the art is effective. If the teacher says it is so, then it must be so. Of course, this has a negative side in that, if the teacher has no actual fighting experience, there is a general watering-down of the skills on offer, and sometimes an air of unreality creeps in. Yet, the majority of well-known teachers have put their art to the test and many of the best students have previously challenged the teacher and lost before deciding to study under him. But the fact that the art is accepted the way it is, as a fighting system, means that the exponent does not have to constantly justify what he does, and is able to get on with the more important business of training.

> **"Training in taijiquan cannot be rushed. When the time is right then the skills you have been striving to develop will manifest themselves."**

Unfortunately, many teachers in the West, bowing to the public's lack of understanding of the art, have changed not only the way they teach their art but also what they teach to make it conform more to the popular opinion of what a martial art should be and how it should be taught.

Amongst practitioners of Cheng style in Malaysia and Singapore, the writings of the Grandmaster are treated like holy scripture. And like holy scripture, they are the focus of much misunderstanding, blind belief, debate, and even conflict. As Master Tan is fond of saying, in *Cheng's Thirteen Chapters on Taijiquan* many of the secrets of the art are revealed, but the student is not told how to train to make practical these revelations. What is needed is the oral transmission and this, by tradition, is only handed down to initiated "disciples."

• • •

Disciple. The very word itself suggests religious devotion, mystic ceremonies, and midnight ritual. Perhaps, however, this is the wrong translation to use; maybe apprentice would be more appropriate, particularly if it is understood in the sense of the mediaeval apprentices of the Guild system in England, who would sign a solemn oath not to reveal the secrets of their trade to outsiders and would owe absolute allegiance to the master craftsman and guild to which they were apprenticed.

Having been attracted to the martial arts of the Orient by the air of mystery that surround them, when I was invited to become a disciple of Master Tan Ching Ngee I jumped at the chance.

Huang Laoshi, in England, coming as he did from the Jing Wu tradition, which had abandoned discipleship and initiation as being an encouragement to sectarianism, had no interest in this practice. But for me it symbolized acceptance and meant access to the highest levels of the art.

When the day came I could hardly contain my excitement. It had been explained to me that there would be a ceremony, after which, in typically Chinese fashion, there would be a celebratory dinner, for which myself and the two other students, who were also becoming disciples, would pay.

Since at that time I was staying at Master Tan's, it was he who drove me to the martial art training hall in the center of the city, where the ceremony would take place. We were met at the door by about seven or eight disciples, clutching offerings of fruit, packs of incense, and the other paraphernalia needed for the initiation.

The training hall itself was on the top floor of a five-story office block and was entered through a wrought iron door, directly opposite which was an elaborate altar dedicated to Guan Di, the halberd-clutching, bearded patron of Chinese martial artists. Turning a sharp right, we came into the training area. One wall was lined with traditional weapons: spears, swords, staves, and so on; while the floor was marked with painted footprints marking out the steps of a form. Against the wall opposite the weapons was another altar with a picture of Cheng Man Ching prominently placed on it. Master Tan swiftly busied himself arranging flowers and fruit on the altar, which he then dedicated by lighting incense and praying to the founder.

I and my fellow initiates stood to one side nervously clutching the lucky red packets in which we had placed our signed and dated oaths of initiation and gifts of money.

Then it was our turn. The milling around of the other disciples who were to be witnesses had stopped as they lined themselves up on one side of the altar. Master Tan took center stage again, demonstrating what we would have to do, including the *ke tou,* the ritual knocking of the head nine times on the floor.

As I was the youngest new disciple I would perform last. This ceremony is based on Qing dynasty court etiquette, and included in the kneeling move is a placing of the hands on the left knee, which would have served both to sweep back the long robes of a courtier and to demonstrate that one was unarmed in the imperial presence.

The reason for the knocking of the head on the floor was explained to us by Master Tan as being symbolic of the disciple laying himself at the complete mercy of the master. This moment is then intended to serve as a reminder to the disciple of how the teacher spared him, when in turn he becomes more skilled than it is the teacher who will hypothetically be at his mercy. During the ceremony Master Tan stood to one side of the altar so that we initiates were actually praying to the photo of Cheng, thus indicating our entrance into the tradition he passed down.

After the ceremony and the meal we returned to Master Tan's flat where he had arranged to teach his three new disciples the first of those "secret" teachings reserved only for the initiated. Despite the fact that it can quite legitimately be argued that none of these are really secret, the fact that they are only taught after teacher and student have formally established their relationship means that they are treated with far more significance than if they were simply taught in an ordinary class.

I believe that the master-disciple relationship is extremely important and its formal recognition in the *bai shi,* or praying to the teacher ceremony that I have described above, symbolizes both the students' commitment to the teacher and their desire to excel as well as the teacher's obligation to improve the student's skill to the best of his ability. But, more than just improving physical skills, the teacher also has the obligation to inculcate in the student a sense of *wu de,* or martial virtue, so that his skills are accompanied by sound moral character development.

In addition, the closeness afforded by the relationship between martial arts brothers and sisters forges connections which extend beyond the training hall and into all areas of life. Because I have become an initiated disciple of Master Tan and several other teachers, many doors have been opened to me that would otherwise have remained closed.

• • •

At the time of this writing, Master Lau Kim Hong is in his late 50s, yet looks 20 years younger. Based primarily in Johor Baru, just across the causeway from Singapore, for the last 30 years, he has been a professional teacher of taijiquan. Whenever I am on my way in or out of Singapore I try to spend a few days at his martial art training hall. Most of the training is conducted outside on the large forecourt which has competition pushing hands circles painted on it and a large galvanized iron, extendible roof which can be pulled out when it rains.

Usually the first thing Master Lau asks me to do when I arrive is to change into my training kit and run through the form so that he can, in his own words, "see what progress I have made." The main area that he pays attention to is leg strength, and so I am constantly aware that it is my stance he will be looking at.

Cheng style taijiquan is deceptive, as it appears that nothing much is going on, with the movements appearing simple and unimpressive. Those critics who regard the shortened form as being easy have either never tried it or have studied with an inferior teacher, for the dual-emphasis on almost-total relaxation and having as much weight as possible on one leg at a time, serves to ensure an extremely uncomfortable experience for the student whose posture is correct.

The author with Master Lau Kim Hong after becoming his disciple.

On one memorable and painful occasion Master Lau took it upon himself to correct my stance so that it was to his complete satisfaction. To this end, he had me do the form while he shouted out corrections and occasionally came over to manipulate me into what seemed to be the most tortuous positions possible.

To start with, Master Lau felt that my back knee, when I stood in a front stance, was hanging in too much. When I obliged him by pushing out the offending knee he shook his head indicating that this was not correct either. The key, he told me, lay in relaxing the hip. This would allow the leg to "hang" naturally, neither forced in nor pushed out.

It puzzled me why we should want the back leg in this position. When I had learnt the mainland Chinese routines, and indeed in the Yang style form, much emphasis had been placed on pushing both knees out to form a bow with the legs. I voiced my concern at this difference.

Master Lau smiled his slow smile and in a characteristic gesture hiked his glasses up onto the bridge of his nose.

"Firstly," he said, "our major concern is with relaxation. If you pay attention to bowing the legs out, there is a great deal of tension in the legs, particularly in the hips. This leads to an increased danger of double-weighting (standing in such a way that you cannot easily change your posture). This, in turn, means that the stance performs the function of pushing you off the ground. In Cheng style we want to sink into the ground, to be rooted. But, of course, in our striving for relaxation we must not forget the function of the art. By allowing the leg to hang just right this ensures that if we have to use the back leg to push off or to support the body when under pressure, it is in the right position."

Master Lau signaled that I should carry on with the form. He then proceeded to move around me looking at my form from every angle, a quizzical expression on his face. When he stopped me it was as I had my left leg forward, weight on it, in a front stance, known in the Chinese as the bow stance.

"You must make sure that your weight is completely on the left, not in the middle," and so saying he shifted my hips accordingly—the pain was excruciating.

"That's it. Now everything is lined up. The left hip is folded in while the right knee points outward. The width of the stance should be about the same as that of your shoulders; while the length is the same as that of two of your feet and one palm."

By way of illustration—just in case I didn't understand—Master Lau measured his own foot, doubled it and added in his palm, then took up a stance of that length.

When my stance was the correct length and width and once again my weight had been shifted agonizingly over my front leg, Lau continued:

"Your right hip should be 'open'. At the same time that you do this and fold in the other one, you must make sure that your shoulders do not turn too far to the left. Now the majority of your weight should be on the front leg but the knee must not protrude beyond the toes. Check that your weight falls through the *yongquan*. Now, finally, your buttocks must be relaxed and tucked under."

By this time I could barely stand the pain, until, at last, I had to stand straight. Seeing my rueful expression, Master Lau laughed.

"Nobody said learning gongfu was going to be easy!"

Since the first seven years of my training in taijiquan consisted almost exclusively of form practice, with little understanding of why exactly I was doing it, you can imagine how great was my relief at finding teachers who could explain, and more importantly demonstrate, what it was all about.

The general belief when I was first training in England seemed to be that if you practiced the form enough then, inevitably, you would be able to use the art. Now while this might be true to some extent, it is only so if your form is correct.

The exponents of Cheng style that I have encountered in the East have always been quick to point out that the form is to taijiquan what push-ups and sit-ups are to Western boxing. That is, they are a way of training the body in aspects of what you will need to apply the art.

In Cheng style the applications of the postures are treated only as illustrations, actual fighting skills are developed at a later stage, albeit based on the foundations of form training. It is, however, necessary to know these in order to judge the correctness of your posture.

This is in contrast to the traditional Yang style. When I was in China, I attended a number of classes in the 108 posture form taught by my baguazhang teacher, Master Gao Zi Ying. Originally his interest in this art had been peripheral, but after he had an accident and broke his hip he started teaching regular classes to a few of his students. Surprisingly enough, considering his own attitude to the art, the majority of these were young men and they were specifically interested in learning taiji as a martial art.

Since he was born into a wealthy family, and his father hired well-known masters to teach himself and his son, Master Gao was deprived access to state facilities. In communist China, after all, to come from a wealthy family is the worst class background one can have. His classes, therefore, took place in a small cul-de-sac outside a cinema. The ideal is to be a peasant or worker. After Master Gao's accident, which happened when he fell off his bicycle, his students clubbed together and bought him a shiny new, green three-wheeler. Perched on this magnificent machine, Gao would shout out instructions in his gruff, northern accent, to his sweating students. Each movement of the form his students practiced was clearly aimed at martial application and it was not a particularly attractive form to watch. There was little grace or flow, but the stances were low and the strikes and kicks precise and focused.

One of my baguazhang classmates was Xiao Liang, a native of Canton Province, whose father was a famous practitioner of seven star praying mantis boxing. His father had instructed him to learn taijiquan while he was in Beijing, and so he was a regular participant in these classes.

It was at the hands of Xiao Liang that I felt the devastating power of the Gao's taijiquan. An innocent bystander at an early morning class in the hot Beijing summer, I was called over by Master Gao and instructed to aim a front kick at Xiao Liang. I am not particularly enthusiastic about such demonstrations as I have learned that the harder you attack, the harder you get hit. But, of course, the teacher who has arranged the demonstration wants it to look good so the attacker is always instructed to attack with power and speed.

Xiao Liang was slight and quite tall, with a toilet-brush haircut and a prominent line of black fluff on his upper lip, which was his pride and joy. He stood in front of me with a trace of a smile on his face, one hand smoothing down the pockets of his navy blue Mao jacket.

I didn't have much choice in the matter so I kicked out at his mid-section as fast as I could. I expected contact but there was none, at least not against his body. The next thing I knew, I was flat on my back with a pain in the center of my chest where his palm had struck me as he executed the move "brush knee twist step."

26

Despite the effectiveness of such a technique-oriented approach to taijiquan when demonstrated in the manner described above, I still had my doubts for I felt that there was not enough actual practice of these techniques against a wide range of attacks. The training just did not seem realistic enough to me.

• • •

It was only when I encountered Cheng style, as practiced in the area the Chinese have for centuries called Nanyang, the Southern Ocean, that I realized I had not really understood what the art was all about.

There is a magic about Malaysia, the wet, sticky heat, the numerous shades of green in the jungle, which is never far away, and indeed the smell of rotting vegetation mixed with the fragrant spices garnishing the cooking odors which seem to hang over even the slightest trace of human habitation. To me, all of these things are inextricably linked with the practice of Chinese martial arts. Countless evenings I have grunted and sweated in training halls from Penang in the north to Singapore at the very tip of the peninsular. Sometimes these training halls have been just that, belonging to any one of the myriad of dialect group or clan associations. On other occasions they have been the living rooms of private houses, the deck of a swimming pool in an upmarket country club, or floodlit basketball courts in small rural towns.

Despite the fact that Cheng style has only been established in Nanyang for less than half a century, it has taken a surprisingly firm hold. The reason for this lies both in the nature of the art and the character of the Chinese immigrants to this region. The history of Chinese migration to this area may be traced back several centuries, but mass migration flourished most under British colonial rule during the 19th century and into the first decades of this century.

The majority of the Chinese in the region were originally from the Southern Provinces of Fujian and Guangdong, both areas which have their own well-established martial arts traditions. Thus, it would be expected that a system such as taiji, originating as it did in the North, would be unlikely to become popular.

The reasons why it did so are probably due, primarily, to the uneasy status of the Chinese in relation to the Malays who form the majority of the population of what is now Malaysia.

On the eve of Independence there was great fear as to what the status of the Chinese would be, and when it was seen that political power would be placed firmly in the hands of the Malays, the Chinese sought both to reinforce their own sense of identity and to acquire practical means of defending themselves by learning their own martial arts. As China, at that time, was undergoing its own momentous changes, Taiwan was the center toward which they looked.

Master Lau Kim Hong who at that time was teaching Fujian five ancestor boxing, said that from the point of view of being a professional martial arts teacher, this was the best time to make a living.

At that time it was not only the martial arts but all aspects of Chinese culture including language and arts that were enjoying great new popularity. The time was ripe, therefore, for the promotion of a martial art that had connections also with traditional Chinese medicine, art, and calligraphy; for the master-founder was renowned for his skill in all of these areas.

The fervent embracing of the culture of a distant homeland is not rare amongst migrant peoples. But at a time of threat such as this, and among a community as conscious of their own ethnic identity as the Chinese, such identification was particularly strong. At the same time many migrants had risen beyond their humble origins and, having reached the top ranks of society through their acquisition of wealth, sought to identify with those aspects of their culture which they felt to be the higher aspects. Taijiquan, with its veneer of philosophical-based, cultured respectability, and its adoption in Taiwan as the martial art of the intelligentsia, was a natural choice.

Cheng Man Ching, himself a former professor of art at the Beijing University of Fine Arts, member of the Guomingdang Senate, and personal art tutor to Madam Chiang Kai Shek, was a figure whose position and accomplishments were fit to command the respect of the new Nanyang Chinese upper class. This, coupled with his reputation as a peerless fighter, ensured that his art would come to their notice.

Possibly the first of Cheng's students to visit Singapore was Huang Hsing Hsien. Originally a practitioner of white crane boxing, having been convinced by Cheng of the value of taiji, Huang became his disciple in 1955. The next year he started teaching in Singapore and soon established a large following. The following year Yue Shu Ting, the man who had introduced Huang to Cheng Man Ching, came to Malaysia. A native of Zhejiang on the Chinese mainland, he had trained with Cheng since the late forties. He taught mainly in the north of peninsular Malaysia, being based in the Penang area.

The third leading figure responsible for the spread of Cheng style taiji in the region was Yue's leading student, Lu Tong Bao. Lu had previously studied white crane boxing but gave this up to learn the internal art of Master Yue.

In 1958 Cheng himself came to Malaysia, and at a public exhibition at the Jing Wu stadium in Kuala Lumpur invited members of the audience onto the stage to try conclusions with him. Cheng's visit did much to boost the sprouting reputation of his disciples and

Master Lu Tong Bao performing taijiquan.

it was while staying with Lu Tong Bao that he taught a set of internal strength exercises which seem to be unique to his followers in Malaysia. Other disciples of Cheng's in Taiwan express doubt that such exercises really originate from Cheng, but one prominent long-term disciple, Master Song Zi Jian, however, seems to confirm the veracity of their origin in one of his books where he makes specific reference to the set of *neigong* exercises that the Grandmaster taught in Malaysia.

These, however, are not the only unique aspect of Cheng style as it is taught in Malaysia. Yue Shu Ting, perhaps feeling that the form needed lengthening, added on a further 18 movements which included those that Cheng had deliberately left out. This prompted Cheng to remark sadly that some of his students seemed to want to add on more, while he with his fifty years of practice only really understood the form as far as "cross hands"!

Another facet introduced by Yue was the practice of the two-person *san shou* routine and the two solo forms derived from it. These he reportedly learnt from a master in China. Cheng, however, felt that any reliance on fixed methods such as those found in the *san shou* routine detracted from the development of true taijiquan skill.

Despite the differences in their curriculum and approach to the art, Yue Shu Ting and Lu Tong Bao in the north and Huang Hsing Nsien in the south, greatly promoted the Cheng style until, by the 1980s, it was the most widely practiced style in both Malaysia and Singapore.

Other of Cheng's disciples also made their various contributions teaching in the area, including Ong Zi Chuan, Chen Zi Chen, and Wu Guo Zhong.

During its years of growth in the region, the style had not been unaffected by the unique nature of its practitioners; for the humble origins of many of the students there ensured that the gongfu of teachers was almost always tested before any commitment to training was made. And, of course, there were plenty of opportunities for such skill-testing.

Thus it is that the present-day descendants of this tradition have not only considerable experience in the practical application of the martial aspects of their art but also the confidence that goes with it. Of the students of Lu Tong Bao that I have trained with, Lau Kim Hong, Lee Bian Lei, and Zhou Mu Tu, have put their art to the test and all agree that their generation really had no choice as Master Lu liked to test them with what he called sparring, but which basically consisted of him beating them up, one by one.

In the early years of their training all of these exponents concentrated on the practical aspects of the art. However, in the last decade or so there has been a return to the theoretical and philosophical foundation of the art.

• • •

One of the younger generation Cheng style teachers who bases his teaching firmly on the example of the founder is Koh Ah Tee. Master Koh has had a somewhat chequered taiji career. As a young boy he first started training with Lau Kim Hong and swiftly rose to become his number one pupil, traveling with him all over southern Malaysia. In this way he managed to meet many martial artists from different backgrounds and to learn about their respective approaches to the arts they practiced.

Master Lau taught throughout Johor state and at various times even had classes in Malacca and Kuala Lumpur. Koh's wanderings with his master also enabled him to gain a

**Master Koh
Ah Tee.**

great deal of experience in pushing hands, as wherever they went Master Lau would introduce him to the local experts and impromptu matches or lessons would ensue.

Like many taijiquan exponents who have risen to the highest levels of the art, Master Koh believes in the importance of tradition and yet his continual striving to improve has compelled him to break the self-same tradition. In his search for even higher levels of skill Master Koh sought out teachers who had studied directly with Grandmaster Cheng. Master Koh then told Master Lau that he wanted to become a disciple of Master Tan Ching Ngee who was, and still is, a friend and training partner of Lau Kim Hong.

How this came about was that Koh had heard about a master from Taiwan called Wu Guo Zhong, a direct disciple of Cheng's who had come to Singapore to teach. At that time, though, Wu had just left Singapore to teach in America. Tan Ching Ngee, however, was serving as his representative in Singapore. Master Lau was incensed that his student should want to become the disciple of another teacher, and ordering Koh to his home, made him kneel in front of a picture of Zhang San Feng, the mythical founder of taijiquan, for three hours. Undeterred by this harsh treatment, Koh went ahead with his plan.

Then, when several years later Wu Guo Zhong returned from the United States and started teaching in Malaysia, Koh went on to become his disciple.

Now it was Master Tan's turn to be furious, but again Koh went ahead regardless. Training with Master Wu, Koh rose to become his chief instructor in Kuala Lumpur.

However, as time passed, Koh sensed that Wu was not all he seemed and feeling that he was not true to the Grandmaster's art, Koh left, taking with him, entirely of their own choice, many of Wu's students.

Now Master Koh is an extremely successful instructor in the capital of Malaysia, where he still avidly pursues his research into the teachings of Cheng Man Ching. When he is not teaching at one of his many classes round the city, Koh is to be found in his bungalow home, reading Cheng's writings or discussing them with advanced students, or else engaged in vigorous pushing hands training.

For several years I had heard about Master Koh from Wu Chiang Hsing, but somehow our paths never crossed. On one occasion I had actually gone with Master Tan to his home, only to find that he was out. Then, one day, I received a phone call from Master Wu saying that Koh had just arrived at his house and they would be coming around to see me.

Master Koh turned out to be around five foot five, of stocky build with the low center of gravity, and the relaxed walk of a taijiquan devotee.

I ushered these two men, my older brothers, into the living room and after the obligatory offering and refusal of refreshments and a smattering of small talk, Master Koh began to ask me about my taiji experience.

As the conversation continued it became plain to me that Master Koh was a true purist. He made constant reference to Cheng, referring to him as *shiyue* (teacher/grandfather), which I later discovered to be an affectionate form of address often used by Cheng stylists to refer to the founder.

Despite his background of study with Lau Kim Hong, who teaches the curriculum handed down by Yue Shu Ting to Lu Tong Bao, Koh has abandoned those things that Cheng himself did not teach.

As Koh is fond of saying: "Form, sword, and gong fu were enough for Shiyue and they're enough for me."

On that first occasion not only did Master Koh expound at length on his views on Cheng style, but he insisted that I test his gongfu by striking him on any part of the body as hard as I wanted. This was something of a specialty of his, demonstrating the strength of his *neigong*. When training with Lau Kim Hong, a greater part of the early years of Koh's study was spent in practicing *neigong*.

All in all, I struck Master Koh more than a dozen times with my fist, the knife-edge of my hand, and with my palm—but to no avail. Koh remained impassive throughout. He then demonstrated his form, which was a masterpiece of "sunk" relaxation.

• • •

One fascinating aspect of the study of taijiquan in a Chinese context is the way that, as a Westerner, you have to adjust to a whole different culture, and sometimes it is extremely different. On my regular visits to train with Koh Ah Tee I stayed at his bungalow, where, due to the high cost of living in Kuala Lumpur, he has to rent out all of the free rooms to cover his mortgage.

So it is that I sleep with him in his large double bed. For an Asian male this is quite normal; in England this is not so common! But many of the most insightful discussions about the art I have had with Master Koh have taken place on his double bed either

during the afternoon siesta or late at night, with the talk often continuing well into the early hours of the morning.

One of his favorite themes is the importance of relaxation. "Without relaxation you have nothing; you cannot develop spring power without this. Your root provides the foundation for the spring, while relaxation allows you to make use of it."

At that he sprang up off the bed, switched on the light, and took up a front stance.

"Look, if you keep your upper body tense this tension is also reflected in the legs and your stance is very unstable. But when you relax your weight and let gravity hold you on the ground—the ankles then become the transmitters of the spring power."

Master Koh's in-depth study of the art of Cheng Man Ching has led him to the conclusion that a clear development may be seen in the Grandmaster's skill throughout his life, and this is reflected in the way his curriculum evolved.

Testing a qigong exponent's neigong skills.

"Shiyue was very fond of saying that you cannot separate form from function. No matter how much you talk about martial arts or theorize, the bottom line is that they are for fighting. In his early teaching days Shiyue taught *san da* (fighting), not the *san shou* A and B forms or the two-person form, but applications based on the moves from the 37-posture form. But, in the end, in his book *The New Method of Self-Study*, Cheng said that the essence of fighting lay in *jie jing* (intercepting power). He also wrote that fighting was not based on fixed methods."

Every morning Master Koh gets up an hour before his classes to practice. His bungalow is situated on the corner of two streets and stands on about one-fourth of an acre of land, all of which is surrounded by a high whitewashed wall. In one corner, opposite the gates which open out onto the road, is a large tree which throws its shade across the concrete courtyard. Of course at 5:00 in the morning there is no sun, but it is still a peaceful place to practice.

On this particular morning as he watched me do the solo form, Master Koh urged me to pay attention to my root. Now this was something I had been working on for quite some time and I had thought that I was doing all right. Obviously not. So I again focused my attention on relaxing and sinking my weight as far as possible over one leg at a time. When I had finished, I could tell by the look on his face that it still wasn't enough.

"The root is the foundation of our skill," Koh advised me. "This doesn't just mean that we must pay attention to the feet. We must look beyond this; just as the feet are the foundations of the body, the 13 forms are the foundation of taijiquan. *Peng, lu, ji, an, cai, lieh, zhou, kao,* forwards, backwards, left, right, and *zhong ding* (central equilibrium): without these our art has no root. So when I say to you pay attention to the root it is all of these things that you must take notice of. Every single movement in taiji must contain elements of these 13 forms. Some people believe that you can take external martial art systems, slow them down and they will be the same as taijiquan. This can never be the case unless they contain the 13 forms. Taijiquan is an art based on the internal, it is not what it seems on the outside. Many people look at the art and completely fail to see how it could be used. But these same people could look at external systems and straight-away feel that they could see their application. Taijiquan is soft on the outside and hard on the inside; the application comes from inside. It is form that trains the inside. That is why it is so important."

> **"Without relaxation you have nothing; you cannot develop spring power without this."**

The first time that I came up to Kuala Lumpur specifically to train with Master Koh, I was accompanied by Wu Chiang Hsing and we had arranged to meet at the office of one of Master Wu's brothers.

Master Koh turned up with two of his senior students and in no time at all we had cleared back the office furniture and were taking turns in going through the form, watched critically by the others. Then, after some strenuous pushing hands, which defied the best efforts of the air-conditioning to keep me cool, Master Koh brought up an aspect of the Cheng style form that I had never come across.

"You must have heard of the demonstration of *yin* and *yang* in the hands," Master Koh asked. Wu Chiang Hsing nodded in agreement.

They were amazed when I said I hadn't, but Master Koh said that it was really very easy and nothing special. Then, taking up the "single whip" posture, Master Koh stood quietly for about a minute and then showed us his palms. That of the right hand was red while his left palm was white. He then did the same thing in several other postures. Each time the red hand was on the opposite side from the load-bearing leg. This he pointed out was in line with Cheng Man Ching's insistence on the cross-connection between left arm and right leg and vice-versa, and simply demonstrated that the practitioner was both relaxed and in the correct posture.

Master Koh is at great pains to stress the importance of the mind in taiji, pointing out that form practice is as much mental training as anything else—for one has to be focused and yet aware of all that is going on around him. By practicing the form with this in mind you are training yourself to have the kind of calm mind that enables you to make effective use of taijiquan in the most extreme situations. Koh notes that Cheng

Man Ching wrote in one of his books that when facing a large man you must imagine him to be a little child, and if training with a little child, imagine him to be a large man. If you can do this then you have attained a measure of taiji's gongfu.

During the time that I have practiced taijiquan I have come across almost as many different approaches to form training as there are teachers. Whereas some teachers aver that during form practice the exponent should adhere to a particular breathing pattern, Cheng Man Ching was quite explicit that the breathing should be natural, as size and capacity of everyone's lungs are different.

As Master Tan Ching Ngee says: "You wouldn't put a Rolls Royce engine in a Mini and expect it to work well."

Having said that, however, after a time the movements of the form themselves will regulate the breathing; that is, of course, if the postures are correct.

Another area of confusion is to whether, when doing the form, the practitioner should imagine an opponent.

Again Master Tan is quite explicit, "The purpose of form training is relaxation. How can you relax when you are imagining someone is about to attack you? We have pushing hands as a training method to teach you how to relax under pressure, but first you must use the form to learn to relax without pressure."

Cheng style taiji practitioners, while acknowledging the important role of the Yang family in the development of their art, firmly believe that their form contains the essence of taiji. While critics say that it is too short to provide any kind of training effect, its adherents reply that you only have to repeat the form several times in order to get all the same benefits as if you practiced the 108 posture Yang style form.

As Master Koh Ah Tee states, "Many people are concerned about the length of the form because taijiquan was originally known as chang quan (long boxing). But they overlook the fact that it is the qualities inherent in the form, not the length, that gave it the title of chang quan. Chang quan is rolling, smooth, and continuous, not broken or interrupted. What we should be aiming for is more in the way of quality than quantity."

Another moot point, even within the ranks of Cheng stylists, particularly those in the West, is whether the form should be practiced on both sides. That is, once you have learnt the form the standard way, you then go on to practice it in mirror image.

Master Tan refutes this, saying that Cheng himself told him that the internal organs of the human body are not symmetrical and if the form is to be treated as a therapeutic exercise then this should be heeded. This is the reason, for example, why the posture "squatting single whip" is only performed on one side.

• • •

When I lived in China, a taijiquan class was opened in the gymnasium of the hotel where I lived. This class was specifically for the "foreign experts," as those of us who worked for the Chinese government were known. The Friendship Hotel in the northwestern suburbs of Beijing was vast, almost a township in its own right, with bars, shops, restaurants, a gym, swimming pool, and a theater. The several hundred foreigners all lived in one compound and throughout the year different activities were organized for them.

Wanting to train as much as I could, I signed up for the class. The form to be taught was the 24-step routine, but I didn't want to let on to the teacher that I already knew it.

On the appointed day, 20 of us foreigners of assorted shapes and sizes and colors were gathered together in the large old-fashioned gymnasium. The main training area was surrounded by a balcony on which stood a dozen or so of the unruly mob of American children who had come with their parents to China, and who had now gathered to watch the entertainment below because, basically, there was nothing else to do.

We stood around in small groups—most of us knew each other anyway—and then all looked to the door as a small, trim woman in a smart, pale blue and white tracksuit came in. She looked to be in her mid-30s and as she looked at us she beamed a large smile and then turned to the stocky figure in the Mao suit who was hovering behind her.

It was Wong, one of the staff of interpreters who worked for the hotel. Most of the interpreters were characterized by their obsequiousness and their desire to foster as many contacts with foreigners as possible, particularly those which might lead to the highly desirable goal of study in the U.S. Wong was no exception, and there were a few muffled groans as we realized he was going to be a permanent feature of the class.

The teacher, Coach Zhen, walked smartly up to the front of the hall and looked around smilingly as Wong shuffled across the room behind her and then plugged in the large radio-cassette player he was carrying. Seeing that all was ready Coach Zhen introduced herself in a tight-lipped, rolling accent that marked her as a Beijing native, and then once again smiled as Wong translated. With this over, the radio was switched on and stirring, martial music with a distinct Chinese flavor filled the room. We were then led through a series of warm-up exercises, all strictly executed in time to the marching beat of the music.

The class continued in this manner with the coach demonstrating and us following, all of course to music. Anyone who has ever practiced the 24-step accompanied by the specially composed music will know how hard it is to ever do the form again without the same tune rattling around in your head even when there is no music.

After several weeks of this, Coach Zhen noticed that I was somehow more coordinated than the rest of the class, and that I seemed to have a better memory. Of course this was not the case, as I had already been practicing the form for several years. But I still didn't tell her.

The third week she asked me my name, and in the disconcerting way foreigners have of speaking in their own—and in my case British—accent, I repeated back, "Noigel." The next week she wanted me in the front row and by the time we had got as far as "step back to repulse monkey" I was her assistant instructor, standing next to her in front of the class. Thus it was that I "taught" taiji in China!

During both the training for the 1986 International Wushu Competition and after, all of us team members got used to being called on to strut our stuff at a moment's notice. When I went to Malaysia the year after, at a time when only retired members of the Chinese population were allowed to visit China, and having won a gold and bronze medal in the competition in China, the demands to demonstrate came thick and fast. By that time it didn't bother me at all.

In my wife's hometown, Batu Pahat, the largest taijiquan class is held under the auspices of the De Jiao Hui (Righteousness Teaching Association). This association was first established in the 1940s in Chaozhou city, Guangdong province; its purpose being to recognize and worship the five major religions of the region, since it was felt that they all embraced some aspects of universal truth. The organization swiftly spread throughout Southeast Asia, wherever Chaozhou Chinese went.

The Association in Batu Pahat has a large meeting hall, five stories high and, in addition to organizing youth activities, religious worship, and community functions, they also run taiji classes. My wife's eldest brother-in-law is the secretary of this branch of the Association and so it came about that I was invited to attend a celebration. Just what the celebration was I wasn't to find out until I got there.

We pulled up en famille outside the large hall, whose lights cut through the steamy fog of the evening. At the main doors was a reception party, maybe ten strong, and we were ushered through the midst of them, shaking hands, exchanging and immediately forgetting names until we popped out of the bottleneck at the door and into the glare of the hall.

It was packed; there seemed to be several hundred people milling around or already sitting on the seats which faced the large stage at the other end of the hall. As we entered, every head seemed to turn toward us, but that didn't bother me; what did was what was written in two-foot high letters on the backdrop of the stage: "WELCOME TO MR. NIGEL SUTTON"

All this it seemed was for me! I was not, however, to be the first attraction. For well over an hour members of the De Jiao Hui taijiquan class gave demonstrations of all aspects of their art. First was a group performance of the Cheng style form, followed by individual senior students performing the *san shou* solo forms and then the two-person form. Finally the assistant instructors, of whom there were about five, came on to demonstrate different aspects of pushing hands. That day the chief instructor was not there. In fact, it would be several years before I met him and, when I finally did, he proved to be an important figure in my taijiquan career. His name: Lee Bian Lei.

Then it was my turn. While the other demonstrations had been going on the master of ceremonies had come up to me and

The author with Master Lee Bian Lei.

The author becoming a disciple of Master Lee Bian Lei (above). The author and Master Lee Bian Lei (right).

asked me what I wanted to demonstrate, and had then insisted that I present at least four or five items.

There seemed to be little choice, so first of all I ran through the 48-step routine, followed by a baguazhang form, a xingyiquan form, and finally a sword form.

This greatly pleased the audience and as I staggered off the stage soaked in sweat and gasping for breath, they applauded long and loud. I do not flatter myself that this was due in any way to the high quality of my performance; it was simply a reflection of the novelty value of a foreigner practicing Chinese martial arts. My performance was also of particular interest to them because I was performing routines that were unique to the mainland and indeed I had visited and lived in China. Something which, at that time, very few of the audience had been able to do.

The situation now, however, has completely changed. As a result of the final surrender of the last Communist guerrillas, Malaysia has resumed full diplomatic relations with China and now all Malaysian Chinese are permitted to visit their relatives there. This has also opened the way for a steady succession of Mainland Chinese coaches to visit and teach in Malaysia. Indeed, the country now has its own successful national wushu team and regular competitions are held at state and national levels.

This increased mainland Chinese influence has led to a certain extent to a decline in the practice of Cheng style, as some of its exponents look to the more aesthetically-pleasing, showy aspects of the Yang, Chen, and other styles. Other practitioners, however, alarmed by the lack of substance and practical application of the modern competition forms, have found a renewed faith in the art of Cheng Man Ching.

Another worry that is commonly expressed by Cheng stylists is that, because of the 10 years of chaos of the cultural revolution (1966–76), the mainland Chinese have, in effect, lost 10 years of gongfu. Since the martial arts were banned as being feudal practices during that time little, if any, training would have been possible. In addition, the communist state's insistence on recreating the arts in their own image has resulted in appearance taking on far greater importance than actual substance.

In my own experience in China I found that only those masters who had trained prior to 1949 had any real understanding of how the arts might be realistically applied. Certainly the new generation could show you what each move was for, but only in an abstract, theoretical manner.

• • •

My desire to get closer to the source of Cheng style taiji led me next to visit Taiwan to meet and train with Cheng style exponents there.

Taipei is a bustling, crowded city, sited in the middle of a bowl of hills, which on a good day when the pollution allows may be seen blue and misty in the distance. Like many cities in Asia, it seems like one vast construction site with new buildings springing up wherever there is even the smallest bit of space. At night the center of the city is a sea of neon with all the latest technology applied to the advertising war.

For the martial arts enthusiast there are a number of "green lungs": park areas where every morning devotees of the martial arts go to practice. The most popular ones are Sun Yat Sen Memorial Park, Chiang Kai Shek Memorial Park, and New Park.

Since at that time Master Tan Ching Ngee was dividing his time between Singapore and Taiwan, he had agreed to act as my guide. He himself held a morning class in New Park close to the downtown shopping area. This was where I got my first chance to see what was going on taiji-wise in Taipei. The entire area is dotted with trees and here and there a traditional-style Chinese pavilion graciously overlooks the carp-crammed waters of the pond which winds through the center of the park

Amongst the trees on the hard-packed earth and along the meandering paths may be seen a wide variety of recreational activities, ranging from ballroom dancing to badminton, from aerobics to *qigong,* and from northern praying mantis to taijiquan. In an area of the park on the side nearest the shops a student of the renowned Huang Hsing Hsian has a class. This starts early in the morning, with the first hour or so spent in form practice, after which the order of the day is pushing hands. At first the students begin quite gently and slowly, running through set patterns of movements, but by about 8:00 things have heated up. Some exponents choose to push on four equally-spaced brieze blocks, attempting to topple each other off onto the dusty ground.

On the other side of the park, just up the path from a noisy and enthusiastic aerobics class, an old man who looks to be in his 70s and whom Master Tan informed me had been a long term disciple of Cheng's, teaches two students who have traveled all the way from Japan specifically to study with him. Slowly they move through the form, posture by posture, holding each stance as the master corrects them.

In the central area of the park a group of students practice northern praying mantis; all wearing the same uniform of baggy black trousers and white tee-shirt. The novices stand for up to half an hour in a low horse stance, fists firmly clenched on hips.

What is most noticeable about the taijiquan practitioners is that even though they may all be Cheng stylists, there are noticeable differences in the way they practice the form. This may in part be due—now almost 20 years after the founder's death—to different interpretations on the part of his different students. It might also be due to the period of Cheng's life during which the student learnt from him, as he himself was continuously progressing and changing his ideas and thus the emphasis of his teaching. Whatever the reason for the differences, they merely reinforce the fact that it is useless to seek for the "true" flavor of taijiquan by looking at form alone, for there can be no absolutely correct form; the only correctness that may be looked for is adherence to the art's principles.

Visiting the Sun Yat Sen Memorial Park early in the morning one may see a great variety of styles of martial art being practiced, including traditional Yang and Chen style taiji.

In this splendid setting the individual exponents are dwarfed by the vast square hall, dedicated to the founder of the Republic of China. The entrances to the building are raised one story above the ground with vast flights of stairs sweeping up to them. The wide walkway-come-balcony area which surrounds the whole building on this level is a favored spot for the practice of taijiquan, and it is here every morning that Master Liao Zhen Xiang may be found.

One of the later students of Cheng, Liao became a disciple only a matter of months before Cheng died. Well-known for his art and calligraphy, Liao certainly looks the part with his long, wispy white beard. He is particularly keen on wall-training, and the enthusiastic thumping sounds of students being propelled back-first into the solid walls of the Memorial Hall can be heard even before you come into sight of the group. That he learnt at a later stage of Cheng's life is immediately evident when you look at him doing his form. The postures are slightly shorter and have a relaxed, rounded look about them.

Just around the corner from where Master Liao's group practices, a Chen style class gyrates and pounds its way through the form, while on the main roadway below, a Yang style class weaves their way through the long form.

The modern mainland Chinese trend of creating new forms and emphasizing grace and form over function and application is also to be found in Taiwan to some extent. The reason for this harks back to developments in Chinese martial arts during the first few decades of the 20th century.

The Jing Wu Association, fronted at its foundation by the great Huo Yuan Jia, started a movement toward eliminating the sectarianism that was perceived to be hindering the continued development of the martial arts of China. Toward this end the finest teachers from different styles were recruited to teach a core curriculum of forms chosen from the different styles. Students who completed the basic course could then go on to specialize in the style of their choice.

A similar format was also adopted by the Zhongyang Guoshuguan (Central Martial Arts Academy) in Nanjing and many of the leading figures in the world of martial arts were recruited as teachers.

The fact that graduates from both of these institutions later went on to become the leaders of the martial arts world both of China and of Taiwan accounts for similarities in developments in both places. In both countries the government has taken a keen interest in the martial arts as a means of promoting an aspect of national culture and also as a way of extending control over a group of people traditionally associated with resistance and rebellion. In addition, increasing foreign interest in the arts has led to them becoming a valuable source of revenue as well as a means of promoting and cementing international relations.

In Taiwan a 62-step taijiquan form, combining different styles, has been put together and now that friendlier relations are being forged with the mainland, people are also beginning to practice the forms developed there. On Taiwan, however, function is still emphasized as much as form and attention is still paid to the classical advice: "If you train form but you don't train gongfu, when you're old you'll be left with nothing." The increasing danger in the world of Chinese martial arts is that this advice is being ignored.

Cheng style taijiquan on Taiwan is relatively strong in terms of the number of people practicing the art, but is divided in terms of attitude and approach. Amongst second generation students, those who studied with disciples of Cheng, there is much muttering that amongst the first generation there were few great fighters. This they attribute to the fact that, because of his reputation and attitude, Cheng predominantly attracted artists and intellectuals to study with him. These same students, however, feel that their generation has potential to reach greater heights in the art.

I do not believe that this view is entirely fair, as many of Cheng's students had reputations as established and accomplished martial artists in their own right. However, it is true that many other of his students were not particularly interested in the fighting aspects of the art. What is true is that the second and third generation students, both in Taiwan and elsewhere, seem to be more interested in learning and testing the effectiveness of the art's fighting applications.

I have visited the Shr Zhong school of taijiquan in Taiwan which was established by Cheng, and certainly the standard there is not guaranteed to inspire confidence in the efficacy of taiji as a fighting art. There is an over-emphasis on relaxation without balancing this by testing the nature of that relaxation in a realistic manner.

So although I went to Taiwan with high expectations, I came away convinced that the future of the art lay in places like Malaysia and Singapore. When discussing this with Master Tan, he pointed out that the more "maverick" second generation students are regarded with dislike and distrust by some of their older "uncles." This, in many ways, parallels the way Cheng was regarded by other disciples in the Yang family, who felt that he had acquired too high a standard and therefore posed a threat to them.

• • •

The aim of the practitioner of Cheng style is to make their whole body conform to taiji principles, which is one of the main reasons why form training is conducted in such a slow and painstaking manner. As a result of the constant attention to detail even after many years practice there is still much to learn.

When teaching, Master Tan Ching Ngee points out the importance of always bearing in mind what he calls the "three essentials." Starting with the legs: the ankle, knee, and hip should always be correctly aligned. Next, moving on to the arms: the wrist, elbow, and shoulder should be coordinated. Finally, with regard to the body: the head must feel as if suspended from above, eyes gazing into the distance while the chin is tucked in; the chest is sunk and the back rounded; and the backside is tucked under so that the lower spine is convex. By just paying attention to these few points you will ensure that when you practice your form you are building a strong foundation.

On the importance of building a solid foundation, Master Tan also stresses that the load-bearing leg should feel like a compressed spring which is only released as the weight is shifted. If you bear this in mind you will find that many aspects concerning the application of power in taijiquan will become clear.

Master Tan likes to remind his students that listening to the teacher is as important, and in some cases even more important, than just watching what he does. He cites Grandmaster Cheng as an example. Apparently, Cheng used to admonish his students that when they sat back from the move "push and turned the body," the forward leg should be kept bent as otherwise it would not be relaxed; yet when he did it his front leg was straight! Similarly, when asked why in photographs of Yang Cheng Fu performing the posture, "single whip," the wrist of the hand held in a hook formation appeared to be unnaturally pushed down, Cheng replied that Master Yang was so relaxed that he could do this and still his arm felt as soft as cotton. This he attributed to the result of years of relaxation practice.

The form may be used by the practitioner as a reference work into which he or she may delve whenever they wish, and which holds an infinite number of lessons for those with an inquiring mind. Cheng himself commented that *chi shi*, the beginning posture of the form, is of vital importance, for within it lies the essence of the art; and that's before you've even started on the form proper!

There are, however, those who take a different attitude to the form from those described above. Rather than making form the center of their practice, they relegate it to a position of secondary or even little importance. One such teacher is Master Lee Bian Lei.

Master Lee relates that he first started studying taijiquan after he was beaten by Yue Shu Ting. Prior to that he had dabbled in external martial arts. So impressed was he by Master Yue that from that time on he spent every waking minute training with him. Then Master Yue left Malaysia to return to Taiwan, where he became a Buddhist monk. From Taiwan Master Yue went to Thailand, where he died. The young Lee, desperate to continue his training, became a disciple of Lu Tong Bao.

When recalling those early training days, Lee talks of being in constant pain.

"Master Lu used to beat me all the time!," Lee remembers. "By the end of the day we were in so much pain that we couldn't walk up the stairs, we had to crawl." This is said with a smile.

Having spent the first two or three years of his training career practicing in this manner, Master Lee now feels that form practice is irrelevant to him.

"I have built a foundation. Now I just practice *qigong* and do a little pushing hands," Lee says with typical understatement.

Lee's students, however, continue to practice form in order to build that all-important foundation.

I have often wondered how the form "purists" that I have met, particularly in the United Kingdom, would regard Master Lee; for they would not be able to judge his taiji by the "correctness" of his form. Such people would then be forced to examine the ultimate purpose of the form: function. And for Master Lee, his art is truly functional.

Master Zhou Mu Tu is Lee Bian Lei's martial arts younger brother, having also become a disciple of Lu Tong Bao. However, because he lived right down in the south, far away from his master, much of his training was under Master Lee.

Master Zhou's prime interest lies in the fighting aspect of the art; indeed, he spent a period of two years training in karate so he could practice free-sparring—this he did as a direct result of there being no such practice in taijiquan. Along the way Zhou earned his black belt and then came back to taijiquan. As senior instructor under Lee Bian Lei at the De Jiao Hui in Batu Pahat, Master Zhou is responsible for teaching the literally hundreds of students that attend the classes there.

Visiting this class is truly an amazing experience, as there are so many students and they occupy every story of the building. On the ground floor the beginners are to be found, laboring their way through the complex movements, which the look on their faces tells you they think they will never master. On the next floor up are the intermediate students learning the start of one of the *san shou* forms. And so this continues right up to the roof, which is covered with corrugated tin, where the advanced students are to be found; some running through weapons forms, others doing freestyle pushing hands.

It is here that Master Zhou is most generally to be found, his energetic, smiling face lighting up as I come in.

"Come, come, join us. Let's practice together." This usually being the prelude to some energetic "playing" at pushing hands.

Master Zhou's attitude to the form is like the man himself: straightforward and direct.

"What we practice is the Yang style. We don't call it Cheng style because at the time Master Yue learnt from Cheng Man Ching he learnt the 108 posture form. Then, in later years, we changed to the 37 because we found that it is better for beginners, in the sense that they are less likely to lose interest before they finish learning the form. Then once they have learnt it, they are more likely to stick to it.

"The purpose of form training is to train your strength; to lay the foundation skills, if you like. Also, it helps improve your health. But perhaps the most important thing is to train your mental intent. In every technique you must train your intent so that not only are you doing the postures with your body but you are also feeling them with your mind.

"*Qi* is a source of strength in the body, but it is the *yi*, the intent, that motivates the *qi*. If *qi* is important to the art, *yi* is doubly important and it is in form practice that this may be developed."

At the De Jiao Hui, students are taught the application of every movement in the form but, as Master Zhou points out, there is little opportunity for them to develop these skills realistically because they are seldom prepared to execute the countless number of repetitions needed to facilitate real understanding.

I asked Lau Kim Hong, another student of Lu Tong Bao, what he felt were the most important reasons for practicing the form, and he replied that it was to train relaxation and sinking.

"If you are not *song* (relaxed) and *chen* (sunk) then you will be forced to rely on brute strength when it comes to pushing hands. One important distinction that must be made, however, is between *song* (relaxed) and *ruan* (flacid). If you are *song* but not *chen*, then in my opinion your softness will be *ruan*, and this is not a quality that is part of taijiquan. If you are both *song* and *chen* then you will have acquired *zhong ding* (central equilibrium). Taijiquan is about action and reaction and unless your relaxation has a firm foundation you can do neither."

As Master Lee spoke, he demonstrated the difference between *song* and *ruan,* in a strong but relaxed stance, when he suddenly went limp, letting his body sag and his head flop.

Hardly surprising, Koh Ah Tee expressed very similar opinions as Master Lau when asked the same question. If anything, however, his answer was even more categoric, as was his tone as he fixed me firmly with his eyes: "The whole of taijiquan can be reduced to one word: *song*. That is the essence, the root, everything. It is absolutely the most important thing. Without having achieved this 'gongfu' you cannot acquire any understanding of *jing* (the application of 'intelligent' power as opposed to brute strength). Without *jing* you cannot reach a high standard of taiji skill."

• • •

One of Master Koh's classes is held early in the morning on the deck surrounding the swimming pool at the prestigious Royal Selangor Golf Club in Kuala Lumpur. This club has a history of over a century and runs courses and classes for its members, as well as the usual golf-related activities.

Being one of the better-known Cheng style exponents in the capital, Master Koh was invited to attend an interview with a view to employing him as a teacher there. How he got the job is best left to another chapter but, suffice to say, Master Koh now teaches the upper echelon of KL society weekly in this beautiful setting.

The white stucco colonial-design clubhouse stands in the middle of the immaculate course which is dotted with beautiful greenery of all shapes, sizes, and varieties. Practicing by the perfect blue waters of the swimming pool as the sun slowly rises is an extremely pleasant experience, to put it mildly.

During one such class Master Koh stopped to explain the purpose of form movements to his attentive students: "The form is like a compendium of the strategy and tactics of the art. If we look at two specific movements, 'step forward move, parry, punch' and 'brush knee, twist step,' we can see how this works.

"In the first move, when punching, we do so to the center of the body, the soft parts. In the second we use the open hand to the face or chest. We are using *yin* against *yang* and *yang* against *yin*. But also if we look at the body mechanics involved we can see that to punch high is unnatural in the sense that it requires tension in the shoulders and upper body; an open-hand strike, on the other hand, is both relaxed and natural. This is the reason for the difference and this same reasoning, in terms of application, may be applied to every movement in the form."

Later on, noticing that one of the students had his wrists flexed and tense, Master Koh once again stopped the class in mid-form and as they gathered around him, held up his own right hand to demonstrate the difference between the shape of his hand and arm and that of the student.

"Look, this is the fair lady's hand; the fingers are not tense, nor are they flaccid, and the wrist is straight, flat, and unbroken. This fair lady's hand is unique to Cheng style and helps to give the art its distinctive flavor. What is important about this is that when you have it right it leads to greatly improved *ting jing* (sensitivity). You will have acquired taiji's 'light touch'."

I asked Master Koh at this point whether it might not be argued that such a soft hand formation could not stand up well to the rigors of fighting.

His look became even more intense.

"No, no. You are missing the point."

Raising his right hand and then bringing it down gently on the chest of the large, burly student in front of him, Koh continued: "See, as it is touching him now, my hand is still in the fair lady's shape, so that I can in a fraction of a second sense his intention, feel his strength and weakness, and then respond."

As the last word left his mouth, Koh pushed his student, who went careening out of control, ending up sprawled against the wall several feet away. When his victim had recovered and returned, somewhat shaken, Master Koh again placed his palm on his chest but this time with the wrist flexed and tense. Again he pushed but this time the student felt it coming and managed to twist away to the side, thus avoiding the full force of the push which only rocked him, slightly failing to significantly unbalance him.

"Now you see the difference. In Cheng style taijiquan *ting jing* is all-important; it is a living skill, not a dead method."

The class resumed their practice with everyone paying a great deal more attention to the fair lady's hand.

While there exists as many different approaches to form as there are teachers, there is no doubt that in Cheng style taiji it plays a vital role. Throughout the world, wherever Cheng's style is practiced, you may be sure students are assiduously training, researching, and discussing the unique legacy of the founder, the 37-posture form.

Chapter Three

On Internal and External

lthough when studying with Huang Jifu and while training in China I had practiced both internal and external styles, when I began intensive study of Cheng style taiji one of the many things that impressed me was the way that the teachers had complete faith in the efficacy of their art. This faith was accompanied by the conviction that the practice of other arts, especially those labeled as "external," would only be to the detriment of the exponent's taiji skills. This became a view that I became an enthusiastic proponent of and, in my school in England, the traditional Yang style form, the 48-step form, and the 24-step form, were all dropped in favor of the 37-step form alone. In addition in my own personal practice, I slowly let slip the bagua and xingyi I had so painstakingly learnt in China.

It was not until I moved to Malaysia and met Master Liang He Qing that I was finally forced to face and question what exactly lies at the root of the Chinese martial arts. The notion of there being two main categories of martial art—external and internal—is a comparatively modern one. Some argue that such an idea originated in the martial art novels that became popular in the early part of the 20th century. According

Master Liang performing a tiger form of hong quan boxing.

to popular theory, the external martial arts are concerned with the development of muscular strength and the judicious use of speed and power, while the internal arts concentrate on the development of the body's *qi* or vital energy and use the soft to overcome the hard.

Cheng Man Ching favored another explanation, that the internal arts were so called because they had their roots in Daoism and originated in China, while the external martial arts were brought to China from India along with Buddhism.

Either way, as any boxer experienced in either aspect will tell you, at a high level the internal and the external are virtually indistinguishable. Taiji boxers are fond of expounding the principle of overcoming "a thousand pounds with four ounces," and yet Shaolin boxers have also been basing their art on this theory for hundreds of years. But I am getting ahead of myself. As I mentioned earlier, it took the teaching of Master Liang to bring about a major change in the way I viewed the Chinese martial arts.

Of all the masters that I have trained with in Singapore and Malaysia, Master Liang He Qing is exceptional for a number of reasons. Not only does he see no conflict between the practice of internal and external martial arts, he continues to practice a wide range of both. In his 60s, he has been practicing martial arts for over four decades and his daily training schedule is such that many younger men would find it difficult to follow. Master Liang gets up at 3:00 A.M., seven days a week, and spends the two hours between 3:00 and 5:00 in his own practice. Then at 5:00 he teaches a class on a grassy playing field by the banks of the estuary of the River Muar. During the rest of the day Master Liang practices as and when time allows before going out to teach again in the evening. His work as a traditional Chinese dentist allows him plenty of time to practice between patients. In fact, Master Liang is a living epitome of one of his favorite pieces of advice: "Gongfu is part of everyday life."

When Master Liang reads the newspaper, he does so in a "standing post" posture; when he watches the television, he practices his *chin na* grips on a piece of sandalwood; and before he goes to bed, he strikes a wooden bar which protrudes from the wall over his bed, practicing a whole range of striking and "bridge arm" moves.

The first art that Liang trained in was Hainan boxing; at the time this was the only art he had access to as he is Hainanese. Then he moved on to train with Master Song Sao Bo, a Cantonese master of hongquan. Song learnt in a direct line from the famed Huang Fei Hong, who is often described as being a kind of Chinese Robin Hood and who lived in Canton province at the turn of the century. Song learnt from Lam Sai Wing, one of Huang's most famous students and who was responsible for taking the art to Hong Kong.

Master Liang stayed with Master Song long enough to become one of his most senior students. Granted his teaching certificate by Master Song, Liang began teaching hongquan throughout Johor State.

In the ensuing years Liang took every opportunity to learn whatever he could, eventually spending a number of years training with Master Yang Ching Feng, a graduate of the Xiamen Jing Wu school.

From Master Yang, Liang learnt the "big three" of the internal arts: taiji, bagua, and xingyi. He also learnt a lesser known internal form, wujiquan. As Liang learnt, and to

style has its own unique flavor, characteristics, and benefits. Once you have identified these then you only have to train them."

Of all the teachers I have trained with, Master Liang is the only one outside Mainland China who practices both internal and external forms and sees no contradiction in so doing.

When learning taiji from Yang Ching Feng,

Master Liang's teacher, Master Yang Ching Feng.

Master Liang performing a crane form of hongquan boxing.

this day continues to practice so many different styles, he has designed for himself a rigorous and systematic training schedule whereby he works on particular styles on different days. In this way he is able to identify and improve on the particular characteristics of each system.

"Chinese gongfu is very simple," Master Liang is fond of repeating. "There are no secrets. The only thing that you have to do is to continue practicing. Each

Liang learnt only traditional Yang style, a 72-step fast form, *san shou* A and B, and two-person forms. Master Yang did not teach pushing hands because he himself had not learnt it. Despite this, Master Liang is still able to make extremely efficient use of his taijiquan. This bears out what Lau Kim Hong once said to me, that you could acquire taiji's fighting skills through learning only form and applications but that pushing hands makes the process much quicker.

With Master Liang, as well as learning a whole range of different forms and their ancillary training methods, I spent a considerable amount of time practicing applications.

As Master Liang pointed out, when he first started training there was no freestyle sparring practice—although later on in his own classes Liang allowed senior students to do so. The results, however, were less than satisfying, for inevitably there were injuries and often the students got so carried away that the resultant fracas in no way resembled the art they were supposed to be practicing, making the whole exercise rather pointless. So it was that Master Liang returned to a method more closely resembling his own learning experience, whereby the students practiced a response to a single attack, gradually adding on additional attacks and counters until a whole sequence of moves could be practiced at increasing speed and power.

It was this type of training that I embarked on with Master Liang, starting with breaking down whatever form I happened to be learning so that Master Liang would attack and I would counter with a move I had just learned. Upon which Master Liang would counter my counter and so on. The resultant exercise resembled a cross between pushing and sticking hands as most of the moves ended up being executed at close quarters. Whatever I tried to do he stopped and very often the whole process ended with me not only locked up but also vulnerable to either one of his vicious low kicks or a strike of some kind, always aimed at a vital target such as the throat, the temple, or the groin. These chains of attacks and counters could continue, and often did, for hours, during which time I received the benefit of his accumulated knowledge and experience. It was obvious from the amount of detail in his teaching that an equally detailed knowledge of the finer aspects of form training is essential to be able to apply any system.

Master Liang is adamant, however, that form training alone is not enough. "Training form and training gongfu are two different things," he asserts, "and require different training methods."

Thus it was that he had me training on a wide range of devices from walls to lengths of bamboo, each designed to complement a particular aspect of form.

The essence of taijiquan, Master Liang feels, is the ability to achieve *song,* and through *song* to develop *jing,* or applied power. This *jing* may be manifested in many different ways. These are most clearly expressed in his Yang style fast taiji form. This Master Liang learnt from Yang Ching Feng, who learnt it from his teacher, Liu Jian Chuan. Liu Jian Chuan had trained directly with Yang Cheng Fu in Shanghai and earned his living as a bodyguard.

Like the *san shou* solo and two-person forms, leading current-day exponents of the Yang family system deny that the fast taiji is a legitimate part of the Yang style curriculum. Whatever the truth concerning this form's provenance, there is little doubt in my mind as to its efficacy in training both the development and expression of power. Through practice the student learns not only how to generate power but also how different kinds of power may be used in different movements. Coupled with these move-

ments is the same kind of explosive breathing used by exponents when practicing the *neigong* exercises. All in all, there is a wealth of information contained in this form, although at first sight this may not appear to be the case.

• • •

I first heard of Liang He Qing from Master Lau Kim Hong, who had been a friend of his for years. Having recently moved to Muar, the small town where Master Liang has lived most of his life, I was looking around for a teacher and for someone who could facilitate my continuing research into the Chinese martial arts. At first I was

Master Liang performing Wu style taijiquan.

unsuccessful until Lau Kim Hong mentioned his friend whose waijiaquan was excellent. Although the external martial arts were not my primary area of interest, I thought that I would go and take a look at his class. He taught several evenings a week at the Guangxi Association Hall, one of the many dialect-based associations set up by Chinese all over the world.

Like many other such classes I had attended, this class was held on the very top floor of the building, and after a long, sweaty trudge up several flights of dusty concrete steps, my wife, myself, and a friend arrived in the large concrete-floored training area. On one side of the room was a large glass-fronted cabinet containing an array of vicious-looking weapons; mute testimony to the often savage past of these clan and dialect Associations. These halberds, spears, and staffs might well have seen use when dialect group fought against dialect group and clan fought against clan; a common occurrence throughout the nineteenth century.

I dragged my attention back from the weapons to the group of 20 or so students who were weaving their slow way through the movements of the traditional Yang style taiji form. At the front of the hall a small, stocky figure called out the name of each posture as he led the group in their practice. This was Master Liang.

Later, when we had been introduced and had talked for a while, Master Liang asked if I was interested in seeing some of the different styles that he practiced.

Master Liang performing Chen style taijiquan.

Master Liang performing xingyiquan.

Then, almost before I could say yes, he had moved to the center of the hall, midway between four large whitewashed pillars that divided up the room.

"Tanglang (praying mantis)," he announced, and immediately his whole demeanor changed. His spine straightened, his shoulders seemed to become broader, and, most striking of all, his eyes seemed suddenly to cut across the room. Slowly at first, he began to move, then faster, interspersing slow rhythmic, almost hypnotic posturings with bursts of sharply-focused strikes and kicks. It was a stunning performance and very different from the taijiquan he had been teaching when we came in; it was almost as if by changing style he had become a different person. This I later found out to be characteristic of his forms practice and an indication of his skill, for he has an extraordinary ability to capture and illustrate the essence of a style.

His next demonstration was of the fast taiji, and once again I was impressed both by the contrast between hard and soft and fast and slow exhibited in his movements. I was also impressed by the visible and manifest power of his movements, some of which were accompanied by the *hen-ha* sounds which the Yang family tradition records as being an accompaniment to the expression of power.

While at the time I thought this form was impressive, it wasn't until I had spent several months practicing it that I really started to understand just how much the form contained. Just as with the *san shou* forms, one of the prime requirements is that you

Master Liang performing northern praying mantis boxing.

should remain totally relaxed and in accord with taiji principles while moving at speed and with power.

"In this way," Master Liang explained, "you can bring the *jing* out through the body. The feeling is that you have no hands, almost as if you are throwing them away on every move."

This is far easier said than done, particularly when some of the movements are jumps, high kicks, or low stances, as inevitably a degree of effort and tension creeps into the performance.

Training with Master Liang has taught me many important lessons, but perhaps the one that he stresses the most is that anyone can acquire the skills of Chinese martial arts—but only if they train hard. This is the attitude that he has always kept—namely, that if the teacher can do something then it is also possible for the student to do the same.

• • •

In the world of Chinese martial arts every teacher has his own specialty and accompanying training methods to develop this specialty. In the past, these skills and the exercises that developed them were carefully guarded secrets, sometimes only being taught to family members or those from the same dialect group. Now, fortunately for all of us, many teachers are recognizing that for the art to grow and flourish it must no longer be regarded as the property of one small group, or even of one race, but that it must be regarded as a part of humanity's cultural heritage.

I have been fortunate throughout my training, in that I have always met teachers who were both willing and open enough to share their art with me. The skills they have developed through their practice of the martial arts, as Master Liang often points out, may be divided into two areas: form and gongfu. When any form is being taught great care must be taken that the student understands each and every move, not only in terms of its mechanics but also its function. The relation of each body part to every other must be understood, as well as the particular mental attitude that each move embodies or requires. Most forms at one point or another require specific attention to be paid to breathing, and this must be emphasized only when the student has become reasonably confident with the movements themselves.

Careful attention paid to all of the above factors will ensure that the student has laid a solid foundation for the acquisition of the more obviously applicable skills. Above all the student will have absorbed the principles and unique characteristics of the form being studied. For example, if it is a xingyi form that is being studied, the exponent will become trained to produce power from vertical circles and to constantly have a feeling of moving forward with the inexorable momentum of a tidal wave.

Accompanying this emphasis on truly understanding form is the need to train gongfu. To paraphrase a Chinese martial arts saying that I've referred to before, "If you train in form but you don't develop gongfu then when you're old you'll be left with nothing." Gong fu in this case may best be defined as the range of physical skills developed through intense training over an extended period of time.

Such ancillary training might take the form of conditioning of particular body parts, the development of grip strength to enable *chin na* techniques to be effectively executed, standing post exercises to develop stance, or specific leg exercises for the training of powerful kicks and sweeps. Without such training the exponent runs the risk of practicing only empty if pretty forms.

• • •

While living in China I tried to learn as much as I could, so it was that I studied with whichever teacher I could find. One system that I spent a lot of time learning was meihuaquan, plum blossom boxing. This art is also sometimes called plum blossom posts because it used to be practiced on logs, sometimes as high as several feet off the ground, laid out in the shape of a five petal plum blossom. The art had its origins in the fighting systems of the Chinese Moslems and, as typifies a northern art, has long, low stances and high, swinging kicks.

My teacher was Xiao Zhang, the son of two clerical workers at the college where I worked. Xiao had been practicing Chinese martial arts since the age of eight and although now, at the age of 19, he was working as a service attendant in a large Western-owned hotel, every minute of his spare time was spent practicing.

A member of the Hui, Moslem minority, Xiao was tall, six foot in fact, with strong features and an aquiline nose. Since his job necessitated using English he was eager to improve his language skills, and so we agreed that he would teach me meihuaquan in return for English lessons.

Our lessons took place outside the main teaching block in the college. This was not an ideal place, as during the Cultural Revolution the college had been closed down and a tobacco factory set up in its place. This factory proved to be very profitable, and so when the chaos of the Cultural Revolution ended and the college was re-opened the factory stayed where it was. This meant that the students and workers had to share facilities and there was always some degree of tension between the two groups.

Outside the teaching area, where we were to practice, were stacked large bales of tobacco, and it was amongst these that our training took place.

Occasionally, when tensions were running high, the students would sneak out of their dormitories under the cover of darkness and move the tobacco away from the college buildings. This, however, would result in reprisals, and the vicious cycle would continue.

One advantage, from my point of view, was that practicing in the aisles between the sweet-smelling stacks kept me out of the sight of inquisitive eyes.

Master Liang practicing "limb knocking" with the author's student Steven Burns.

From the outset of our lessons Xiao Zhang was very keen to impress upon me the efficacy of his art, and when I expressed some skepticism as to the value of the high, straight leg ax kicks which were an integral part of his style, he was at great pains to show me exactly how they worked.

Ordering me to square off and attack him, Xiao stood with his back very straight, feet in a kind of short cat stance, and arms extended with open hands as if inviting me to come forward. Mindful of my painful experience at the hands of other teachers intent on proving the value of their style, I was cautious and shuffled around him looking for an opening. Then he moved forward, his rear arm swinging toward me in a kind of extended arm roundhouse.

Smartly moving to one side, I drove in at his exposed ribs with a front kick. My mistake! The swinging arm suddenly changed direction and the fist slammed down on my kicking leg as I desperately attempted to withdraw it. Then his leg was scything through the air toward my head in a straight leg, inside crescent kick. As I tried to move back just out of the way of the kick as it continued on its arcing journey, Xiao Zhang pivoted and the other leg swung round in the same extended fashion.

Now I was in full retreat, for had I stayed where I was I would have required extensive hospital treatment. But I had run out of space for my back was up against a stack of tobacco and it was then that Xiao Zhang swept his leg straight up, this time in a vertical arc, which had he been an inch closer would have deprived me of any hopes of enjoying fatherhood, and then just as swiftly brought it down to stop a few centimeters from my nose.

54

A smile creased his face as he brushed his fringe away from his eyes.

"That's how we use these kicks," he said.

I believed him.

• • •

Arrival for the first time in Malaysia is a full-scale assault on the senses. When I stepped off the plane in July 1987 it was six in the evening and already getting dark, but the wet blanket of tropical air still wrapped itself around me with enough force to make me feel I had taken a wrong turn into some kind of sauna with a broken thermostat. All around were the twinkling, multi-colored lights that make night in Southeast Asia forever Christmas. I could taste each breath as it slid down my throat and the smells instantly clogged my nose.

Layer upon layer of sound seemed to be jostling for the attention of my ears: the underlying rhythm of the cicadas, the ever-rising clamor of Chinese voices in a confusion of dialects, and the ever-present soft slapping of fans and the humming of air-conditioning units as they fought their incessant battle against the heat.

A car ride and a night's fretful sleep later, punctuated by dreams of turbulence and rapid descent, and I was sitting in the cool shade of the large family living room of my father-in-law's house. Since he had built it to accommodate his six sons and their future families, the house is very large indeed and the living room is about 30 feet long and 15 feet wide. When I say it is cool, this is a statement I now recognize to be true, but, at that time, jet-lagged and sapped by the humidity, I felt oppressed by the heat.

My fifth brother-in-law, whom Chinese custom dictated I call fifth elder brother, had told me that a friend of the family, who was a master of martial arts and a teacher of taijiquan, among other things, would be coming to visit me. So it was that I was perked up a little, after all that was what I had come to Malaysia for, although my wife would probably have her own opinion on that. The master's arrival was heralded by the shouting of the dozen or so nephews and nieces who always seemed to be everywhere at once.

"Uncle Nigel, Uncle Nigel, the *shifu's* here, the *shifu's* here!"

And then in that agony of Chinese politeness referred to as "calling people," Master Tan Swoh Theng greeted and was greeted by all the members of the family in descending order of importance. Indeed, on his arrival family members seemed to erupt out of the bedrooms adjoining the living room, pour down the stairs and flood out of the kitchen, so that the guest was surrounded by a sea of solicitous would-be hosts.

"Have you eaten?" "Drink some tea." "Please be seated." "Would you like brandy?" The assault of Chinese politeness washed over the guest.

After I had been introduced and we were sitting with the beverage of our choice in front of us—it was, finally, after some gentle verbal sparring, Chinese tea—the topic turned to the question of what exactly it was that I wanted to learn.

When I explained that my desire was to learn pushing hands his face took on a slightly distant look which seemed rather dismissive of my plan.

"Look, look," he stood up and enlisted the aid of fifth elder brother in moving the furniture out of the way so that a bare patch of wall was exposed.

"There is no great secret to taiji pushing hands!" So saying, Tan led me over to the cleared space and positioned me so that I was standing in a front stance with my back about a yard away from the wall.

"Come, we'll push."

He started off in a straightforward double-hand pushing pattern, which I quickly followed. Then, just as I was getting into the rhythm, his arms slipped through mine and pushing against my chest, Master Tan propelled me at great speed into the wall. So hard was the impact and so unexpected the attack, that I thought I would vomit.

Master Tan stood back and surveyed the damage, as fifth elder brother remarked that I had turned green. My wife, ever solicitous, covered her mouth and laughed at my dazed expression.

"Is that what you wanted to learn," she tittered.

After we had rearranged the furniture and I had drunk several glasses of water, the conversation continued.

"You see, pushing hands is a matter of timing and surprise: if you can achieve them then it is very easy."

Master Tan seemed to wonder whether I had gotten his point. I had.

"But what I can teach you is my special gongfu; this comes from wuzuquan (five ancestor boxing, a popular southern style originating in Fujian Province). That will be of benefit to all the arts you train in."

Still stunned and shaken, I agreed. And thus it was that I embarked on my training career with Master Tan, during which time I was not only to learn five ancestor boxing but also his unique approach to taiji pushing hands, *chin-na*, fighting skills, and bone setting.

After this first painful encounter, word was passed to me by fifth elder brother that Master Tan wished to teach me but only if I was willing to become his disciple. This was a dream come true—I felt as if I was stepping into the world of "Gong Fu." Of course I accepted, and a propitious date was fixed.

On the appointed day Master Tan himself appeared at the family home to pick me up. We drove to a large, up-market housing estate on the edge of town where his senior disciple lived. The large semi-detached house was fronted by a neat garden and the front room was plushly decorated. The floor was tiled with what looked like marble and the fabric of the brightly colored furniture was cool to the touch.

Shijie (martial arts older sister), the name I have only ever known her by, invited us to sit, and refreshments were duly brought out.

We were waiting, it turned out, for another two of his disciples to act as witnesses at

**Tan Swoh Theng, master of
five ancestor boxing.**

the ceremony. When they arrived I saw that one was a large man, over six feet tall and with a heavy build, who looked to be in his late 30s. The other was a diminutive, attractive girl with her hair cut short in page boy style. They were introduced to me as elder brother and sister and then we were ready for the formalities to begin.

With the sofa, armchairs, and coffee table pushed to the side of the room there was now enough space to perform a whole taiji form if you so wished.

Master Tan disappeared into the kitchen and then reappeared carrying a large bundle of incense sticks. Handing me 11, Master Tan directed me to light them and go outside to pray to Heaven. He accompanied me and this was duly done by holding the incense between my joined palms and waving it up and down three times in a supplicatory manner. Three of the sticks were then planted in offering in the front garden.

Next we went inside to the altar of the Earth God, which was on the floor in the kitchen, where the same procedure was repeated with another three sticks being placed in front of the altar. Finally we moved over to the fridge on top of which an altar to the Five Ancestors was set up. After praying, the remaining five sticks were placed there. The praying this time, however, required that I kneel to the ancestors before planting the incense. Then, with my right hand raised, I repeated the oath of loyalty recited by the eldest *shijie*.

Master Tan, resplendent in the formal silk suit he had donned especially for the occasion, then took out a charm written in the customary red ink on yellow paper and burned it, scattering the ashes into a cup of Chinese tea which he offered to me to drink. The burnt flavor of the tea made drinking it an effort, but I gritted my teeth and swallowed it down in one hasty gulp.

It was then back to the living room where the final part of the ceremony was to be carried out. First I presented a red packet containing a gift of money to Master Tan,

Master Tan Swoh Theng with his disciples.

then I poured tea into four small cups and, in order of seniority, starting with the master, presented the tea to each of them.

My new brother and sisters broke out in a spontaneous round of applause and shook my hand in congratulation. A camera was produced and a whole film used up recording the start of our relationship for posterity. First the obligatory photo with Master Tan sitting stern and straight in his chair, me standing behind his left shoulder. Next were all the various combinations of me with Master Tan and one or other of my elder wushu siblings, then without Master Tan, and finally the whole group together. It was an exhausting business.

After the photos were over Master Tan gathered us on the sofa which had been pulled back to its original place and talked about the responsibilities inherent in the master-disciple relationship.

"You are now a part of our five ancestors martial arts family. As such, we will look after your progress in the art and help you in whatever way we can. Your duty to the teacher includes not forgetting him on his birthday and Chinese New Year. Just a token of your appreciation in a red packet will do.

"A student can never repay the debt he owes his teacher, for without the teacher you would not have access to the art. So if the teacher is in trouble it is your duty to help. Your final responsibility is to be present at the teacher's funeral. To see him on his way and thank him for all he has done."

Master Tan's son performing a five ancestor boxing form.

Our gathering ended on that somber note.

To his advice, I would add for the benefit of the Western student some more: Never go empty-handed to your teacher's house, just a gift of fruit will be enough; when he has given up his time to teach you, always repay him with a red packet, it will mean that you learn more next time; never forget how much a good teacher invests in his students, for he invites you into his life freely and without restraint.

When it works properly, the master-disciple relationship is truly a special one.

The five ancestor fist system traces its history back to the Fujian Shaolin Temple and has its origins in the student of one Shaolin monk. The student was not satisfied with the boxing that he had learnt and so he traveled around learning the finest aspects of the best systems that he could find. Synthesizing his knowledge he combined Da Mo boxing, white crane, monkey, Taizu (a Chinese Emperor), and xiannu (female immortal) boxing. The result was a system that contained scores of empty hand forms and dozens of weapons forms.

Master Tan taught that forms were to teach basics. Above and beyond that, however, they served as an advertisement for the style. As such, the exponent is expected to master one or two forms which may be used for demonstration purposes.

The stances in wuzuquan are generally quite short and the arms are kept close in to the body to protect the vital areas under the ribs and armpit. By executing short-range techniques with the elbows kept tight in to the body, the muscles of the upper arms, shoulders, and back are strengthened. Just a few repetitions of the basic forms, when done properly, results in extreme discomfort in all of these areas, and after a while it is all you can do to lift your arms.

The most basic forms are known as *sanzhan* which in Japanese is *sanchin*. Indeed, a connection between these forms and Japanese *kata* may be seen both in terms of stance and technique.

There are very few kicks in the five ancestors system and Master Tan advises that it is best not to kick but rather to get in close and use your fists and body.

All in all, it is an unadorned, simple, yet brutally effective art.

• • •

Over the years that I have been studying Chinese martial arts I have trained with a number of teachers who come from what might be termed the "modern tradition." This particular approach is a product of the late 19th and early 20th century movement to overcome and destroy the sectarianism present in the arts so that they might serve as a tool to strengthen and unify the Chinese people. This approach was institutionalized at two major centers.

As I have described, one was the Jing Wu school in Shanghai whose famous chief instructor, Huo Yuan Jia, has since been immortalized in films, books, and television series. This school taught a curriculum which necessitated that students should master a number of basic forms from different styles before going on to specialize. In its heyday, the best masters of the time were employed to teach their specialties and before long branches had been established in several major Chinese cities as well as throughout Southeast Asia.

Following a similar pattern, the Nanjing Central Martial Arts Academy was established in the early part of the 20th century. Again, students were expected to learn a variety of basic forms before specializing. In both of these schools the master-disciple relationship was abolished because it was felt that it was an obstacle to progress. The emphasis was very much on demystifying the arts and making them available to all.

Huang Jifu trained in his youth at Ipoh Jing Wu. Later he went on to train in Singapore with Chen Yu He, who had attended the Nanjing Central Martial Arts Academy and was working as an instructor for Singapore Jing Wu.

Under Huang Laoshi I learnt the basic Jing Wu routines of 12-routine tantui, jiequan, and gongliquan. At the time I was teaching martial arts to a class of children at the school where I taught and these forms seemed ideal for basic training. I cannot say, however, that I had any great interest in them at that stage.

The tantui or springing leg forms originate in the boxing systems of northern Chinese Moslems and are practiced in low horse and front stances and characterized by large, sweeping, swinging movements of the arms and cripplingly effective low toe kicks, which are aimed at the opponent's shins and are known as "inch kicks."

Huang Laoshi used to tell the story of how as a kid he and his classmates used to dare each other to run up to the Sikh guard at a local factory and test the efficacy of their inch kicks on his tree trunk legs. Actually, to hear him tell it, such practice did more to improve their sprinting skills.

Later on I learnt the 10-routine tantui from Tan Ching Ngee. This varied only slightly from the 12-routine version, still placing great emphasis on low toe kicks and large arm movements designed to develop optimum strength and coordination.

Finally, having in the meantime forgotten the 12-routine tantui, I re-learnt it from Master Liang He Qing. As a form, tantui is easy to overlook because of its simplicity and also because of the discomfort involved in repeatedly holding the same, low stances. Hard practice, however, rewards the practitioner with a solid foundation in the basics of the northern school of Chinese martial arts.

When learning 10-routine tantui in Singapore from Tan Ching Ngee, he took me to train in the finer points with one of his leading students, Liang Chee An. Liang Shixiong at that time was in his mid-30s, of medium height, but was a very slim, almost skinny man who owned and managed his own hawker's center, situated on one of the large housing estates which proliferate on the island.

I was to train with him at a small privately-owned temple administered by another of my *shixiong,* Chen Yi Biao, who also served as a priest at the temple. Here, Master Tan held a taiji class twice weekly.

The temple is situated just outside the main city area and on a road flanked by, as yet, undeveloped land. It is set back about 500 yards from the main road and fronted by a large concrete area where the training takes place.

A single-story wooden building with sleeping-quarters at the back, the temple housed a myriad of Buddha images lit by candles. This, together with the constant turning of the prayer wheels, accompanied by a recording of Buddhist chanting, made the whole place seem like a set from the old "Kung Fu" television series. In fact, every time I went there I expected to see David Carradine appear, barefoot and with flute in hand.

When I arrived at the appointed time there was already a taiji class taking place and much of the area in front of the temple was occupied by the 20 or so students who were moving from posture to posture under the attentive eye of Master Tan. Seeing me, he waved and motioned me over to one side of the temple where I could now see Liang Shixiong squatting down with one leg stretched straight out to his side. As I came over he stood up and finished his warm-up by bending over and rotating his knees a few times.

Master Tan's idea was that Liang Shixiong would fine-tune my performance of the forms and also teach me the applications in detail.

Liang Shixiong's movements were crisp and clean with all of the stances held long, low, and steady before he would burst into powerful motion, then once again sink into the stability of a rock-steady posture.

In the past, many masters, it is said, practiced tantui as a complete art in itself, for it contains all the basic techniques necessary to reach the highest levels of skill. Each routine consists of a number of movements repeated a number of times. This ensures that the student establishes a strong foundation. The forms progress logically from simple punches and kicks to more complex high and jumping kicks, footsweeps, and combination blocking, parrying, and striking motions. Also contained within the forms are both methods of applying and countering locks and holds.

Within no time at all I was drenched in sweat as Liang Shixiong urged me to go lower, hold the stances for longer or to punch harder. I tried, but sometimes although the spirit was willing the flesh was just too weak. Several times while trying to go lower

> **"In tantui you use the power of the whole body so that when you use a swinging punch, the waist and shoulders rotate to add power."**

I fell flat on my backside which, while it caused a nun watching from the side door of the temple to laugh, elicited no response from Liang.

"In tantui you use the power of the whole body so that when you use a swinging punch, the waist and the shoulders rotate to add power. The kicks are delivered low and without telegraphing so that the opponent is doubled over by the sudden and unexpected pain and so is vulnerable to your swinging, pounding arms," Liang Shixiong explained while I tried to catch my breath.

To illustrate his point he asked me to square off and spar with him. I took what I hoped was an appropriate stance but, before I could even think to launch an attack at him, he was in motion and I felt a sharp pain in the middle of my shin; then his arms were whirling and scything in front of me and it was all I could do to keep out of their twisting flight path. He stopped and I gulped in air. It reminded me of Xiao Zhang and his meihuaquan: frightening!

Relearning the 12-routine tantui with Master Liang He Qing, I found that although his emphasis was different from that of Huang Laoshi, the routines were essentially the same.

As with all the other styles that he practiced, Master Liang insisted that tantui should be used not only to train solid basic stances but also the "springy" *jing* of the form's name. In order to allow the development of such *jing* the waist must be relaxed so that it can be the originator of the power; at the same time the shoulders and the arms must also be kept loose.

One oft-repeated criticism that he made of my performance of tantui was that I ran through the moves too quickly.

"When you practice make sure that you have a definite purpose in mind before you start. Perhaps you are developing a low stance, or training *jing*, or increasing the height of your kicks. Decide on one thing and then practice in the way which best suits your purpose. You cannot race through the forms every time and expect to significantly increase your skill. Forms must be practiced slowly and precisely. Every move must be correct, then you will develop the skills which the form has to offer and the learning process will be natural."

Thus Master Liang advised me as I massaged my aching hip; the result of rushing through the eighth routine which includes a series of high kicks as well as several rapid changes of direction.

The fact of the matter was that the low stances and extended postures of tantui were so excruciatingly painful that it was far easier to speed through them; so it was that I was constantly being admonished by Master Liang to go slower.

Master Liang also pointed out how even the smallest moves were there for a reason. Right at the beginning of the tantui the fingers of both hands are extended sharply downwards then slowly clenched into fists only to be released again before the exponent moves into the first recognizably martial move.

"This move," Master Liang stated, "trains the fingers for *chin-na*. When you clench the fist you do so one finger at a time, starting with the little finger and then the next and so on, always steadily increasing the pressure."

Chin-na was one of Master Liang's specialties and he spent a great deal of time training finger strength. This he did by kneading a length of sandalwood or rolling a pair of metal balls in his hand practicing various grips as he did so.

In order to teach *chin-na* he favored having students work in pairs, performing an exercise similar to pushing hands where the object was for one exponent to put a lock on his partner, who then sought to escape and counter, and so the game continued. This he preferred to the teaching of specific techniques other than those already contained in forms, because it was natural and relied on changing patterns and responses.

Although I prided myself on my taiji-trained ability to relax and ease my way out of even the most expertly applied lock, with Master Liang my efforts invariably proved to be in vain, so quickly was he able to change from one technique to another. This really was *ting jing* in action.

Chapter Four

Pushing Hands

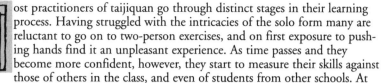 ost practitioners of taijiquan go through distinct stages in their learning process. Having struggled with the intricacies of the solo form many are reluctant to go on to two-person exercises, and on first exposure to pushing hands find it an unpleasant experience. As time passes and they become more confident, however, they start to measure their skills against those of others in the class, and even of students from other schools. At this stage the desire to beat others and become good at pushing hands becomes predominant and often form practice is neglected or even abandoned. Finally, if they have the help of a good teacher, they come to view pushing hands in a more balanced perspective, seeing it as just one of the training methods used to develop taiji skill.

During the time that I spent training in taijiquan in England, very little emphasis was placed on pushing hands. There were a number of reasons for this. Many of the teachers training at that time had not learnt the complete art and consequently spent most of their time concentrating on what they did know: the form.

Huang Jifu taught basic single-hand and double-hand pushing patterns as well as the *si zheng tui* (basic four technique pushing hands pattern) of the Cheng Man Ching school, but he was not particularly keen on allowing his students to do freestyle because of its potential both for injury and for creating misunderstanding as to the nature of the art.

While in China, I learnt some pattern work but the freestyle pushing that I learnt was all in the context of other styles. It was not until I went to Malaysia that I was exposed to pushing hands in all its free-flowing excitement.

To trace the history and development of pushing hands is as difficult a task as any relating to historical research concerning the Chinese, due to the intermingling of fact, fiction, and "official histories" which are dependent for their "truth" on the dynasty sponsoring them. The most commonly accepted story, however, is that pushing hands was developed as a safe way of learning and practicing the art's close-quarter fighting skills. Actual application in sparring situations of taiji *jing* having resulted in too many serious injuries, pushing hands became a substitute for punching hands and kicking legs!

Whether this story is true or not, pushing hands as it has evolved today is certainly an extraordinarily effective method for training the student to preserve his balance at close range, while disrupting that of his opponent. At the same time the student is learning to avoid and neutralize attacks while maintaining a favorable position for counters.

At that time, however, I knew none of this, only having a vague idea that teachers who could push their students a long way away had a reputation as being high-level exponents. There was, and still is, a great deal for me to learn.

It was Wu Chiang Hsing who gave me my first real taste of the flavor of freestyle pushing hands. In his top floor training hall, after he had watched me perform the 48-step routine and the 108-step Yang style form, Wu invited me to push with him. I explained that I had never really done any freestyle; he just grinned and said that it didn't matter. It did. After the opening few rounds of double-handed pattern, Master Wu slipped inside my arms and sent me reeling toward one of the pillars that were spaced regularly around the hall. Moving faster than he had seemed to do when he pushed me, Wu caught me and pulled me back toward him and we started again. It seemed that wherever he touched me he was able to put me off-balance. I, on the other hand, was unable to get my arms into his body and on the few occasions that I did he simply relaxed, rooted, and turned his waist so that I was unable to find his center of gravity.

After a while the whole situation became ridiculous because I was just being thrown, literally, from pillar to post. We stopped and Master Wu went over to a table where he poured out a glass of water for both of us. I needed it for I felt seriously dehydrated.

"Your main problem is that you have no root. That's why it's easy for me to throw you about," Master Wu said. I agreed, there was no disputing that fact. The problem was exactly how was I to develop this elusive root. Master Wu was noncommittal.

"If you practice the form correctly then you will develop a root, but there are also auxiliary exercises that can help."

Being a typically impatient Westerner I asked him how long this would take.

"One or two years if you train hard," he replied with a smile.

This was not what I wanted to hear and I was not convinced; there was doubt in my mind as to what exactly he meant by "root," let alone the training methods necessary to develop it.

In answer to my questions Master Wu invited me to push with him once more. This time he started off much slower and as he executed each attack, he used his arms to guide me into the correct response. So, as Master Wu pushed with his left hand, with the other he showed me how to turn my waist and then how to use this movement to counterattack.

Working in this way we continued for the next couple of hours so that by the time we had finished I had some understanding of the body mechanics involved. As Master Wu introduced new movements he also taught me basic two-person exercises to train these same points. Most of these maneuvers, however, were based on the upper body and the waist, so the whole issue of root still remained something of a mystery to me. But I was not content with the idea of it being something I would have to wait years for. I had heard similar statements about different aspects of the Oriental martial arts over the years I had been training and had found it generally true that hard work and application could considerably shorten these estimates of time. First, though, I would have to find exactly what I needed to do.

Many of the practitioners that I encountered during those first few months training in freestyle pushing hands expressed surprise that I had been studying taiji for so many years and yet still had no root. Lau Kim Hong, Tan Ching Ngee, and Wu Chiang Hsing, in turn, took me from place to place to push with their friends, associates, and students, so that I could get the maximum experience and exposure to different styles and techniques.

It was Master Tan Ching Ngee, however, who first pinpointed the source of my problem, when he noted that in my practice of the 48-step form I "rooted" through my heel; that is, I kept most of my weight over this area. By simply adjusting my stance so that the weight fell through the *yongquan* point in the center of the foot. I immediately felt a difference as my ankles started to do the work instead of my thighs. At that time I had not yet made a commitment to the Cheng style, but I adjusted my stance in the other forms that I practiced so that my center of gravity remained over the correct part of the foot.

At the same time, Master Wu taught me the *xiong jing* or "bear's swing," which is a

Cheng style exercise designed specifically to train the root. This I worked on day and night and still I continued traveling around southern Malaysia pushing hands with whomever I could. By combining the methods of twisting and turning that I had learnt from Wu Chiang Hsing with the new approach to "rooting" shown me by Master Tan, I made gradual improvement.

As I began to feel more confident I made a point of returning to push with those who had first noticed my lack of root and I took great delight in asking them whether or not I had now gained a root. But I still had a lot to learn.

• • •

In Beijing I had searched high and low for a teacher of pushing hands, but without the right *guanxi* (connections) or *yuanfen* (fate), finding a genuine teacher in China is not an easy task. As part of my bagua training I had to take part in their unique form of single-hand pushing, which was practiced to develop the skin of the wrists and forearms so that even the slightest contact with an opponent would cause enough pain to serve as a momentary distraction, which would open him up to further attack.

There was one area beneath the walls of the Forbidden City where a large group, mostly of old men, met to practice pushing hands patterns—but this was not what I wanted to learn. Coach Peng had taught me several of these patterns, but his explanations as to their purpose were at best half-hearted and it was plain that he wasn't convinced of the efficacy of these exercises.

Wherever I went I asked about pushing hands. Then fate intervened. I had been contracted to give a series of lectures on England and the English to a group of Chinese Trades Union representatives who were due to visit England the following spring. My grateful students—they always seemed to be grateful—asked if there was anything they could do for me. I trotted out my, by then well-worn, speech about wanting to learn pushing hands. After the class was over and most of the erstwhile students had left, the leader of the group came up to me and announced that he had a friend who practiced what he thought was taiji pushing hands, and that he could arrange for us to meet. This was exactly what I had been waiting for and a meeting was fixed for the following day.

We met in the hotel complex and retired to the coffee shop of the main building, where we talked over cups of strong coffee.

Comrade Liao, as he introduced himself to me, was a typically tall Northern Chinese with high cheekbones and a long, straight nose. He was also well-built, but his relaxed movements belied this and even gave him a slightly hunched appearance. He wore the standard blue Mao suit and a matching cap which all the time I knew him he never took off. He explained to me that it was not taijiquan that he practiced but rather a style called dachengquan. This style I had heard of but he was able to fill me in on more details. Founded by Wang Xiang Zai in the early part of this century, it was based on his training in xingyiquan, but cut down to what he considered to be the essentials. These included a series of static standing-post exercises, pushing hands, and a set of application exercises.

The reputation of this art was not, however, based on its content alone. The founder traveled the length and breadth of China challenging experts of all systems and, in most cases, winning. Wang was critical of the majority of Chinese boxing methods and he let his actions add substance to his words.

While I was disappointed that I would not have the chance to learn taiji pushing hands at this time, dachengquan seemed a fair substitute. Liao was quite happy to train me twice a week in the pushing hands of his method.

The basic pattern started with the partners linking hands at the wrists, one high and one low, and then rotating the arms in opposite directions. Out of this basic pattern any move could be executed, provided the exponent remained sticking to his partner. Unlike taijiquan pushing, most of the techniques were executed against the arms rather than the body.

Comrade Liao was both soft and relaxed and there was no telegraphing of his intentions. Indeed, the first thing I generally knew of his attacks was when I went flying through the air! As well as the two-person method, he taught me two of the basic standing-post exercises and a method for developing pushing skill while training solo.

With the hindsight of the training in pushing hands I have since received, I now realize what a high level of skill this quiet and modest man actually had and I am grateful for the opportunity I had to learn from him even though, at the time, I did not realize how lucky I was.

• • •

As a result of Singapore's connections with Mainland China at a time when just across the causeway Malaysian Chinese were not even allowed to visit as tourists, a steady stream of instructors of a variety of styles have visited to hold courses and spread their knowledge; many of them staying for months at a time. Many Malaysian Chinese traveled south especially to study with these teachers. Taijiquan has proved particularly popular and leading exponents from all styles, as well as of the new combined forms, have taught in Singapore. Graduates of their courses have then gone on to open classes of their own. This has resulted in there being an over-emphasis on form and many instructors have little or no experience of applications or pushing hands. To remedy this situation the Singapore Martial Arts Instructors Association organized a pushing hands class especially for instructors.

I was first taken to this class by Tan Ching Ngee one Thursday evening. The light was just fading as we turned into the compound of the association's headquarters, behind the Geylang Stadium. On the matted training area on the left an aikido class was whirling and tumbling, *hakamas* forming fan-like patterns in the air as the wearers were upended and then righted themselves. Directly in front of this area was a large concrete playground-like area flanked by a row of trees. In their twilight shade a san cheen do class was practicing techniques on the rank of wooden dummies set in the ground. San cheen do is one of several composite systems established in Singapore, and combines elements of traditional Chinese arts with karate and taekwondo. Its practitioners wear *gis* (karate uniforms) and colored belts, and are well-known for their enthusiastic participation in the regular full-contact fighting competitions held on the island.

Across the car park from this area was another tin-roofed training area where I could see a few people already practicing pushing hands. In the open space in front of this a silat class was in progress. Most of the students seemed to be Malay girls in their late teens and the sweat glistened and gleamed on their brown faces as they leapt and pirouetted through the graceful yet deadly movements of this indigenous Malay art.

Reluctantly, I pulled myself away and over to the area where the taiji class was being held. It was not due to start for another 10 minutes and Master Tan was talking to a thin, elderly man clad in a pair of khaki shorts and a batik shirt. This turned out to be his instructor of 25 years, Master Chen Yu He. Master Chen had studied at the Nanjing Central Martial Arts Academy during the 1930s and counted as personal friends and acquaintances many of the leading martial arts figures in China. Well-known, particularly for his skill with the *jian*, Master Chen was now the internal martial arts adviser to the Instructors' Association and was always present to oversee training sessions.

The three instructors for pushing hands were Master Tan, one of his students, Koh Ah Seng, and a large, tanned man everyone simply called Ah Cheuk. Ah Cheuk had trained with Lu Tong Bao and in the 1970s had won a pushing hands tournament in Singapore and, as a result, was nominated as the Chief Instructor for pushing hands. There was no finesse in his techniques; instead, he simply wrestled his opponent out of the way, if possible throwing them to the floor in the process.

By occupation a seller of fish in the market, it showed. The Fujian dialect he spoke was scattered with obscenities and he made his dislike of foreigners plain.

On that first evening he used me as an object lesson, picking me out and asking me in heavily-accented Mandarin whether I had done any pushing hands before. I shook my head and before I knew what was happening he had pulled me by the elbows into a front stance and then, while all the time explaining to the students around him exactly what he was doing, he threw me here and there as if I were a sack of potatoes to be hurled about. Quite frankly I was extremely pleased when he had had enough. The class then followed what I presumed to be its normal course with the students practicing a whole range of pushing hands exercises, followed by a swift run-through of the *san shou* A and B forms.

Training in these classes was surprisingly organized, perhaps reflecting Singaporean life. At the start the students lined up and bowed to the three instructors. This was followed by warm-up exercises which were actually quite strenuous and included standing-post exercises as well as chain-punching while standing in a back stance. It was Koh Ah Seng who supervised this part of the training, his huge, round body

Master Chen Yu He demonstrating xingyiquan.

trembling in time with the movements of his ample waist.

"Come on, train your gongfu. That's what we're here for," this said with a beaming smile on his sweat-tracked face. The students who varied in age from their early 20s to the late 60s would grimace as they painfully continued. Many of these students were instructors of the new Chinese combined forms and found much of this work extremely difficult.

After the warm-ups the class paired up to run through the series of pushing hands exercises which were used to introduce the students to the type of movement they would encounter in freestyle pushing. Where exactly these exercises come from is uncertain, but most of the variations of Cheng Man Ching style taught in Malaysia practice them in some form or another. They vary from single hand pushing to complex maneuvers that involve pushes, counters, and evasions, all performed in quick succession.

Every five minutes or so, at an order from Koh, partners would be changed and the series would be started all over again. Then when everyone had practiced with as wide a range of partners as possible, it was time for freestyle. Again, partners were changed regularly. Finally the evening ended as it had started: with gongfu training. This time as well as the punching there were countless repetitions of movements taken from both the solo and the *san shou* forms.

By the time the class had finished some of the students, particularly the older ladies, were visibly wilting, but Koh Ah Seng was still going strong and still with that damned smile on his face.

• • •

Wu Chiang Hsing had his own series of exercises similar to those taught at the instructors class in Singapore and it was these that he first taught me in an effort to introduce me gently to the complexities of freestyle pushing.

One morning, before dawn, we were practicing on the rooftop of the building which houses Wu's training hall. We came up there because it was especially cool and the view as dawn broke over the surrounding town and the jungle-clad hills beyond was quite spectacular. As we were running through an exercise which involved each partner pushing their partner's hips in turn, Master Wu suddenly switched tactics and pushed against my stomach. I tried to neutralize his attack by turning my waist, but it was no use. His hand just stuck to me, following my movements until I had nowhere to go but fall over.

"When the opponent attacks your stomach with a push you can yield two ways," he observed. "This, depending on where his hand is placed. If it is in the center of your stomach or to the right (that is when you have your right leg forward), turn your waist to the right and use your left hand to push it away. If, on the other hand, his attack comes to the left, you should use your left hand to push it down and away, turning your waist to the left at the same time."

As I tried to comply with Wu's instructions, he showed me how, if I turned my waist more than 45 degrees away from him, he could easily topple me by pushing against my buttock and shoulder simultaneously. I had in effect "given" him the straight line to push against while the principles of the art demanded that when attacked with straight lines I should defend with circles, and vice-versa. By defending with circles I would give my opponent nothing to push against.

Another point that Master Wu observed was that often I was giving him opportunities that he would not otherwise have had. For example, faced with a push against my back shoulder, I would turn so far that I was left vulnerable either in the manner described above, or because he was able to stick to me until I was completely off-balance and needed only the gentlest of nudges to cause my downfall—literally. My own body would uproot itself. Slowly as I followed his instructions I learnt to move only enough to neutralize my opponent's push; by so doing I was able to give the impression of never being there, yet at the same time my movements were controlled enough that I remained in position for a counterattack should the opportunity arise.

At the same time that I was coming to terms with the way the leg movements of the Cheng Man Ching form developed rootedness, I was learning, in pushing hands, how to pay attention to the waist, the hips, the knee, and the ankle; for the correct alignment of all of these parts was essential in order to develop spring-power in the legs.

• • •

In addition to training with Koh Ah Seng at the Instructors Association, I also spent some time with him when he visited England. Eager to learn all that I could about pushing hands, I quizzed him at every opportunity. Whereas the advice of both Wu Chiang Hsing and Tan Ching Ngee was firmly founded in taiji philosophy, Koh's pushing was concerned solely with the practicalities of effective application.

Since it was Summer we were able to train outside most of the time, ruining the back lawn of Huang Laoshi's house, where Koh was staying. For such a big man he was able to move with startling speed and to change direction at a moment's notice. This he confided to me was one of the key points both in pushing hands and in fighting; the ability to push or pull in one direction, then to sharply change direction or angle, thus causing the opponent to go flying.

It was Koh who showed me how to change, press, or push into an elbow strike, which could cause a great deal of discomfort to an unwary opponent. "Good to use against people our size," he said with a smile and a wink. Indeed he had lots of advice on tactics for use against opponents of all shapes and sizes.

For people who were proving difficult and were large in stature, Koh recommended crossing the hands at the wrist, clenching the fists, and pushing hard against their chest as you stepped in. While not being exactly the most subtle maneuver, it was certainly effective.

"One problem that many people have," Koh said to me one day, "is that they try to use exactly the same tactics on every opponent irrespective of build. Against people who are shorter than you it is a waste of effort to try to push them upwards. Push them down. They're nearer the ground anyway, so that is the natural way. Against taller people, of course you can push them up because they are nearer the sky."

While he was in England Koh taught pushing hands in both evening classes and weekend seminars, and since I knew him and we had practiced together before, I was always chosen to be his partner when demonstrating either freestyle pushing in general, or specific techniques in particular.

One evening at a class at the Ealing Youth Judokwai, where Huang Laoshi held his class, Koh called me up to aid him in introducing the class to pushing hands. The students all sat around the walls of the room, which were decorated as a traditional *dojo* for the practice of Japanese martial arts, complete with a matted floor and photographs of famous masters.

I was quite glad about the floor as I knew that such demonstrations required a great deal of "giving of face" on the part of the junior partner: me! What this practically entailed was that I had to let him throw me around the hall. Many Westerners not familiar with the respect and courtesy demanded between senior and junior exponents of the Oriental martial arts take such demonstration at face value. I have been asked by shocked students how my seniors and/or teachers have been able to throw me around so easily (for do not students always believe that their teacher is the best?). And I have found them quite disturbed when I explained that for me to throw myself is a token of respect for my senior. Such politeness, however, has a positive benefit, for if you are able to give your teacher "face" he is far more likely to teach you more, for you have demonstrated the correct attitude. This is not to say that the teacher cannot do what he is demonstrating, but rather that if he has done a good job in teaching you then it is going to be harder for him to do in a "clean" fashion than if you were untrained. There are still far too many practitioners of taijiquan and other Chinese martial arts who are taken in by demonstrations. There is only one "real" way to determine an exponent's level of skill, and that is to "taste" his art for yourself.

· · ·

Meanwhile, back in Ealing, I allowed myself to be hurled from wall to floor and back again, and the students, duly impressed, avidly took in all that Koh had to teach. In giving him "face" I in no way detracted from his level of skill but instead aided in creating an atmosphere in the class which would best enable the students to learn, as now they "trusted" his gongfu. What every serious student of the martial arts has to learn at some stage in their training career, however, is that sometimes the senior students, or even the teacher, must be tested for real. If the teacher is honest and values this quality in his students then he will welcome such a test, provided it is not in front of juniors or outsiders who might misunderstand. For that reason Master Tan Ching Ngee advised me never to turn down an opportunity or challenge to push hands, but always go somewhere private to do it as this avoids potential misunderstandings.

The first red streaks of an Asian dawn crease the sky and slide their way across the lake. As it gets lighter the trees and shrubs begin to emerge from the shadowy hills that gently slope down toward the water. All around there is sound and movement. In a dim, distant pavilion, a Chinese opera group are warming up, coughing, and then stage-laughing, trying out the occasional high note. Old ladies practicing walking *qigong* shuffle along the paths, arms twitching antenna-like, from side to side like so many ants on the march.

The area where we were is beside a jetty which extends out into the lake, ending in a small pavilion. In front of us the path winds around the bank of the lake away from the open space where we are practicing our form. The ground is hard-packed earth under what will later prove to be the welcome shade of a large oak tree.

Master Tan, myself, and two other disciples were not the only taiji practitioners there. On the other side of the tree is a group of 10 or so people running through the 48-step combined style form. In front of us, at the water's edge, several individuals are practicing a whole range of different taiji styles—including Yang, Chen, and Wu—so that as the light started to fill the shadowy nooks and crannies around the park, our corner seemed to be some strange slow-motion world.

We were not there, however, just to practice form, for this is the place that taiji devotees come to every Sunday morning to practice freestyle pushing hands, and if you turn up you're fair game.

Tan Ching Ngee had brought me down there so that he could show off his latest acquisition: the foreigner who could speak Chinese and do Chinese martial arts.

Also present that morning were Grandmaster Chen Yu He, and after we had exchanged greetings the first overtures were made. A large, burly man approached Master Tan and whispered in his ear. Master Tan turned and gestured toward me; his meaning was unmistakable: he's all yours.

The man came forward and we started pushing. I was tentative at first, feeling him out, content to let him make the first move; a tactic which I have always found to be advisable with an unknown opponent. After the first few moves, he seemed eager to get it over with and to prove to his friends, who by now had formed a small but appreciative audience, that Chinese expertise could overcome foreign brawn.

By this time, however, I had acquired enough skill to neutralize his best efforts and he became increasingly desperate. Sweat broke out in large beads on his brow, and a trembling borne of the effort to appear that he was not making much effort, spread from his body to his arms. Finally, deciding it was no good, he had to stop.

"You very big-size," he muttered in pidgin English as he stumped off shaking his head.

Now there were a dozen or so spectators who had been attracted by the show we had put on and, at the center of the crowd, one gentleman was holding court in a loud and authoritative voice.

"You see, the problem is that the red-haired fellow is using strength and so his opponent also used strength. But if you use the soft to overcome the hard then you will have no problem."

I resisted the urge to smile for the red-haired fellow—that was me—had understood every word of his Mandarin.

Now the expert was nudging one of his cronies forward.

"Go on, have a go. Remember four ounces overcomes a thousand pounds."

His companion stepped toward me in what I felt was a slightly reluctant manner. He was thin and bony and his face was set in a serious mask. I put out my arms and we began. At first we were both tentative and consequently were content just to stay connected to each other. But all the while his companion instructed him in a loud voice to use four ounces, to seize the moment, and to use the soft to overcome the hard. Emboldened by all this advice, he threw caution to the winds and attacked with a frantic forward push. Now, although successful forward pushes are invariably most spectacular, with the recipient flying through the air, they are very hard to execute against an opponent with even a modicum of skill. So it was that as he pushed, I countered, and he fell to the side, only just recovering his balance at the last moment before he hit the ground.

His mentor was not amused. More exhortations to only use four ounces and to find the needle within the cotton followed, as my now desperate opponent resumed his pushing. His arms had now become tense and his feet were shuffling around on the ground as he frantically tried to topple me. But of course the harder he tried the easier it was for me to redirect his attacks. At last he gave up, begrudgingly shook hands with me, and walked back to where his loud-mouthed friend stood.

This worthy fellow immediately looked at the crowd around him and said, "Well it's obvious, the foreigner's so big and he's using strength. It's not taijiquan."

He was surprised when I laughed—surely I couldn't have understood?

Many of the people that I have pushed hands with in the park were sincere and genuine, and in those cases pushing hands with them became truly a learning experience. But still there were always the gunslingers, eager to make a reputation for themselves and equally as eager to find excuses for their failure to do so.

• • •

In the last decade or so, pushing hands has been lifted from the training hall and placed unceremoniously in the competition arena, with events being held all over the world, from Florida to Canton, from Bognor Regis to Beijing, and from Huddersfield to Penang. As with any major development, opinions are sharply divided as to its value and many different sets of rules have been experimented with in an attempt to make contestants conform to the principles of taiji; or in some cases just to make the contestants appear to be practicing taiji when locked in competition.

The debate as to the value of such events has now raged ever since the first competition and it shows no sign of abating. Those who are in favor of competition argue that it promotes the art by attracting young people to learn; for they have something to aim for, some glory to acquire. Also it enables more people to be exposed to the art, whether as spectators or by reading about such events in the local press. The argument is also made that it keeps the art realistic, enabling students to test their skills in a situation that is challenging yet controlled.

On the other side, opponents point out that competitive pushing hands with its weight classes, timed rounds, and restrictive rules encourages battles in which the strongest and fittest win with little room for use of taiji principles. Furthermore, the new students attracted by competition come for all the wrong reasons. Here is the most sweeping argument for training in pushing hands, and indeed in taijiquan in general. The art is concerned not with winning or losing but rather with the development of the highest human potential in its exponents.

Koh Ah Tee, for example, a dedicated opponent of competition, argues that pushing hands is a training method designed primarily to develop and improve sensitivity, or *ting jing.*

"In taijiquan," he states, "the hands must not move."

What this means in real terms is that the practitioner of taiji never initiates the first attack but instead waits for his opponent to move and so expose himself to a well-timed counter.

"If both competitors followed this philosophy, then there would be nothing to see at all, and certainly not the bull-like grappling that you see in most competitions," Master Koh contends.

There is also the question of ego-involvement which is inevitably heightened by the central issue of competition, the desire to win. Koh argues that the taiji exponent should be struggling to completely overcome the ego so that there is no desire to win and so ultimately neither should there be any desire to compete.

On hearing this, one of my students questioned me as to how Master Koh tests his art, and how he knows whether he's on the right track or not. I, in turn, replied as follows: "There's nothing wrong with pushing hands with other people to see what level your art has reached compared to theirs. For in such a situation there is not the external stimulus of a trophy, an audience, and the resultant overriding desire to win. Remember, however, when you compare skills with someone else in this way, that you do not want to waste time; don't be so foolish that you let your opponent play with you. Instead, wait for him to move, and when he does, throw him. This, then, becomes a way of testing the *ting jing* you have been developing through your previous pushing hands practice.

In the same way, if you meet people who want to test your fighting skills, then let them. Just follow the same simple rules: keep calm, let them come to you, and then take advantage of their moment of weakness."

Wu Chiang Hsing, on the other hand, has different views on the issue of competition. A keen participant in competition himself, Wu asserts that doing so gives him an opportunity to test his courage.

"Competition is nerve-wracking, but taijiquan teaches us to be calm and to use relaxation to overcome whatever confronts us. I look upon competition as a form of training. But I am not concerned with winning or losing, I just use it as a test," he says.

Master Tan Ching Ngee, who has successfully participated in national-level pushing hands competition, agrees but goes on to say that the competitor must be careful to assess what is actually going on.

"If you win," he advises, "you must ask yourself whether you won because you used taijiquan methods. If not, you have won nothing. If you have lost, you must also question whether you lost because your understanding of taijiquan was inadequate. In that way, competition gives you even greater opportunities to improve your skills."

• • •

In 1988 I was invited by Master Tan Ching Ngee to be a referee at the First Johor State Taijiquan Championships. This was the first of what has now become a bi-annual event, held on each occasion in a different town in Johor state. This first competition was to be held in the largest town in the State, Johor Baru.

Johor Baru, or JB as it is locally known, is the town closest to Singapore and consequently is the most expensive town in Malaysia, with prices pushed up by the constant stream of visitors from Singapore on the lookout for a bargain.

Master Lau Kim Hong's club was to be the hosts of this event and it was at his training hall that the referee training was held. The rules were based on those used in Taiwan, whereby the competition, which was moving step, takes place in a large circle and competitors are awarded points based on their ability to push their opponent back two or more steps, out of the ring, or in such a way that any part of their body other than their feet touches the floor. Sweeps and judo-type throws are not allowed, nor are prolonged clinches. Following the Taiwan pattern, the referees were expected to conduct themselves in a quasi-military fashion. We were all provided with uniforms and

every judging decision had to be accompanied by the appropriate stance and an ear splitting blast on a whistle.

Just a few hours after arriving weary and jet-lagged from London, I was whipped across the Causeway in Master Tan's car, at the front of a convoy of his students, all of whom were also serving as referees. By the time we had gone through all the appropriate procedures it was already getting dark and when we finally rolled up outside Master Lau's clubhouse, those of his students who had gathered to "act" as competitors for our training, were practicing under arc lights on the large, concrete outdoor training area.

Master Lau Kim Hong practicing push hands with Dave Spencer.

Master Lau had invited his old friend Master Tan to provide a team of neutral referees from neighboring Singapore. Since these were all Master Tan's students and the Johor State Taijiquan Association was paying all expenses, the referees' training had something of the feel of a family outing about it.

There had already been a half-dozen or so of these sessions prior to my arrival. Since I was coming in on the last three days of training, much attention was understandably focused on my abilities, or lack thereof, as a referee.

After a 15 minute briefing, accompanied by diagrams, demonstrations, and whistle-blowing, I was thrown in at the deep-end, refereeing one bout after another while the rest of my brothers/referees sat or sprawled comfortably around the training area and shouted out what was, generally, less-than-helpful advice. "Relax, Nigel, you're trying too hard." "Stand up straight. No, it should be the other leg forward!" And the like.

I was exhausted, embarrassed, and soaked with sweat and so, when a temporary halt was called to the proceedings so that I could be measured for my uniform, I was greatly relieved.

While I rested the tailor fumbled around my person and asked me how wide I would like the flares on my uniform trousers. I tried to decline flares but Master Tan stepped in and informed me that it was what everyone was wearing! Not in England, I thought, but there was no choice. Thus it was that on the day of the competition I stepped out into the arena wearing a pair of smart flares and a natty, matching Mandarin jacket.

But that is jumping ahead.

The next item on the agenda for that evening was a rehearsal of the demonstrations that were to be given. I was to perform sword-sparring with Master Tan and, in front of our appreciative audience we skipped and cha-chaed our way through the fast-moving footwork that characterizes the use of the straightsword. All the while I desperately tried to avoid the mercifully blunt end of Master Tan's wooden sword. Every time he actually hit me there was a smatter of applause from the spectators. By the end of the evening—actually, it was early the next morning—I was not only physically exhausted but also bruised and battered from Master Tan's tender ministrations with the sword.

Three days later when the day of the competition dawned, however, I was as ready as I would ever be. Unfortunately for all present, we were in the middle of a heat wave and even at 8:00 A.M., when we gathered for the opening ceremony, the temperature was well in the 90s and climbing.

The previous night we had stayed in a hotel paid for by the Association and all the referees were in high spirits after their expenses-paid meal and entertainment the night before, which had included dancing and singing to the small hours in a plush hostess bar. So now as we lined up on the playing field outside the large hall where the competition was to take place, my fellow referees had tired eyes but smiling faces.

The event was being held at the Number One Chinese High School, a prestigious private school, which stands on the side of a hill overlooking the town. The actual competition was to take place in the main gymnasium which, with its stage at one end for guests of honor and its tiers of seats for the audience on either side, was ideal for the event. The end of the hall farthest away from the stage opened onto the school playing fields. There was only one snag and that was the heat. With the intense heat that we were "enjoying," the battery of fans high up on the walls of the hall were less than adequate for the task of cooling not only the competitors and officials but also the several hundred spectators.

As we lined up outside, referees behind the student marching band, followed by the competitors arranged in their club teams, we were not to know how much hotter it would become. All we knew was that it was already uncomfortable and nobody seemed to know exactly why we were still standing outside and when we'd be going in. Then at a signal from one of the reception officials standing at the entrance to the school, the band began to play. We could see a flurry of activity at the main gate about 70 yards uphill from where we stood, sweating.

"The Minister of Sport," someone whispered near me as the pool of activity disappeared through a side door into the hall and the band got into full swing. After the band had marched once around the field and into the hall, we followed, closely pursued by the competitors until we were all standing in neat rows inside the hall which was already sweltering hot.

The next hour seemed like one of the longest in my life as a seemingly endless parade of VIPs and local dignitaries gave one speech after another while we fidgeted and yawned and mumbled, until Master Tan was called up on stage and, raising his right hand, led us referees in a refrain of the referees oath, which little ceremony was followed by a similar one for the competitors.

Then, at last, the competition finally started. At first I was extremely nervous, but as the day wore on I became more comfortable—not that the competitors were always happy with my decisions. This was the first pushing hands competition that I had attended and it soon became apparent that it was not necessarily the most skilled exponents who won. Equally important factors seemed to be strength, stamina, and just plain guts. This certainly seemed to bear out the Chinese idiom about the components of fighting skill: *"dan, li, gong, yi,"* which translates as "guts, strength, skill, and art," in that order.

In one match a tall, lanky man in his mid-30s, who looked as if he wouldn't last the first round, confounded his opponent by extending his long arms and repeatedly seizing his wrists; in this way he denied his opponent the opportunity to get in close. Then when his opponent was exhausted from his attempts to get away from the wrist-grasping, the lanky man pushed him, step-by-step, out of the ring.

Perhaps the most bizarre matches occurred in the heavyweight division. Many of the competitors were so unfit that after the first 30 seconds or so of frenetic activity they just leant against each other.

During one particular match which I was refereeing I could hear the two participants talking to each other, "Look, I won't push you if you don't push me, that way we can both rest."

I separated them and then they started again with a few more seconds of frantic activity, after which they once again leaned against each other like fat old stags with locked horns.

When it came time for the forms competition, for which I was also to serve as one of the judges, Master Tan handed me a sheet of paper with a list of all the categories to be judged and the criteria to be used. It was completely useless for me, however, as it was all in Chinese and at that time I could not read Chinese.

The competitors came out into the area six at a time and ran through their form together. The only way I could work out where to write what, was by asking one of my fellow judges, and so it was that I muddled my way through 50 or so performances. I thought I did a pretty good job, but later on when I compared the scores I had given with those of the other judges, my marks were almost the exact opposite of theirs. This can partly be explained by the fact that I was used to competition in mainland China where aesthetics were prized above all else, whereas the other judges were looking for things that I was not yet experienced enough to see: the quality of the exponent's root, whether they were sunk and *song*, and whether their movements conformed to the principles of taijiquan.

The day ended with a series of demonstrations by the master instructors present. A large man, Master Zhu, who had been a student of Yue Shu Ting, performed his fast taiji routine, one which he himself had put together. This was followed by a demonstration of flying crane qigong by a lady teacher from Singapore.

Then it was my turn. To my embarrassment Master Tan had arranged for me, as his pet "turn," to do not just one demonstration but several. First I performed broadsword, then straightsword, and finally baguazhang. By the end my fine referee's costume was a soggy mess. Then I had a few minutes rest while Feng, my wife, was trotted out to demonstrate the 24-step taiji routine.

At last it was the part I had dreaded most: I was to perform sword-sparring with Master Tan. This specialty of the Cheng school is rather like pushing hands with swords, the idea being to stick your blade to that of your opponent, following his movements until you can flow naturally into an attack. We were using wooden swords, but with the fast-moving nature of the exercise accidents were always possible.

Although we had been rehearsing for some time now I was still apprehensive as I marched out behind Master Tan, in time to the Chinese music which he had chosen for our signature tune for this particular demonstration. Reaching the designated spot we both came smartly to a halt and Master Tan spun round to face me. We bowed to each other and both took up our ready position, sword points menacing each other.

For the next three minutes, that actually seemed more like hours, we sped backwards and forwards; the bursts of frantic movement only interrupted by our resumption of the "ready" position after each time that he had successfully "cut" me: once across the shins, once a long slash across the stomach and, finally, in a move that elicited a gasp of excitement and bloodlust from the audience, across the face.

After this move, as we resumed the ready position, Master Tan nodded to me and we came to attention, bowed and marched off. The relief almost made me forget the dull pain of my aching cheek bone and the smarting of my shin.

Although the competition was over that wasn't quite the end of the day. Later that evening there was a large party at a local restaurant for the competitors and the officials.

And so that was my first experience of pushing hands competition. Since then the debate over the value of such events, and their effects both positive and negative on the promotion and development of taiji, has raged on.

• • •

In the United Kingdom, a definitely British form of such competitions has evolved—although for its format it has borrowed the idea of *leitai* or competition on a platform from the martial tradition of China. The matches take place on a platform approximately eight feet by four feet and points are scored by removing your opponent from the platform or by causing any part of his body other than the soles of the feet to touch the platform. The rules are rather less restrictive than those followed in Asia, with both footsweeps and throws being allowed.

While some authorities have argued that such competitions could easily be won by wrestlers or judo players, they have obviously not experienced such contests firsthand. Certainly, I know of a number of extremely competent and experienced wrestlers and *judoka* who have fared badly on the platform.

A less easily-answered criticism is the one that avers that such competitions do little to encourage or promote the use of "real" taijiquan skills.

It seems to me that skill is definitely needed to survive and succeed in such events and that if one is using principles encompassed in the range of knowledge known as taijiquan, no matter how low-level those skills may be considered by "experts," then such competitions have value. And if they serve to attract newcomers to the art and give them the motivation to want to learn, then they are also of value. Furthermore, if such competitions allow martial artists to realize that not all practitioners of taijiquan spend their time in abstract philosophical discussions or "floating like clouds," then they are, again, worthwhile.

During the time I have practiced and taught taijiquan, I have seen quite a number of my classmates and students take part in competition, aim at competition success, and finally achieve the success they desired. Then, satisfied with the progress they have made, but recognizing that taiji has far more to offer them, they have stopped competing and renewed their efforts to get to the heart of what the art is really all about. Looked at in this light, competition is just one step along the path of some, but not all people's taijiquan journey.

• • •

Ever since I first met Wu Ching Hsing and Tan Ching Ngee in 1987 I have struggled and agonized over both the theory and practice of pushing hands. As mentioned earlier, first it was the problem of acquiring a root, which perplexed me. Next it was the question of how to counter specific attacks to particular parts of the body. It seemed that every time I solved one problem to my satisfaction, another one popped up. Of course, although I didn't realize it at the time, this is all part of the taijiquan learning process. The only acceptable, positive, and long-lasting solution to training problems lies in coming to terms with the fact that when you seem to be having the most problems and making the least progress, that is in fact the time when the seeds of further progress are being planted. If you are dedicated to the martial arts you will keep on training, and that is the only answer. The only real secret: more training.

What I found at each successive stage was that whatever it was I particularly wanted to learn, or was having difficulty with, became an obsession with me. So I would wrestle with trying to devise new ways to train to acquire the skill I wanted. I would try to analyze the component parts of this skill and generally fret, worry, and work at the problem until the solution came.

Of course the magical ingredient was and always is time. If you are doing everything right and to the best of your ability and yet you are not getting the desired result, then you just have to keep at it and let time do her work.

Many times since I have been teaching Chinese martial arts, I have seen my students make seemingly sudden bursts of progress and invariably when I ask them what special training they have been doing they reply, "nothing much." Indeed, in some cases they have even stopped practicing for a while. Usually this is as the result of them having trained hard and intensively to improve in some area and then becoming discouraged when they seem to be making no progress, they take a break for a while. Their hard training, however, has planted the seeds and so it is that after a period of time they find that they have made the improvement they desired. In this respect the Chinese martial arts in general, and taijiquan in particular, resemble a pot of tea: unless it is left to brew for a while the full flavor is never found.

Another problem faced by the teacher is coping with his students' success for it is axiomatic that a student should surpass his teacher. Indeed, all of my teachers have been adamant on this point, stressing that just as a father wants his children to do better than him, so should a teacher feel about his students. Easy to say, but in the world of martial arts where you have achieved all that you have through hard work, it is easy to get into the habit of doing everything you can to protect your position; particularly if that position involves people treating you as if you were special. This temptation to always want to be better than your students, at any cost, is further magnified when you realize that your students learn in two years what it might have taken you six years to learn, and, in matters like pushing hands and sparring, you actually "feed" them your gongfu as you work with them.

At various points during my early teaching career I used to get quite desperate when I found that I could no longer throw such-and-such a student as far as I used to, or as easily. Often my desperation would spur me to midnight phone calls to Master Tan Ching Ngee in Singapore, which luckily he accepted with good grace, doing his best to reassure me that this was natural, and then giving me further tips on how to progress.

Of course, with the vantage of hindsight I can see that the fact that some of my students progressed rapidly not only impelled me to try to reach higher standards but also gave me a number of training partners to facilitate this process. Indeed, I feel honored to count those students from the early days among my best friends, for we have grown together.

Sadly, however, there are some teachers who believe that the only way they can keep ahead of their students is by trickery, holding back of knowledge, and the abuse of exaggerated systems of "discipline" and "respect," which serve to protect the teacher from ever being challenged. This is unfortunate because such people not only fail their students but also themselves, as a by-product of their selfishness is that they deny themselves the opportunity to learn from their own students, which enables the knowledge to be kept fresh and alive.

• • •

Taijiquan is an art without limits, for the individual practitioner can continue to practice and improve throughout his life without ever feeling that the end has been reached. Along the way, however, it is easy to forget this and substitute a number of "ends" for this unending path. For me one such "end" was becoming good at pushing hands. Since there are certain approaches and techniques that can be used to acquire a "base" level of skill which then enables the exponent to beat those who have not acquired such skills, the feeling can grow that one has "got" pushing hands skill.

It is a sad fact that many teachers of the art have learnt these basic skills then jealously guard them and use them to maintain their edge over their students. This is a dead-end street, simply ensuring that neither teacher nor students make any real progress.

I have been fortunate in that all of my teachers have always been extremely open with me and I have tried to be the same with my own students.

• • •

After several years of pushing hands practice there came a time when I began to feel bored with it; being able to handle most opponents with comparative ease, and where I did have difficulty quickly being able to analyze my errors and devise a way to correct them. In short, I was getting blasé about the whole thing while consequently making no progress.

It took Koh Ah Tee to simultaneously destroy my false sense of security and restore my interest and enthusiasm. I had first pushed with him several years before and while I felt that he was quite "sunk" and rooted, I felt that had I wanted to I could have thrown him from pillar to post.

Such a judgment, it later turned out, was not a reflection on the level of his gong-fu, but rather a reflection of my lack of understanding of exactly what pushing hands was all about.

When we renewed our acquaintance when I called on him one Chinese New Year in his family home in Northern Johor, I once again had the opportunity to taste his gong-fu. Since I now felt that I "had" pushing hands skill, I was less interested in imposing my will on him and instead just "listened" and followed. What I had entered into out of politeness became a fascinating exercise as I could find no gaps or holes through which to enter and attack. Then I was flying through the air, for in my eagerness to find his weaknesses I had exposed my own. So "clean" was his push that there was no warning and no feeling until, suddenly, my feet were no longer beneath me and I was accelerating toward the nearest wall, which I hit with a teeth-rattling thud.

As we continued pushing Master Koh pointed out to me that I tended to rely on arm strength, which resulted in my not making use of the power of the whole body. There was no feeling of "one moves, all moves," as it says in the Classics.

What he said made sense and it was chastening indeed to realize that I still had much to learn. On this occasion I made little or no attempt to push him, concentrating as I was on trying to put into practice his advice.

When I left, it was with a definite idea of what it was that I needed to work on. For the next few months I concentrated on coordinating the whole body and waiting for opportunities rather than trying to impose my will on opponents. But, as the months passed and I reviewed the occasion in my mind, doubts again began to creep in; after all, I had not really been trying. Surely it would have been a different story if I had put him under pressure?

So it was that on the next free weekend I arranged to travel up to Kuala Lumpur to stay with Master Koh for a few days and put my theories to the test.

The furniture in the front room of his bungalow at that time—what might be called "garden furniture"—was made of metal tubing and white plastic, but most important of all it can be folded and stacked away, leaving plenty of room for pushing hands. With the room thus cleared, and under the stern gaze of Cheng Man Ching looking down on us from a large portrait painted by Master Koh himself, we faced each other and joined hands.

I was determined this time not to give him the least opportunity to attack and also to do my best to test his defensive abilities. As always his touch was soft, yet at the slightest sign of attack on my part his arms transformed into a pliable yet controlling shield. Undeterred I pressed on, seeking an opportunity and then when I thought I had it, stepping in to push.

The result? Nothing. It was like trying to uproot a cliff. My arms collapsed and next I was flying through the air with what seemed like ever-increasing velocity. Before I could go too far on my uncontrolled flight, Master Koh had grabbed my arm and pulled me back to earth. It wasn't supposed to be happening like this. I tried again and again. The end result was always the same: I flew.

On the odd occasion when I was able to find something to push against I was sometimes able to lift his front foot off the floor, but the back foot remained firmly rooted and his counter was always swift and effective.

In the end I had to stop because I was getting nowhere. As we rested and I reflected on my lack of success, Master Koh advised me on what I should be doing. "The first problem is that you attacked too much," explained Koh. "Every time you attacked you gave me an opportunity. I just used your own strength and movement against you. Once I had neutralized your attack you had no choice but to go backwards to avoid over-extending. At that point I just followed you and let you go. Because I was at the back of my stance after your attack I then had the whole length of my stance as I moved from the back leg to the front to develop power and momentum. In the process, I kept my hands and arms relaxed so that you were unaware of what was happening and also to ensure that the power came from my whole body and not just the arms.

"You, on the other hand, almost always attacked when your weight was already on the front leg. This resulted in the power emitting from the arms only; such power is not only less effective but is also usually telegraphed by tension in the hands."

He looked to me for a reaction. All I could do was nod in agreement, for everything he said was true.

"Earlier on you told me that you were worried about not having a partner to prac-tice pushing hands with," he continued, "but, you know, I don't think that this is so important. I feel that I have made the most progress over the last few years when I have had no one to work with other than my own students. I know that many teachers say you must push with people better than you if you are to retain your skill or to contin-ue developing it, but I don't feel this is necessary after you have acquired basic pushing hands skills. I have made progress through thoughtful research."

I found this information not only interesting but also inspirational for I had often worried about how I could continue to improve without others to practice with. A note of caution must be introduced, however, because Master Koh did make the provi-so that such thoughtful research was only of benefit after the necessary foundation skills had been laid. He himself had suffered a tough and intensive apprenticeship at the hands of Master Lau Kim Hong and from which he had aquired a store of experi-ences to rely on in the process of his research. In addition, Master Koh continues to test his art at every opportunity.

As a result of this experience I came away convinced that provided I followed Master Koh's road I could, and would, continue to make progress.

• • •

In Malaysia and Singapore freestyle pushing hands is an important part of taijiquan training, yet many taiji exponents in Britain had never encountered such practice until the advent of pushing hands competition. Then the accusation was leveled against this training that it was something invented by those who first organized these competitions.

That this is patently untrue may be seen in one of the earliest films of Cheng Man Ching, where he and his students are practicing push hands. While the majority of them are practicing the *si zheng tui* pattern, there is at least one pair who are obviously enjoying a freestyle "tussle."

The artificial division of approaches to push hands into those who practice routines and those who practice freestyle is a mistake as they are two sides of the same coin.

Without training in fixed patterns, the student will never develop the precise and basic skills which are the foundation of continued progress; without freestyle, the student will never really put these skills to the test in a free-flowing and unpredictable situation.

Cheng Man Ching placed a great deal of emphasis on the *si zheng tui* and there is no doubt that as well as introducing the student to the intricacies of "ward-off," "roll-back," "press," and "push," it also develops great strength in the legs and flexibility in the waist and hips.

Master Tan Ching Ngee describes it as an exercise in perfection. As he says: "If you wish to make a perfect object, say a container, you must ensure that all the parts are made perfectly, so that where they have to interlock they can do so. In this way the container can fulfill its purpose.

"It's the same with taijiquan: if you seek to acquire the genuine skill you must ensure that all of the factors that contribute to make up that skill are perfect. Therefore, *si zheng shou* is a means of training whereby the four basic skills of *peng, lu, ji,* and *an,* together with the drawing of a clear distinction between substantial and insubstantial, emphasis on an agile and mobile waist, and all the other cardinal movement principles may be perfected."

Another important function of such pre-arranged sequences of movements is that the discipline of adhering to the pattern conversely allows the exponent the freedom to concentrate on fine-tuning their skills.

One vital aspect of such fine-tuning is learning to relax the mind. Without a relaxed yet aware mind, the body cannot take on the same quality of alert relaxation. The development of such ability is closely connected with fighting skill, for when you fight you can't have an opponent in mind or be afraid that you are going to get hit, as either will result in increased tension and consequently slower and less powerful movement.

As the practitioner moves from fixed patterns to freestyle pushing it requires more practice to remain both mentally and physically relaxed. At this stage, the inexperienced exponent will find that his mind becomes fixed on trying particular techniques or avoiding others.

With time, however, you learn to just follow the opponent and make the mind, as Master Koh is fond of describing it, "like a pool of still water." The water responds to whatever affects it, be it a breeze ruffling the surface or a stone dropped into it.

• • •

The living room of Master Tan Ching Ngee's 21st floor flat in Singapore is L-shaped, so that as you walk in the front door, to your left is one part of the L, while the other faces you. In order to create better *feng-shui,* a large trophy cabinet has been placed jutting out from one wall so that it partially blocks the way from the door to the large window at the other end of the room.

The area facing you as you enter and beyond the cabinet contains a suite of heavy rosewood furniture in the traditional Chinese pattern, and a TV. The other part of the

L is used for dining. The walls are decorated with pieces of calligraphy and traditional paintings; many of them gifts from fellow martial artists.

In the dining room area a large glass-fronted cabinet contains hundreds of bottles of different kinds of wines and spirits from all over the world; gifts from students, which as Master Tan seldom drinks, perform a decorative function. Once an English student and myself made an estimate of the value of this collection, deciding that it was worth several thousand pounds.

Whenever I stayed with Master Tan I slept in the small room that doubled as both office and treatment room. One wall was completely covered with shelves full of books and medicines, and the combined acrid-sweet smell made the air in the room somewhat "exotic."

When it was time for training, which might be any time of the day or night depending on Master Tan's mood, the heavy furniture in the living room would carefully be lifted and placed against the walls leaving a space large enough for two people to do form, pushing hands, or sparring.

Since we were on the 21st floor a breeze constantly blew in through the open windows, sometimes causing the wooden weights on the wall scrolls to clatter noisily against the walls.

On this occasion I had asked if we could work on pushing hands and Master Tan was only too happy to oblige. His arms, almost totally hairless and tanned dark brown by the sun, are incredibly light and the skin and the muscle has an elastic resilience which I have noticed as common to most teachers of taiji. There is also a quality of natural relaxation about his "fair lady's hand" which is very different from the almost rigid stiffness required in the practice of the newer combined taiji forms.

Stepping into a characteristically long front stance and hiking up his shorts with his left hand, with his right hand he invited me to join in some basic single-hand pushing. This was the usual prelude to freestyle pushing.

"No, no, your arm is too heavy," he chided me. I had not been concentrating.

"Remember in the Classics the passage where it states that the body should be so light and sensitive that a fly landing on it would set the body in motion. This is the kind of sensitivity you are aiming for."

Master Tan next noticed that I had a tendency to turn my waist more to the left than the right. With the right leg forward, of course it is easier to turn to the left and so, without realizing it, I was giving in and going the easy way.

"When you're training pay attention to the right side, the difficult side. By doing this your waist will become more flexible and your *fa jing* will benefit."

I was still trying to control the lightness of my touch, but finding it very difficult until it was pointed out to me that if I just concentrated on following the opponent, trying to match exactly his force and direction, this difficulty would fade away.

Master Tan stopped and stood up out of his stance.

"You know, you have to be really clear in your own mind about the difference between *rou* and *ruan*. If you can understand this and also know what *song* is, then these principles may be successfully applied to your training.

Rou is to be elastic or pliable like bamboo, so that when stretched and released it springs back—inside there is action and reaction.

Ran, on the other hand, is like chewing gum which, when stretched and released, collapses.

To say that something is *song* it must appear to have substance, but when you attempt to strike it or grasp it, it escapes from you. It's rather like trying to grasp water. Indeed, *song* is very like water; if released on you from somewhere nearby it is like having a shower, but if it descends on you from a great height you won't be able to withstand it.

Some people when pushing hands say that you must be like water, so they play as if they were playing in a warm shower; but when you use the force of a tidal wave or a waterfall, they complain that this is using strength. This is not the case; rather, it is the speed with which the *song* comes at you that gives it the power.

We started pushing again, slipping out of the single-hand pattern into freestyle. Sensing an opportunity I pushed, but like a snake Master Tan's body twisted and suddenly was no longer there. He smiled, and now I knew what he meant by *song* being something that appears substantial and yet suddenly is insubstantial.

Again I pushed, and this time he allowed my hands in to push against his shoulders. At last, the perfect opportunity. I stepped in slightly with my front foot and continued the push, but although I could feel his body I could not find his center of gravity. The harder I pushed the more he leaned over backwards away from me until my arms were also locked straight. Then I could feel it; a kind of fluttering, tearing feeling deep inside his body. The triumph welled up inside me. Master Tan's body then seemed to catapult upright and I was thrown abruptly through the air.

The grin on his face was so wide that it almost stretched from ear to ear.

"This is our tradition, when pushed, we snatch victory from the jaws of defeat. Just like a bamboo bending before the wind, I let you push me backwards until you had over-extended yourself and then I snapped back."

"You see," he went on, "you allowed your arms to become straightened and locked, so it was obvious that you had nowhere to go but backwards. Your force was finished, so I simply followed you and helped you on your way."

As always, I understood what he said, but putting it into practice proved more difficult. For example, however hard I tried just to wait for him to attack, after a few minutes impatience and nervousness would take over and I would rush in.

This time things followed the usual pattern and after the initial circling I attacked. This time, as Master Tan countered, I somehow sensed what he was going to do and managed to "block" his attack. This I did, mainly by dint of using brute force and ignorance. But as soon as he felt his attack was blocked, Master Tan relaxed and my tense force caused me to slightly lose balance. That was enough and, once again, I was flying through the air.

The pushing hands of Master Koh Ah Tee is probably the most refined I have come across. His insistence on adhering strictly to both the letter and spirit of the Classics ensures that every moment spent pushing with him is extremely valuable.

Master Koh's favored teaching method is for students to practice the *si zheng tui* repeatedly, all the time striving to ensure that they just follow their partner's movement and do not allow the slightest bit of force to creep into their practice. Such training often goes on for half an hour to an hour, until the students become so "tuned-in" to each other's movements that they seem to blend into one with their partners.

Through such practice, Master Koh's students develop a refined sensitivity that allows them to just touch an opponent and know his intention.

Having often fallen prey to the desire for a good, sweaty, muscle-wrenching wrestle passing as pushing hands, this training is initially frustrating. However, after some time a feeling of having found a quiet centredness takes over and the practice becomes quite satisfying.

By ensuring that no force is placed on the opponent, Master Koh is always surprised by any attack, as there is no muscular telegraph. Similarly, the insistence on a light, sensitive touch necessitates maximum use of the waist to neutralize the in-coming movement. Additionally, through continued practice the ankles are stretched and strengthened, thus enhancing the exponent's *fa jing*.

It is not necessary, however, to have a partner to glean the benefits of this exercise as it may also be practiced solo. With care and imagination, both flexibility and sensitivity may be trained.

When practicing this exercise with Master Koh you feel as if you are being led ever so gently into a trap; every advance on your part is met with retreat, but a retreat so cunningly timed that unless you are careful you over-extend and fall into what feels like a black hole. No sooner do you find yourself propelled backwards with gathering velocity until you find yourself either on the floor or smashed into some inanimate object.

In executing the *si zheng shou* it is important that you bear in mind the maxim, "in taijiquan there are no hands." Every move is carried out by the body, the arms simply follow like antennae sensing the opponent's intention, or like hoses conveying the body's power to the opponent. While this sounds easy, it is actually quite difficult and requires constant attention to every movement. When the mind wanders away, the hands tend to take over, placing more force on the partner's body than is necessary and moving ahead of, or separate from, the rest of the body.

Master Koh repeatedly points out that taiji comes from *wuji*, or a state of nothingness. As such, it should be without form or shape. Such natural elements as wind and water are good examples of how the formless and shapeless can produce great destructive power.

Good taijiquan should look like nothing special, he insists. It should be performed in such a manner that you don't notice it—you should just walk past someone who's practicing in this manner, without really noticing them.

On the other hand, taijiquan forms that contain spectacular movements, high kicks, and low crouching postures all performed with lots of "martial spirit" are, Master Koh contends, far removed from the real thing.

When I heard him say this I suddenly realized—almost as a sudden burst of enlightenment—why it was that when I was pushing with him I felt so keenly that his skill was what I wanted, but as soon as I went away I forgot about it and returned to a more "external" form of practice. This was precisely because he was in the process of making himself like the wind and water, neither of which you normally notice until the storm wind is blowing or the tidal wave is sweeping down on you.

• • •

In the years since I became a disciple of Master Lee Bei Lei, I have had a number of interesting and painful encounters with him.

One day, after an extended period during which I had not seen him, I received a phone call from Master Zhou Mu Tu, saying that Master Lee had just arrived in Batu Pahat from his home in north Malaysia. On these infrequent visits Master Lee stays for several weeks, holding "open house" in his hotel room in the daytime, and teaching classes every night. The phone call amounted to an order to attend Master Lee's "court," and I duly complied at the earliest opportunity.

Master Lee was staying in the "Happy Hotel," which is situated in the middle of Batu Pahat. The hotel is located on one corner of a square of shops and bars, and visitors to this area in the evening will notice the number of open windows at which "casually dressed" young ladies sit, back-lit by red lights. It is that sort of hotel.

Master Lee's room was on the third floor and by the time I had trudged up three sets of stairs he was standing outside on the landing clad only in a pair of black training trousers.

His torso was, if anything, more muscular than I remembered and his gap-toothed grin of welcome seemed to contain even less teeth than previously.

My hand was engulfed in the powerful grip of two palms, both of which were not much smaller than my head, or so they felt.

"You've got fatter," he rasped. I had forgotten just how difficult it was to understand his heavily-accented Mandarin.

Master Lee ushered me into a large room, to one side of which were placed two double beds. The center of the room was clear, with all the furniture pushed to the sides. Obviously the room had been chosen for its usefulness as a training area.

There were half a dozen other people sitting around the room who got up as I came in. I knew at least four of them as *"shixiong."*

Then came the calm before the storm. I was shown to a seat, and for the next half-an-hour or so we caught up on each other's news—all the taiji gossip, who had pushed hands with whom, whose standard had improved or declined, and who was regarded as being the man to challenge.

One of the people I had not met before was a small but solidly-built man in his early 30s. As we were talking he pulled on an elastic knee-bandage, a sure sign of what was about to follow.

"Why don't you let Ah Hen have a play with you?," Master Lee suggested.

I knew it to be an order not a suggestion and, not wishing to appear reluctant, leapt to my feet.

We squared off and joined hands. Ah Hen was phenomenally strong, nor was there any subtlety or finesse in the first contact. He simply gripped one of my arms at the wrist and locked his other arm under my armpit. He then pushed with what seemed like all his might.

I was taken completely by surprise as I had been expecting some tentative "probing" before the launch of any all-out assault. It took nearly all my strength to hold him off and for the next couple of minutes we wrestled back and forth. It was not, however, just a case of brute force and ignorance—he was able to use *ting jing* to avoid any attempts I made to counter, and when I sought to soften the contact in order to escape his grip he simply followed my motion. Finally, as he attempted to swing me around, he committed himself enough that I was able to execute the same attack on him, compelling him to sit on one of the chairs at the side of the room.

At that point we both stopped to rest. I certainly needed it. Over the previous few months I had been doing a lot of stamina and fitness training and had this not been so I think that I would simply have collapsed in the face of his attacks.

But my respite was to be all too brief, for the next "contender" stepped up, having first visited the bathroom, then emerged taking off his belt and rolling up his trouser legs! For a moment I wondered if he was some kind of Chinese freemason.

This man, Ah Kune, was the chairman of Master Lee's club in Batu Pahat, but, unlike the majority of other Chinese club officials that I had come across, he obviously did not regard his role as being that of an honorary official. He was a large man with the kind of puffy-skinned face that usually denotes too many hours spent in smoky bars enjoying fine brandy and the company of maybe less-fine women.

His solid body, however, denied the tale told by his face and although his initial contact was soft, it was swiftly followed by a ferocious attack. I held him off as best as I could, his occasional softness allowing me to move him backwards from time to time.

This epic struggle finally came to an end when, with a ghastly ripping sound, his shirt split from armpit to waist. This was unfortunate, as he was due to go straight on to a business meeting in Singapore. So now it was a case of him having to leave early so as to call in at his house to fetch a new shirt before embarking on the two hour drive south to Singapore.

Throughout these two encounters Master Lee had sat on the sidelines, occasionally growling out advice in Hokkien to my opponents, or in English to me.

Now, obviously the urge for action got the better of him and he stood up and came over to where I stood panting.

"You sound like a steam train," he said with a laugh and extended his arms toward me. Almost immediately on making contact he slammed me backwards through the air so that I ended up sprawled on the sofa behind me. He pulled me to my feet and repeated the process, this time sending me to one side so that I ended up in an arm-chair. There was just no time for me to prepare myself, for his initial contact was gentle. The third time I turned to the side but he followed. A couple more times I was able to thwart his attacks by dint of sideways movement, but then he caught me straight on with a tremendous push that propelled me through the air. I hurled backwards, losing my footing and smashing down on to one of the beds. On impact this metal and wood structure exploded, leaving me on the floor entangled in a mess of mattress, sheets, wood, and twisted metal.

"Oh, sorry, sorry," Master Lee repeated. He didn't sound it, as he pulled me out of the wreckage.

When I expressed my concern about the bed, Master Lee dismissed it with a wave of his hand, "Never mind, never mind." And we continued our pushing. That is to say he pushed while I, for the most part, flew through the air.

Abruptly he stopped and returned to his seat.

"Walk around a bit and then drink some water," he commanded.

I did as I was told.

The afternoon passed in this manner: bouts of muscular pushing hands interspersed with periods of rest spent discussing training methods and the comparative skills of various well-known exponents. As usual, the talk turned from pushing hands to fighting and it was then that Master Lee got to his feet again. Somehow I knew that this was not going to be something that I would enjoy. Sure enough, it was me that he wanted as his partner.

"It's a mistake to make fighting out to be something complicated," he rasped. "Attack me!"

I lunged at him with a punch to the face which he parried with a vast, meaty paw, sending pain shooting up to my shoulder. He continued his attack with a backfist, which I was just able to parry. Mentally I congratulated myself on this, but all too soon, for the next thing I knew a wave of pain from my gut sent all the air shooting out of my lungs and doubled me over, gasping for breath.

His backfist, which had not been designed to do anything more than to get my attention, had been immediately followed by a sidekick to the stomach.

I looked up to where Master Lee stood, his feet together and arms folded across his chest.

"See, it's simple," he said as the gaps between his teeth seemed to widen with his smile.

● ● ●

Master Tan Swoh Theng's approach to pushing hands is colored by his background in five ancestors boxing, which also features a number of similar two-person practices—although much more use is made of the physical strength of specific body parts. Since five ancestor boxing is also a close-quarter art, with strikes being delivered from close range as the opponent is trapped and unbalanced, Master Tan sees many similarities between the two arts.

Thus, when pushing he is prone to use locks and strikes as well as throws and sweeps. Although this makes the training process less relaxed, it does give you a good idea of the realities of fighting at such a range.

"It is not enough," Master Tan notes, " just to focus on using the soft to overcome the hard; we must also have the ability to use the hard to overcome the soft."

One of the innovations he has made in order to better teach his students how to use their arms to trap and control the opponent, is to practice pushing hands while sitting down.

By making the two practitioners sit down, the necessity of always paying attention to the stance is removed, so more attention can be paid to the role of the waist and the upper body. Master Tan is quick to point out that this exercise is not a substitute for conventional pushing hands, as the development of a firm, rooted stance is vital; rather, this exercise supplements and complements such training.

The participants sit on the edge of stools opposite each other with their feet placed more or less as they would be if they were standing. Arms are then joined and the fun commences. The only rule is simple: the two students must keep both feet on the ground and their bottom on the stool.

The Master's favorite tactic is to lock up his opponent's arm in such a way that he has no avenue of escape than to fall off the stool. He pays much attention in his teaching to ensuring that the student is able to change quickly and automatically from one technique to another. The pushes he delivers depend more on generating power over a short distance which shocks the opponent's whole body, as opposed to the "long" force most usually associated with taijiquan.

When practicing the more conventional standing pushing hands, whether fixed step or moving, Master Tan emphasizes the importance of a long, strong stance.

"When your opponent closes with you just relax and let your whole body become like a bag of water. How can you grab a bag of water? No matter what you do it will escape. Then, when the time is right, lock him up so he has no escape and then push him over."

Such advice is always followed by a practical demonstration and it is not long before I'm flying through the air or having close encounters of the painful kind with the furniture.

"Control of the opponent's elbow and shoulder is very important when pushing hands, for it prevents him from attacking and also makes him vulnerable." So saying he grabbed my arm, simultaneously pulling and twisting, his fingers like spikes digging into nerve clusters.

"Attacking the body's weak points is useful, particularly when attempting holds and locks, as it serves both to distract your opponent and to set him up for your finishing techniques."

Master Tan releases my arm and I try to shake and prod some life back into it.

"I don't agree with some aspects of pushing hands competition," he says, sitting down and indicating that I should also do the same.

"For example, many times, whether in pushing hands or in actual fighting, you have to take a step backwards or to the side in order to counter. With the rules as they are presently here in Malaysia, if the opponent pushes at the same time as you step you can end up losing points. Does it not say in the classics that you have to go back to go forward? By taking that backward step the opponent's attack may be neutralized and then his force may be 'borrowed' and returned."

I agreed that this was true, but replied that I failed to see how the rules could be changed.

"Well, the most important thing is not just changing the rules but rather ensuring that the referees are adequately trained and know enough to identify whether the participants are actually using taiji methods. All of this embracing and wrestling is boring to watch, does not represent what taiji is all about, and if it becomes habitual it would get the exponent seriously injured in a fighting situation."

Such attention to the realities of fighting, both armed and unarmed, is characteristic of Master Tan's teaching. And although it makes training sometimes painful and unpleasant, it also serves to keep it realistic.

● ● ●

For several months Koh Ah Tee had been trying to arrange for us to do some pushing hands with exponents of the Chen style. In Kuala Lumpur there is quite a large school with Chen Xiao Wang, a descendant of the founders of the style in the Chen family village in China, as its chief instructor. Master Chen is regarded in China as the lineage holder of the style. Currently based in Australia, he makes regular visits to his schools in Malaysia and Singapore. He and Master Koh have met on several occasions and on the second, Koh asked him if he could do some pushing hands with him. At first Chen Xiao Wang seemed eager to accommodate him and they parted with the understanding that a suitable date would be arranged. A few days later, however, Chen phoned to say that he was willing but the committee members of his association felt that it was not a good idea and, therefore, he would have to call off the encounter.

Master Koh was extremely disappointed and could only speculate that Chen Xiao Wang being famous in the world of martial arts had too much to lose should he not be seen clearly to "win."

When he told me this story, Koh was at great pains to stress that he was not out to "beat" Chen Xiao Wang or to tarnish his reputation; rather, he sought to determine for himself the level of Master Chen's gongfu and to try to learn from the experience what he could about the comparative merits of the Chen and Cheng Man Ching styles.

Since I, too, had never had the opportunity to push hands with Chen stylists, Master Koh next contacted the chairman of their association to see if a pushing hands session could be arranged with interested exponents, seeing as it was not possible to push with the chief instructor. He explained that he had a friend from England who was a pushing hands enthusiast and who would very much like the opportunity to gain some experience. But it was all to no avail. The chairman said that it could not be done.

Our last resort was to go to where we knew there were Chen stylists practicing and see what would happen. In the meantime, however, the man responsible for popularizing Chen style in Malaysia, Master Wong, had fallen out with the association and left. This, Master Koh felt, might well prove to be an avenue worth exploring.

So one Saturday morning we set out for the famous Tian Hou Gong temple, a landmark tourist attraction built on the summit of one of the hills overlooking the city of Kuala Lumpur. We were not sure that there would be anyone there practicing Chen style, but Master Koh had heard that there was a class being taught there.

As the car completed its laborious climb up the narrow, wriggling road to the top of the hill, the ornate blues and greens of the temple's tiled roof decorations gleamed in the sun.

Around the car parking area in front of the temple stood an array of life-sized, painted clay figures from Chinese mythology—ranging from the Eight Immortals to characters from the classic *Journey to the West,* including the mischievous monkey.

In the open area underneath the temple's main steps I could see several people practicing Chen style. We were, for once, in the right place at the right time.

After parking we walked over to take a closer look. There were three people of markedly different shape and size practicing. The largest one, a man well over six feet tall and weighing about 200 pounds, looked the least expert; while the smallest, who was about five-foot-four and on the skinny side, seemed to be leading the group. As we watched, they twisted and spiraled their way through the moves of the first form of the Chen style. This form, some taiji historians have it, is the forerunner of the Yang style long form, being smooth, slow, flowing, and continuous.

The second Chen form, *pao chui* or cannon fist, by way of contrast, contains jumps, high kicks, a full range of explosive actions, and is far more obviously martial both in content and execution.

As we watched they came to the end and then, while the large man rested, the small senior student and the other member of the trio, a man of average height and build, began to stomp and pound their way through *pao chui.*

Master Koh turned to me and remarked that one of his students, a Taiwanese businessman, had studied Shaolin *pao chui* when he was young and not only were many of the moves similar to those of the Chen style, but their names were also almost identical.

I knew what he was getting at. What we were seeing being performed in front of us seemed very far removed from the Cheng style approach to taiji.

With a final flourish and a stamp of their feet they were finished and it looked like their training for the morning had come to an end.

Master Koh ambled over to the senior student, who was wiping his neck and face with a towel, and opened the conversation by asking if it was indeed *pao chui* that they had just been performing. Seeing his interest the other two came over to join in the conversation and Master Koh introduced me and himself as being two enthusiastic practitioners of the Cheng style, adding that I had come all the way from England to gain experience in pushing hands.

This was true, but he had neglected to mention that I had left England a couple of years before. By intimating that my time was limited he hoped there would be more chance for some actual pushing.

At this point the big guy excused himself; he had not been studying long, did not know pushing hands, and, besides, he had something to do!

Then there were two.

Surprisingly enough, in view of his self-confessed seniority, the little man was next to go; he too, apparently, was very inexperienced at pushing hands and also had a pressing appointment. Maybe some other time in the unspecified future!

The third member of the group, on the other hand, was quite keen to stay and chat and would certainly like to "exchange" experience.

Mr. Chen, an appropriate name, had been doing taiji for 11 years, having started off training under a student of Huang Hsing Hsian before switching to the Chen style. He explained that he preferred this style as, being a young man, the more martial emphasis suited him.

After a half-an-hour or so of talking we retired to one side of the temple where a small road giving access to the temple kitchens came to a dead-end.

Here, out of sight of inquisitive eyes, we were to do some pushing.

Since I was junior, it was my turn first. This was something I was looking forward to as I had never before encountered a Chen style exponent in pushing hands.

The first surprise was that Mr. Chen took up no obvious stance, instead he stood with his legs about shoulder-width apart and with his left leg forward, knees not noticeably bent. Then he gripped my extended arms quite hard at the wrists.

This was not what I had been expecting, for from what I had seen of films of Chen Xiao Wang and other members of the Chen family doing pushing hands, they normally took up a long, low stance. In films they also seemed to keep their hands open even though at wrist height, rather than the elbow height I was used to.

In order to counter his grip I took a longer stance, sank down, and turned my waist, causing him to reach out on his left side. For the next few minutes we just moved, with Mr. Chen attempting to jockey for a position where he could make use of his grasp on my wrists, while I just sought to prevent him from getting comfortable.

Then, all of a sudden, he changed tactics and charged straight in at me.

That was the opportunity I had been waiting for and he fell over and to one side. Recovering, he attempted the same tactic several times, each time with a similar result.

Trying another approach, he attempted to put a wristlock on me, which caused me to instantly relax my wrist and then roll him back with the other hand. By now he was panting hard, because he had been doing most of the work.

In order to save face all round I started to breathe heavily myself, and asked if we could stop.

"Very tired," I gasped.

He looked incredibly relieved and paced up and down swinging his arms as he attempted to get his breath back. He didn't notice the smile exchanged between Master Koh and myself.

When he had recovered, it was Master Koh's turn. Once again Mr. Chen took up his non-stance and gripped the arms, but rather than staying in this position as he had done with me, instead he charged straight in.

Master Koh let him come in and rode the force, shuffling backwards untidily several times.

To the uninitiated spectator this backward movement would look quite sloppy, but I knew what he was doing: feeling, sensing, and getting the measure of his opponent. By now, however, Mr. Chen was getting wise and he switched tactics, going for an arm lock.

In one fluid motion Master Koh sank into his stance and seemed to fling away his opponent's arms. Mr. Chen was left no recourse but to charge in again, only to be neutralized by a stance as rooted as the cliched "mighty oak."

At this point I should describe the place in which we found ourselves. On one side was the temple and blocking off the end of the road a high wall surrounding an outdoor storage area. This wall extended right to the edge of a sheer, though grass-covered cliff, which dropped sharply about one 150 feet down to a mini-plateau, on which was built a large house complete with tennis court and swimming pool. Over and away from the side of this hill stretched the suburbs of Kuala Lumpur, out as far as the distant, mist-wreathed highlands.

Meanwhile, back in the fray, Master Koh neutralized one more gigantic shove and then turned his defense into offense, sending Mr. Chen hurtling, at terrifying speed, toward the cliff.

Without allowing Mr. Chen to become disconnected from him, however, Master Koh followed his rootless retreat and caught Mr. Chen a fraction of a second before he made his first parachute jump without the aid of a parachute.

Mr. Chen looked behind him and down and the blood drained from his face as he began to shake. Bending over, he tried to get his breath and recover his composure.

I felt sorry for him as I, too, had been on the receiving end of Master Koh's seemingly relaxed pushes—and they were terrifying enough without the realization that you had only been a fraction of a second and a short stumble away from almost certain death.

Not surprisingly, after that Mr. Chen no longer wanted to continue. So we all retired to a local coffee shop for breakfast.

During the meal time conversation Mr. Chen mentioned that his first Chen style teacher had been Master Wong but, after the latter's split with the association, he had lost contact with him. Chen did tell us, however, that he thought Master Wong still practiced with a small group of students at the temple every Sunday morning.

So it was that the next morning found us once again heading for the Tian Hou Gong temple. When we arrived, since we were not sure exactly where they would be practicing, we made a quick, circular tour of the outside of the temple complex.

It was in the car park at the rear that we finally struck lucky. Practicing Chen style form in one corner was a tall, well-built man, whom Master Koh told me was Master Wong, and another man who seemed to be his student.

While Master Koh went round to the front of the temple to fetch his car I waited and watched. It was straightaway evident that Master Wong was at a higher level than the exponents we had watched the previous day. His movements were smoother and more rooted in appearance, while the power of his waist was evident in the techniques where the *fa jing* was released.

Every so often he would stop and correct his student's movements. Sometimes he would explain the application in order to clarify the way a particular technique should be performed. It was obvious that he was a careful and painstaking teacher.

I thought back to what Koh Ah Tee had told me about Master Wong; how he had taken part in both form and pushing hands competitions in China, where he had enjoyed some success. Always eager to improve his own standard Wong welcomed opportunities to push with people from as wide a range of backgrounds as possible. All of which augured well for our coming encounter.

By now Master Koh had arrived and we moved over a little closer to watch as teacher and student continued and then concluded the lesson.

This was the moment Master Koh had been waiting for and he walked over to Master Wong to introduce himself. They had met before at several taiji functions, he explained, but it was obvious from the puzzled look on his face that Master Wong did not remember him. Then Mmaster Koh introduced me, as he had done so many times before, as an enthusiast from England intent on seeking more pushing hands experience. Surprisingly enough in view of his reputation, Master Wong did not look overjoyed to hear this news.

The conversation continued as they talked about mutual acquaintances—myself and Master Wong's student were left to stand on one side. I was used to these long periods of inaction and comparative boredom, which were more than made up for, usually, by the action that followed.

Now Master Wong came over to me and speaking in excellent English asked me some questions about people I had trained with—it seemed we, too, had several mutual acquaintances. Then it was down to the nitty-gritty. It appeared that I was to be served up to the student first. I looked over at him more carefully.

He was not a big man, maybe five-foot-four and of slender build. In fact, the sort of person I least like pushing hands with.

From bitter experience I have learnt that what such people lack in size they make up for in aggression and sheer tenacity, moving in and sticking to you like a love-starved Jack Russell.

I tried to get these thoughts out of my mind as we joined hands. Like his fellow-stylist of the previous day, he engaged at the wrists and kept his body further away than I would normally have expected—obviously he wasn't a Jack Russell.

Rather than attempting to stay fixed in one place he shuffled around, occasionally jerking at one or other of my wrists, attempting to make me lose balance to the side.

One thing I have learnt from my pushing hands experiences over the years is that people are most often vulnerable to the techniques they themselves prefer. This proved to be the case as I stepped in and with one hand on his shoulder, the other using his grip on my wrist, I rolled him back to the side. Both his feet came off the floor and I just managed to catch him before he fell over. We continued, and a few moments later I was able to do the same thing to the other side. So it went on until to save his face I begged exhaustion and we stopped.

Then came the major disappointment. Despite all we had heard to the contrary, and despite Master Koh's coaxing and ultimately less than subtle hints, Master Wong would neither push with me nor with Master Koh. Instead, he talked about his experiences and his expectations, which was all very interesting but not what we had come for!

Chapter Five

Applying the Arts.

t the heart of all martial arts systems lies the premise that the original *raison d'etre* of the art is as a system of individual combat, whether armed or unarmed. For a number of reasons, as these arts have emerged into the 20th century, in some cases this premise has been submerged so that the art's are primarily presented as a system of therapy, a spiritual discipline, or a sporting endeavor.

Having started my martial arts career studying karate, where at least the applications of the art in fighting seemed obvious, I had the expectation when taking up Chinese martial arts that the martial aspects would be as obvious, and the necessary skills would be developed in the same manner. Unfortunately, this was not the case.

First, there seemed to be no sparring, at least not as the term is understood in karate or taekwondo. Instead, there seemed to be an overemphasis on forms and occasional mention of ancillary exercises which never seemed to be practiced in class. Second, the training seemed to be conducted in a far less serious manner. There was no obvious external discipline as there was in karate. People rested when they wanted to and there was little in the way of exertion.

Of course as time passed and I learnt to look below the surface of things—an essential skill when dealing with things Chinese—I began to see that very little of the real learning went on in class. Indeed, these were only a kind of public front and very often served as a kind of screening process to enable the teacher to identify the students with either the right attitude or a genuine ability, or ideally a mixture of both. Such students were then encouraged to seek extra tuition from the teacher. This might involve becoming a disciple, or in the case of teachers coming from a more modern tradition, just in forging a closer relationship with the teacher so that he would take more notice of the student.

Very little, if any, in the way of application and fighting training is conducted in regular classes as, apart from any other considerations, the majority of students, particularly in a taijiquan class, do not attend to learn these aspects of the art.

While training with teachers in China I had often asked about applications of the movements. The younger ones such as Coach Peng were happy to demonstrate the way in which each particular move could be applied, but there was never any attempt to systematically practice such applications.

My baguazhang teacher, Master Gao Zi Ying, on the other hand, who was then in his 80th year and who had been fighting challenge matches before my father was born, insisted that not only did I know the applications intellectually, but also that I was able to do them physically. He also insisted that I practice a whole range of auxiliary exercises such as specific weight training to build up my forearms, kicking a post set in the ground to develop powerful, low scooping kicks, and standing post exercises in which force was exerted against young saplings, thus developing a springy, tensile strength.

Despite these additional exercises, form lay at the core of the training and it was at the college where I taught that I received an object lesson in the value of intensive form practice.

• • •

Knowing of my passion for Chinese martial arts, some of my students invited me to train with the college wushu team. At that time the team had only just been formed and was composed of a number of individuals with different levels of experience and ability. There was no official coach so the third year student who was deemed to have been training for the longest time was elected as informal team leader.

A slim, tall youth, Hou He Ming had trained since childhood in tongbeiquan (a northern style with loose, flailing arm motions based on the movements of an ape), which he performed with flawless ease. Using the arms in a relaxed whip-like manner, in performance the exponent of tongbeiquan wears a tunic with extra-long sleeves which are flicked out at the imaginary adversary.

The other members of the team came from a variety of backgrounds, including changquan (long fist), meihuaquan (plum blossom boxing), nanquan (southern box-ing), baguazhang (eight diagram palm), and xingyiquan (form and will boxing); and it was at the hands of an exponent of xingyiquan that I received my lesson.

Xiao Chen was not a student at the college but was the 17 year old son of two lec-turers and thus, as a member of the *danwei* (work unit), was eligible for the team. He had trained in xingyiquan for the previous three years.

All of this I found out the very first time I met him, for he was brought up to me and introduced as someone who would like to "spar" with me. This sparring, it was explained to me, would be "soft touch," which I took to mean light contact.

As I watched Little Chen warm-up, Xiao Huang, another member of the team and the one who had affected the introduction, told me that Chen was a great fan of Bruce Lee. Just how this had come about I wasn't sure, for all of Lee's films were banned in the People's Republic of China at that time. But Xiao Chen had obviously seen or heard about them, for as we faced off to start he adopted a Lee-like pose and even began to make meowing noises. We both moved around each other, him hopping from leg to leg, me shuffling cau-tiously. Then he attacked, launching a front kick at me that if he had connected would have left some nasty bruising on my lower abdomen. So much for soft touch!

I managed to sidestep and deflect the kick, sending him slightly off-balance, but he recovered quickly—very quickly. Now it was my turn to take the offensive.

When practicing karate, my favorite technique had been a fast roundhouse kick off the front foot which sent the top of the foot slamming into the opponent's face, usual-ly with enough force to set them up for a follow-up technique. Obviously this was not something that the aspiring "Little Dragon" was used to, for my foot not only connect-ed with his face but did so with enough force to knock him to the ground.

My first reaction was one of panic. I imagined being deported or worse for phys-ically abusing a Chinese teenager. But such thoughts didn't last for long for the Little Dragon got up, but now with fire in his eyes. Instead of the leaping about which he had previously favored he now took up a steady stance and then rapidly advanced on me with a series of low-level punches. His attack was too fast for me to do anything other than move backwards as fast as I could and desperately try to parry down his inexorable attacks. He was advancing too fast, however, for me to maintain the distance between us at which I could comfortably counter. He just kept closing in; then came the pain.

One of his low punches, backed by the weight of his body and the speed of his advance, had thudded into my groin. Now it was my turn to sink to the ground clutching my injured extremities. Even as I was going down I heard Xiao Huang say quite clearly:

"That's xingyi; he's using xingyi."

That was little comfort to me.

Some time later, when I had recovered somewhat, Xiao Chen told me that he hadn't done much sparring before, as his xingyi teacher had said to him that it was more important to practice form. I would vouch for that, for once Xiao started putting into practice what he knew, he completely messed up my fighting distance, put me on the defensive and finally finished me off.

Over 18 months later and back in England again, after having spent most of my time in China only practicing form, application, and auxiliary exercises, this lesson was reinforced when a fellow student of Huang Laoshi's invited me to spar with him. Prior to learning taijiquan and northern Shaolin from Huang Laoshi he had studied choy lay fut (Cantonese romanization), a southern style developed in Guangdong Province.

My classmate, Peter, was a tall, stocky man in his mid-20s who shared my passion for Chinese martial arts in all their varied forms and manifestations. We met regularly to train.

On this occasion we faced off and Peter took up a long, low stance, while I stood in a more upright bagua stance. Knowing by now that the best thing to do was to wait for my opponent's attack, I just stood my ground. Then suddenly he was moving in; his arms sweeping through the air in large circles. I managed to avoid the first two blows and then in an instant the angles changed and he was thrusting a straight punch at my face. My forward hand came down to parry and control the attack and as it did so I stepped forward and the other hand slid up his captured arm to attack his throat. I don't know who was more shocked, him or me. There had been no idea in my mind of executing this particular technique; it had just happened. The nature of the technique, however, was not accidental. It was the first move from the 64 hands form of baguazhang. This beginners' form was the one that Master Gao Zi Ying had especially emphasized when teaching me. During the time I had spent training with Master Gao in China I had probably repeated the form and this move thousands of times. All that training had obviously had an effect, as Peter could testify. Luckily, I had been able to "pull" what was essentially an extremely dangerous strike.

Above all, this incident convinced me of the efficacy of forms training, for at that time I had been concentrating almost exclusively on form and application and had done little in the way of sparring. It also reinforced my respect for the windmilling arms of the choy lay fut practitioner, for had one of Peter's strikes landed I would, at the very least, have suffered a nasty headache.

These two incidents caused me to question the assumption I had made, based on my years of karate practice, that sparring was essential to the development of combat skills. In my subsequent research I have found few Chinese masters of traditional arts who agree with the kind of sparring often found in karate and taekwondo schools in the West. Those who said that they had practiced sparring usually turned out to be describing something amounting to almost all-out fighting, with the teacher calling up his students one-by-one and then beating them, often quite severely.

Many students of Lu Tong Bao describe such an experience and often, in turn, went on to mete out similar treatment to their own senior students. This was done to give their students the courage to face any challenges they might meet when teaching themselves.

The idea of pulling punches in this process was almost unheard of. After all, what is the point of training differently from how you would actually fight!

The most important lesson I learned from these experiences and, as later training subsequently reinforced, was that the range at which real fights occurred was subtly different from that to which my previous sparring training had accustomed me. The Chinese internal arts in particular train the student to work comfortably at close range and to use tactile sensitivity to flow through, flood over, or sweep under the opponent's defenses. In that paradoxical manner which is the way of so many things in the internal martial arts, the flowing fun of pushing hands, which seemed so far-removed from the violent realities of fighting was actually far better preparation than hours of "soft tap" dancing.

• • •

Huang Laoshi was keen that his students should learn the applications of the moves they were practicing, but he often confided to me that he had never met a taijiquan master who hadn't done some other martial art before, and who could use his art; and I could tell by the way that he said this that he wasn't totally convinced of the efficacy of the art.

Then I met Tan Ching Ngee. Here was a man completely convinced of the efficacy of his art and willing to prove it to unbelievers. Prior to meeting him I had already heard of his exploits: how he had challenged a teacher who had ridiculed Cheng Man Ching style taijiquan in a newspaper article; how in establishing himself as a teacher in the pragmatic world of the Indonesian Chinese he had had to fight people trained in ju-jutsu, muay Thai, and Western boxing.

At first I went to him to learn pushing hands, but as time passed I began to pester him about exactly how taijiquan might be used. Initially he insisted that I concentrate on improving my pushing hands and learning the Cheng Man Ching form, but then one day as we were running through the self-same form in the living room of his high rise apartment he relented:

"If you really want to learn about taijiquan as a fighting art there is one vital lesson that you have to learn." So saying, he shrugged his shoulders, planted his feet, and pointing to his cheek and said, "Slap me."

I was extremely reluctant to do so, but he insisted and so, somewhat tentatively, I gave him a half-hearted slap where he had indicated,

"No, harder!"

There was no mistaking that tone of voice so I hit him harder. He turned his cheek and ordered me to hit him repeatedly, first one cheek then the other, every so often pausing to ask me—no, order me—to hit him still harder.

I was not very happy about this because not only were my palms beginning to hurt and red marks to show on his face, but also I could not help but feel a nagging fear that there was going to be some sort of "pay back" involved.

"Enough," he said. "Now when I do it to you just try to relax and each time I slap take one step backwards."

My God, it hurt, and each successive impact seemed to make it worse. Then, slowly, as I had done to him, he increased the power. It was at that point that I felt a surge of red, blinding, almost uncontrollable rage which must have shown in my eyes, for Master Tan stopped, smiled, and said, "Now you know what learning to fight is all about."

The adrenaline rush slowly subsided and I nodded in rueful acceptance as he pointed out that to apply any fighting art you must be familiar with such a rush of anger, but also must be able to use it to your advantage, not allow it to control you.

Having explained to me how to use this burst of adrenaline, he commanded me to attack him. Not wanting to get too close I figured that I would open with a kicking attack, so I initiated a front leg roundhouse kick and attempted to follow it up with a front kick. "Attempted" being the operative word because Master Tan had already stepped inside my first kick, jammed the second, and his hand was in my face. The pain was more shocking than his previous slaps because not only was he moving forward but his whole body was behind the technique. The first strike had bent me backwards and the following ones forced me to step, then stagger, back. I tried to throw a punch in his direction but my arm was thumped down, I momentarily wondered where he had got the iron bar from. Now the force of his blows was so great and I was running out of space. Some instinct of self-preservation compelled me to bend down, both arms covering my head where the pain was worst, he stopped.

I once read a description by Robert Smith of an occasion on which he asked Cheng Man Ching to demonstrate how his art might be used. The way in which he described Cheng's inexorable advance and his feelings of panic described exactly the experience I had just been through.

Since that day I have spent many hours studying not so much the techniques themselves but the principles underlying them—for with an understanding of principle one technique can become a thousand.

One thing that often surprises people about the application of taijiquan as a martial art is how simple and uncomplicated it actually is. Indeed, as Master Koh Ah Tee is fond of saying, when a teacher makes the art seem complex he is usually doing so for one of two reasons: either he, himself, doesn't really understand the art or he wants to drag it out to make more money from his students.

When I had recovered from the onslaught I asked Master Tan what exactly he had done.

"The first thing you've got to understand," he replied, "is that there is no fixed method. I don't have time to work out that my opponent used attack A so I must use defense B. Instead, when it comes time to use your art you must trust your training. From form you have learnt balance, coordination, and how movement in one part affects the whole; from pushing hands you have learnt how to make the whole body sensitive, you have learnt how to defend your own weaknesses and exploit those of your opponent, and you are not afraid of being close to him; from weapons training you have learnt footwork and timing; and finally *neigong* has given you the courage and the ability to use the opponent's strength against him. So you see everything that you have learnt comes together in those few seconds when you are under attack."

"But you seemed to be doing specific things," I questioned.

"Yes, of course there are certain rules you've got to follow. For example, against kicks there is little point using your hands or arms to block because their strength can never compete with that of the legs. Instead, you have to move out of the way, but in doing so always try to move forward. This is because both kicks and punches develop greater power as they move out. If you can intercept them closer to the opponent then the effects will not be so dangerous."

"You will have noticed that I attacked your face a lot."

I nodded, rubbing my jaw.

"This is because people live in their faces—go directly to the point, for when your opponent's brain is processing pain messages from so many nerve endings in his face he will have no time for anything else. The other important thing is to constantly maintain pressure through forward movement. Once your opponent is moving back, unless he has a very high level of gongfu indeed, he is lost."

"But surely there must be some situations where you have to move backwards?" I asked.

"There are, if for example the opponent attacks suddenly from close range or is too big or fast for you; but even then, as you go backwards you must have the idea of going forwards."

"Like 'step back, repulse monkey' in the form," I interrupted eagerly.

Master Tan smiled. "Exactly like that. But you notice that in the whole of the form that is the only move where you actually step back. If you can, however, when you go back try to move to the diagonal so that you do not lose too much ground which you will have to make up when you counter."

He motioned me to the center of his living room floor and I tried to position myself so that I didn't have my back to the open window. Twenty-one stories down, people looked minute and the South China Sea stretched to the horizon, interrupted only by the occasional oil rig or cargo ship.

"Now attack with a strong front kick."

As I complied, he stepped back and to one side and with a simple flick of the leg nearest me his extended toes came up and caught me under the thigh. His kick wasn't hard, but it still hurt.

"See, a kick may be used against a kick, but in reality I would kick the back of your kneecap. After that it would be extremely difficult to walk, let alone fight."

I agreed, but remarked that to do such a thing your timing must be perfect.

"Exactly," smiled Master Tan, "and that relies on having the taiji mind."

• • •

Master Lau Kim Hong likes to laugh. Indeed, he laughs a lot. When he's pushing hands, he laughs. When he's teaching form, he laughs. Even when he's doing fighting techniques, he laughs.

Having been convinced that taijiquan was an effective fighting art after being soundly beaten by an exponent, Master Lau has had no qualms throughout his career about actually putting his art to the test. When he first started teaching, school closing was common and any class could become an arena where reputations might be made or destroyed.

On this particular afternoon Master Lau was laughing as he told me the story of one such incident. We were sitting in the living room of my house, Master Lau having called in on his way up to Kuala Lumpur, as it was his habit to do about once a month. The overhead fan was making a desultory effort to cut through the heavy air and in the distance thunder echoed across the jungle-clad hills.

"I used to teach a class near here," he said, "in Pontian. Do you know it?"

I replied that I did and he carried on, again with a laugh.

"I hadn't been teaching there long, a few weeks, but already there were quite a few students of all ages. I was teaching at the Guanxi Association Hall. The students were practicing the first few movements of the form when three young men entered. Even though they were at the other end of the hall I could tell that they hadn't come to make friends." Another laugh.

"So I walked down to where they were and asked them if they were interested in learning. They expressed a vague interest; or rather one of them did. In fact, he was the one who did all the talking. He asked me a few questions. The usual things: what did I teach, how long did it take to learn. Then suddenly looking directly at me he said that he didn't see how taijiquan could be used as it was so slow. Now he laughed and point- ed at the beginners practicing just behind me—what if they had to face a Western boxer. Now finally I thought he was getting to the point. I asked him whether he had done any boxing and he shook his head no, but pointed to one of his silent compan- ions and said that he did. This was the signal for the boxer to take his watch off, empty the pens from his pocket, and start jogging on the spot, shaking his arms and rotating his head. This made me angry, but I laughed."

I could clearly imagine the scene: the would-be challenger tense and expectant, his talkative companion excited and ready for some action, while Master Lau just laughed.

"What happened?" I prompted.

"Well, I asked him if he wanted to try his boxing on me. It was obvious that he did. The boxer just nodded; in fact the only noise he made the whole evening was a series of groans, but they came later.

So I stood and waited while my opponent raised his clenched fists in front of his face and started to dance from toe to toe, the way boxers do. Then he attacked, coming in with some kind of combination of punches. I stepped forward, pushing his punches away and to the side and slapped him in the face. I only meant to hit the side of his face just to teach him a little lesson, but unfortunately he turned his head to the side at the last moment and my palm hit him full in the face, across the nose and eyes. He crumpled to his knees clutching his face and groaning. Seeing this his two friends rushed over and attempted to get him to his feet, but he wouldn't get up. In fact he stayed on his knees for the next 15 minutes. I expressed my regret over what had happened, but what else did he expect?

"I went back to my class; in fact they'd stopped to watch the show. Then a few minutes later I went back to see how the boxer was getting on. I managed to pry his fingers away from his face and get him to stand up. His face was a mess: both of his eyes had swollen up and there was a perfect red palm print etched across the center of his face."

When I asked Master Lau what happened after that he said that the trio had left, but he continued to say, "You know, they weren't gentlemen."

Master Lau Kim Hong demonstrates a takedown.

"What do you mean?" I asked.

"Well, I beat the boxer but none of them ever came back to study with me."

As he said this it wasn't just Master Lau that was laughing.

Incidents like Master Lau's encounter with the boxer are common in the world of Chinese martial arts. However, many people in the West are surprised to hear that these things happen to teachers of taijiquan. This is first and foremost because even those Westerners who accept that it is a martial art have a distorted, idealistic idea of how it should work; often imagining beautiful, flowing movements resulting in a non-aggressive even non-violent solution with the opponent somehow peacefully subdued with his body intact and his feelings unhurt.

The reality is somewhat different, particularly in Malaysia where many of the exponents were highly-qualified experts in other martial arts before they were "convinced" of the value of taijiquan. The "convincing" usually took the form of a sound beating at the hands of a taijiquan practitioner. So it is that such exponents have no need for high-sounding philosophical explanations or long-winded exposition of theory. They know that the art works and that is enough for them.

• • •

Master Lau Kim Hong demonstrates "roll back."

Lee Bei Lei is well-known in martial art circles throughout Malaysia, for in his youth one of his favorite occupations was "school-closing." Whenever a teacher opened a new class and Master Lee was in the area he would go to "call on " the teacher to offer a challenge. If the teacher lost he would have no choice but to close his school.

Lee is a big man, although now considerably "calmer," in his own words, than in his youth. According to those of his martial arts brothers that I have spoken to, he employed a unique tactic when fighting: namely that of holding both his arms up so that his elbows covered his face, and then charging in at his opponent, allowing them to strike his body at will until when they were exhausted, at which time he would drop his arms and counter. That usually spelt defeat for his opponents.

"Of course," he said to me, "you have to train the *neigong* so that you are not afraid of your enemy's blows!"

Master Lee's not insubstantial stomach is like a steel drum and anyone so ill-advised as to hit it is likely to suffer damage to both fist and wrist, so those stories seem extremely believable.

In my constant search for more knowledge about taijiquan, and also prompted by the requirements of my academic research, in 1991, five years after meeting Master Lee for the first time, I approached him to ask if I could become his disciple. After the usual protestations of humble and unworthy status he accepted and it was arranged that the ceremony should take place two days later at the house of his disciple Chen Han Seng.

After the formalities had been completed in the living room of Chen's plush, almost mansion-like house (the centerpiece in the main hall was a large waterfall cascading down from the first floor into a large rocky pool complete with valuable Japanese koi carp), we retired outside to do some practice. To one side of the house there was a full-size badminton court and it was here that we gathered to train. Present were 15 of his disciples from Batu Pahat who had traveled down to Johor Baru where they had been staying for the past three weeks, training for the Johor State wushu championships in which they were now in the middle of competing. The following day was the finals and since most of the team had already fought their way through to this stage they were

At the Guangxi Association Hall. Note the traditional weapons.

exchanging last minute tips on tactics and technique.

It was at this stage that Master Lee emerged from the house and called me over. His very strong Fuzhou accent combined with a constantly rasping voice, whether the result of too many cigarettes or one too many blows to the voicebox I don't know, but even his long-term students found it very difficult to understand him.

I knew what was going to happen next and I was not looking forward to it. I knew that he was a man with considerable gongfu, but of course he wanted to prove it to me. I could not refuse.

"Why don't you attack me?" Well, unfortunately I had understood that. I could not help it, I had to express my reluctance.

"Come on, I won't hurt you," he urged.

I tried to laugh but it was a poor effort: "I'm frightened to attack you, Master Lee."

He also laughed, but it was a laugh with an edge; the time for excuses was over. Knowing what would happen but not how, I had no choice but to launch a punch at his head.

Surprisingly, I was able to follow the action quite well for I saw him use his front hand to slap away my attack. Then, almost in slow-motion I saw the same hand, from my perspective a vast palm getting larger by the moment, as it closed in on my face. The pain was massive and there was no way I could have carried on any kind of attack after that.

Master Lee's next action was almost as fast. Looking over his shoulder at the smiling audience he grasped me by the hand, a look almost approaching genuine concern on his face and said, "Sorry, sorry. I only used a little force, sorry."

"Never mind," I mumbled, "It's only a little pain."

The headache lasted for the next three days.

• • •

As with many other areas relating to the study and practice of taijiquan there is a certain amount of controversy over the origins of the *san shou duai da,* solo and two-person forms which are also sometimes referred to as the fast forms.

While nominally belonging to the Yang style, such noted experts as Fu Zhongwen, the nephew of Yang Cheng Fu, as well as the latter's youngest son, Yang Zhenduo, both deny the existence of such forms.

Described in detail in one of his books, Chen Yen Ling, a student of Yang Cheng Fu's, according to the story is supposed to have stolen the training manuscripts from his teacher. Jou Tsung Hwa, in his book the *Tao of Tai Chi Chuan,* asserts that Chen told him he was given the documents by Yang. Jou, however, is not terribly reliable as a source.

Still other teachers aver that the forms are a more recent creation, possibly attributable to the late Sha Guo Zheng, a master renowned for his invention of new forms. Certainly there is on the market a commercially-made video showing Sha and a colleague demonstrating a form very similar to the one practiced in Singapore and Malaysia today.

Making inquiries in Malaysia I was told that the form was introduced at the same time that Yue Shu Ting first came to the country. It was taught by an elder brother he had brought with him who had studied Yang style in China. Certainly Cheng Man Ching did not teach these forms, saying instead that fighting was based on application of principles and that if the exponent understood *jie jing* (intercepting power) then any technique might be used.

In Singapore I was told that Chen Yu had taught the form to Lu Tong Bao, but that he himself had learnt it from Chen Ten Ling's book and undertook last minute revision just before Lu arrived for his lessons.

The *san shou* forms are taught in Hong Kong and more rarely in Taiwan, but there, as everywhere else, confusion reigns as to their exact origin.

Such research, however, is probably of interest to martial arts historians alone. The fact is that the forms exist and they are useful in training the exponent in a wide range of skills required in order to effectively cross the gap between pushing hands and anything-goes fighting.

I was first introduced to the solo version of these forms which are somewhat less than prosaically known as A and B by Koh Ah Seng. During his first visit to the United Kingdom Koh taught me both of them. When Koh practiced these forms he "thundered" through them, attacking them with the gusto with which he approached all aspects of his taijiquan. On each stamp one of his massive legs would drive into the ground. And even if we were practicing on grass you would swear that you felt the earth shake.

Of course such a training style was not to everyone's liking. One crisp Autumn morning as Koh and I were running through *san shou* A on the lawn of Huang Laoshi's West London home, Chen Yu He, who had accompanied Koh on this trip, came out of the conservatory, cocked his head to one side, and then launched into a tirade in his native Hokkien dialect. Koh, at whom this broadside was aimed, gave a slightly abashed smile and then out of the corner of his mouth muttered, "He doesn't like the stamping; you don't have to do it if you don't want."

"This is taijiquan not Shaolin," Master Chen said in English. "You don't have to make a lot of noise." He was frowning and shaking his head as he said this,

"Not Shaolin! Not Shaolin!" Abruptly he turned and went back inside.

Koh shrugged his shoulders and laughed, "It's up to you."

I continued with the stamping. There are a number of reasons given for this stamping; one being that it aids in the process of sinking the *qi,* another that it serves to distract your opponent, while yet another avers that it is literally a stamp on your opponent's foot. Whichever explanation or explanations you favor I have always personally thought of it as a dramatic way of emphasizing the change from insubstantial to substantial, for as the raised leg lands the other leg is freed to do whatever it needs.

Having learnt the forms from Koh Ah Seng I then had to forget them in order to learn those taught by Wu Chiang Hsing. The A and B that Wu taught were different in several significant details than those taught by Koh, and to try to practice both versions would ultimately result in confusion. Since Koh himself had admitted to me that he wasn't sure if his version was completely correct as he hadn't practiced it for a long time, this seemed to me the best thing to do.

In order to learn first the solo forms and then the two-person routine my wife Feng and I got up every morning at 4.30 A.M. so that at 5:00 A.M., bleary-eyed but reasonably awake, we could meet Master Wu, who obligingly drove around to pick us up and take us to the large playing field where training took place. Since it doesn't get light in Malaysia till at least 7:00 A.M., and the heat seems to make the darkness more impenetrable, I always find such morning training a rather surreal experience. It is, however, a rewarding one, for even though it is often still hot, it is a few degrees cooler than in the light of day and on occasion a gentle breeze conspires to make a sweating Westerner feel a little more comfortable.

There is also something very refreshing and even romantic about the practice of martial arts as the sun rises. Of course the Chinese believe that the *yang qi* given off by the earth and the trees at dawn and at sunset to be particularly beneficial for human beings. So perhaps this contributes to the general feeling of well-being engendered by such training.

Another factor in favor of early morning training is that there is always a feeling of accomplishment at having been able to get up at all, and there is so much more time left in the day afterwards. All of this, however, does not negate the awful feeling when the alarm goes off and the air around is dark, still, and heavy.

At 5:00 A.M. prompt Mr. Wu's *qigong* class started—dozens of mainly middle-aged women in lines shaking, twisting, and noisily inhaling and exhaling to the count of their teacher's stentorian voice.

On these occasions I like to cause as little commotion as possible, so under the cover of the dark I would sneak to the back where my less than enthusiastic and grumblingly arthritic movements would hopefully be less noticeable.

After *qigong* it was time for taiji practice and well over half of the women would move away from the training area, congregating in gossiping clumps which merged, mingled, and then separated as they set off for breakfast or home. Those that were left stood in depleted ranks behind Mr. Wu and followed as he ebbed and flowed through the 37-posture form.

Then finally when my legs were aching, my throat parched, and my T-shirt dripping wet, it was time for *san shou*. Now the red streaks of dawn were cutting a pathway across the lightening sky. Mr. Wu was just teaching myself, Feng, and one of his senior students named Ah Li. Every day we would religiously run through the moves we had already learnt, practicing them at varying speeds from slow to the cracking pace at which Mr. Wu habitually performed them. On each new move he demonstrated the application and some time would be spent attempting punches, throws, and locks on each other. Then it would be more repetition.

"*San shou*," said Master Wu, "is relaxation in action. You have to take all the principles you have learnt from the solo form and make sure that they can be applied when each movement is not measured and deliberate. This is not as easy as it might sound, for even to avoid double weighting while moving at speed is no easy thing. Coupled with that is the fact that you must not give in to the desire to put hard strength into punches and kicks that now, because they are being practiced at speed, seem much more martial than they did when performed in slow motion."

Every move from the traditional Yang style is contained in the *san shou* forms. When put together with one person performing A and the other B, a whole range of emphases are possible. For example, one might choose to train locks, holds, and escapes so each partner would try their hardest to apply the numerous locks and holds contained within the routine, thus giving their partner practice in countering such techniques.

One of the key skills taught by these forms is movement. The exponent learns how to move in every possible direction as well as learning how to use *zhong ding* or central equilibrium to counter the opponent's movement.

They also perform a useful function in illustrating the connection between the skills developed in pushing hands and those relating to fighting. For by practicing the two-person routine the student is enabled to change from defense to attack, from locking to striking to kicking to throwing, and all at the same range as pushing hands is practiced. Furthermore, skills that the student has developed through pushing hands practice, such as the ability to preserve their own balance while disrupting that of their opponent, may be seen in relation to punching and kicking.

The force developed through long-term practice of the solo *san shou* forms is known in Chinese as *chang jing* or long force, and the effect when using a punch is likened to that of a ball and chain. The fist is the ball and the arm is the chain, with the rest of the body as the handle. In order for this force to be developed effectively, the whole of the body must remain as relaxed as possible so that no tension can impede the flow or speed of the movement. Only by practicing the slow, solo form can this ability to relax the whole body be acquired. So once again, everything rests on the foundation built through form practice.

• • •

One of the fastest teachers that I have met is Master Zhou Mu Tu. Master Zhou, a disciple of Lu Tong Bao and a martial arts younger brother of Lee Bei Lai, takes great interest in the fighting applications of the art. When he was younger and frustrated by the lack of sparring practice in taijiquan, Zhou took up karate and trained for two years. This was just long enough to get a black belt and as much karate sparring experience as he needed to convince him of the true value of taijiquan's pushing hands—the closest equivalent there is to the type of sparring that he had been doing in karate.

The day we had arranged to meet to "talk" about his experiences was an exceptionally hot one, even for Malaysia in June. As his car drive up outside my father-in-law's large house and I went out to meet him, the questions were already buzzing around in my head.

In the cool gloom of the large living area we talked for some while before the words ran out and it was obvious that more practical demonstration was needed. I was particularly interested in Master Zhou's assertion that he wasn't really interested in pushing hands per se, but rather only in its application to the development of fighting skills. This surprised me because it is quite common to find exponents of taijiquan who say that they are not interested in pushing hands usually do so because their pushing hands is no good, but Master Zhou has consistently entered and won pushing hands competitions over the last few years, even though he is in his 50s.

As we got up and went outside, choosing as our training area a shady corner under a large tree, Master Zhou explained that whenever he does pushing hands he tries to imagine that he is fighting, and so his main priority is to deny his opponent any opportunity to strike. He then proceeded to graphically illustrate what he meant as we squared off and started pushing. Every time he felt an opening he lightly struck me, sometimes with his palm, sometimes with the back of his hand, and sometimes with his closed fist. On the other hand, when I attempted to punch him or even just push him, his defense was sure and was always executed in such a way that I was left off-balance and vulnerable to his counterattack.

"This kind of training," he explained, "is used to build a foundation for the development of fighting skills, for not only does it teach you how to relate pushing hands to fighting but also you will find that if you are relaxed enough movements from the solo form and the *san shou* will naturally manifest themselves."

I replied that this was all very well but how was the student to develop power, as it could not safely be used in such practice—soft taps being the only acceptable way if you were not to swiftly run out of training partners.

"The answer was that, as with so many other things in taijiquan, it lies in *yi nian* (mental training)," he responded. "*Yi nian* forms the habits which you need to rely on in order to be able to apply the art successfully. Power is dependent upon speed and one of the best ways to develop speedy reactions is like this."

Standing in a relaxed posture Master Zhou's eyes suddenly fixed on a point in the air and his fist shot out in the direction he was looking. Then he looked in another direction and did the same thing.

"What I'm doing is mentally deciding upon a point and trying to hit it at the same time that the thought enters my mind," he explained. "There should be as little pause between thought and action as you can make."

Next, he asked me to punch at his chest as fast as I could. Every time, his arm interrupted mine and I was unable to get anywhere near the target. Having given this kind of demonstration before myself, I knew what was coming and thought I would be able to thwart his intentions. Sure enough he asked that we should reverse roles with him punching and me parrying. Most people place all their attention on making the block a conscious action instead of simply letting the body reflexively defend itself. So I tried to relax as much as possible and felt quite confident that I would be able to stop him.

With an audible thud his fist hit my chest; I was not as relaxed as I had thought. And again . . . and again. He really was incredibly fast, but without any unnecessary motion or wind-up. And how was his speed achieved?

"*Yi nian.* It's all *yi nian.* Just use the method I told you."

• • •

Training with Master Tan Swoh Theng is never a gentle experience, and over the years I have accumulated more than my fair share of bumps and bruises, strains and sprains in the process of learning his art.

After I had been training with him for some time he suggested that I should learn bonesetting with him. This is a field that most Chinese teachers of the martial arts have an interest in for a number of reasons. Firstly, it is useful to have a knowledge of first-aid so as to handle training injuries. Secondly, it is an area in which many old-time masters made a living, as securing enough income from teaching martial arts was seldom a viable option. In addition, there has always been a connection between the knowledge of the art's killing potential and its curative value, the idea being that those who have an in-depth knowledge of how to destroy the body should also have developed an understanding of how the body works and, therefore, how its health and well-being may best be promoted.

Master Tan Ching Ngee had also approached me about learning bonesetting, but I put him off, in part because of squeamishness and also because I felt that I had more than enough things to practice without adding another whole area of study.

Now, however, it seemed like a good idea to acquire some basic knowledge, so I arranged to visit his house in the evenings when he gave treatment and learn "on the job," as it were. This was a good decision, for not only did I learn the rudiments of bonesetting but I also got to spend a lot of time training with him in the intervals between patients.

Tan Swoh Theng's solid build and somewhat fiery character ensure a unique flavor to his fighting applications. When I first knew him and was studying wuzuquan with him, he expressed his doubts as to the efficacy of baguazhang's circle walking, stating that were someone to attempt to circle him in that manner he would simply step around with his back leg and then adjust his front leg so that he was constantly facing his opponent. I felt that it was neither the time nor the place to explain to him that circle-walking was not designed to be employed in this manner, but rather was a training method to strengthen the legs and develop a kind of elastic strength throughout the body.

Taking my silence as a sign of disagreement, Master Tan ordered me to commence circling him, which I reluctantly did, while he adjusted his stance in the appropriate manner. I was then commanded to attack him whenever I felt like it. Of course I didn't feel like it, but that was irrelevant. So I continued to circle and then moved in, feinting an open hand attack to his head and following through with an attack to the groin. They never landed. Instead, he heel-kicked me in the stomach, driving the air out of my body with a whoosh. As I started to double up his back hand followed through with an uppercut that stopped mercifully just short of my throat. His other hand then chopped down on my exposed neck.

"You see, bagua, all that circling, a waste of time," he uttered in a tone of satisfaction.

Like many other southern boxers, Master Tan was disdainful of what he considered to be the too philosophical and over-theoretical approach of systems from the north of China. According to his interpretation, the application of taijiquan became a series of brutally effective strikes, kicks, throws, and locks, all delivered at close quarters.

One evening in the small back surgery room of his single-story terraced house, after he had finished treating a patient who had supposedly fallen out of a lorry (as a black society member, one of Master Tan's roles is that of physician to those injured in street fights), Tan became eager to expound upon the use of different target levels in taijiquan. I suspect that this enthusiasm had been sparked off by the lorry driver, a large man with the permed swept-back hair and pencil mustache that at that time were popular with triad members. His injuries, massive bruising to the center of the chest, seemed to me to suggest that he had been fighting rather than falling out of lorries. And when I asked Master Tan, his rather cryptic answer—that if the man said he had fallen from a lorry then he had fallen from a lorry—served to convince me that his injury was the result of violence of some kind.

Anyway, for whatever the reason, Master Tan asked me to run through the moves of the taiji form from "snake creeps down" to "golden cock stands on one leg." After I had done this several times he pointed out that the initial deflection took the attack from high to low, thus unbalancing the attacker. Then when your opponent attempts to regain his balance the defender takes advantage of his upward motion to deliver a knee strike.

I was fairly familiar with all of this and so was maybe a little more blasé than I should have been. Master Tan attacked with a face punch, which I parried and pulled down, dropping my hips as I did so. As he pulled back I followed up with the required knee strike, but pulling it well before it made contact with his lower abdomen. For some reason this displeased him and Master Tan told me to try again. This I did several times, and although I tried to put more force in the knee strike it was not enough for the by-now-visibly impatient Tan Swoh Theng.

"This time you really hit me!" His voice contained more than a hint of menace and his fist flew toward my face with a speed and intensity sufficient to trigger a similarly fast reaction on my part. My knee pounded into his gut, and for a fraction of a second a feeling of satisfaction and self-congratulation nudged its way to the front of my thoughts. But it lasted only for a nanosecond, for the next thing I knew my knee was forced out by the elastic expansion of his gut and as I toppled backwards, leg still upraised and his elbow ground down onto the top of my thigh, causing a pain so intense that it seemed as if every nerve in my leg had been galvanized into agonizing action at that moment of impact.

For the next 15 minutes or so Master Tan manipulated pressure points, punched, and pummeled my leg in an effort to reduce my agony. Throughout the whole process, however, he smiled and his eyes sparkled.

"Do you know what I did?" he asked.

I clutched my injured leg and, looking at him in consternation, replied, "You hit my thigh with your elbow!"

"Yes, yes, but which move was it?"

I admitted that I didn't know, omitting to mention that I didn't care; all I wanted was for the feeling to return to my leg.

Master Tan stood on one leg in the posture known as "golden cock stands on one leg."

"You see, I used the elbow coming down instead of the hand rising at the same time that you were trying to do the same move." His grin broadened.

I had to admit that it was a novel application, and one that was definitely effective.

When I first met him, Master Tan was still working in the market selling vegetables and only practiced medicine part time. Now, however, he has opened his own clinic and it is there that I go to train. His specialty is bonesetting and the treatment of muscular and skeletal injuries. The front of his clinic is a shop selling medicine, surgical aids, and appliances. Customers in need of "inner fortification" may choose from a wide range of herbal and medicinal teas which are dispensed from large metal urns at the front of the shop. Like the majority of such shops the front is completely open to the street, being covered with sliding metal doors only when the shop is closed.

Whenever I am in town I visit his shop and have spent many hours training in the back storeroom, helping him treat patients or just sitting around drinking endless cups of tea and putting the world of martial arts to right.

It is also in the back of his store that I have spent a great deal of time exploring his own "unique" approach to sparring. What he likes to do is to break down forms into their component parts and then practice these individual moves against as wide a range of attacks as possible. Although at first the attacker pulls his punches, as the defender becomes more proficient the attacks become more realistic.

All of the applications that he teaches are direct and to the point, usually commencing with one or two punishing blows and then flowing into a limb break or takedown. Master Tan's fighting experience has taught him that it is the simplest things that work best and that any encounter is usually over in just a few moves.

Master Tan first started learning Chinese martial arts when in his early teens. As he tells it, he was fond of fighting and in search of greater skill, so the martial arts were an obvious choice. The very first system that he became involved in was one that is slightly outside the mainstream of what Westerners would consider to be martial arts, but it is part of a rich Chinese tradition. This was shen da, or spirit boxing. The exponent trains under a spirit medium, usually in a temple and, before practice, engages in various purification rites. This usually culminates in the burning of a charm, the ashes of which are then mixed into a cup of Chinese tea which the practitioner drinks. The practitioner then goes into a trance and performs according to the dictates of the god which visits him in this trance state. People I have witnessed doing this perform routines that closely resemble a number of traditional styles, although on questioning when they come out of the trance state they deny ever having learnt them.

I asked Master Tan whether he believed such practice was of value. He laughed and said that it really depended on what you had inside you for the gods to bring out.

This answer notwithstanding, spirit boxing was not enough for Master Tan and he went on to learn hongquan and then Fujian white crane. Finally he joined a class where

The author with Master Tan Swoh Theng, Master Gan of Singapore, and two visiting masters from China.

five ancestor boxing was taught by Master Gan He Chiang. Although there were over a hundred students in the class, the young Tan was singled out for special attention when Master Gan told him that he wanted to teach him medicine and bonesetting.

At first he was not interested; it was fighting that was his passion after all. However, one of his *shixiong*, hearing of their teacher's offer, scolded him for turning down the opportunity to acquire such precious knowledge. So it was that Master Tan started studying privately with Master Gan, but not before he was initiated as a disciple in the wuzuquan tradition, for without such initiation the knowledge could not be passed on. Slowly Tan became more interested in the healing side of the art, spurred on perhaps by the realization that the knowledge used to heal could also be used to harm—two sides of the same coin.

While in his early 20s Master Tan set off to travel around Malaysia and make his living as an itinerant medicine seller. This is a tradition of five ancestor boxers referred to as "walking the outlaw path." He traveled right up north as far as the Thai border and then back south to Singapore before going on to Sabah and Sarawak in East Malaysia. Living in such a way there were plenty of opportunities for him to gain experience in both the medical and the martial arts and on his return he continued to teach five ancestor boxing, sometimes holding as many as five classes a day.

Now, however, Master Tan concentrates on his business, only teaching public classes in *qigong*, which are free and open to all. Taijiquan and five ancestor boxing he teaches only to a small group of disciples who train with him on a one-to-one basis.

Tan is a dedicated teacher and spares no effort to ensure that his students not only understand what they are doing but also acquire a measure of gongfu, all of which means that training with him is extremely hard. In demonstrating applications, techniques are slammed in so that there can be no doubt about their effectiveness.

"If a student has no respect for the teacher, and if he does not trust his teacher's ability, the teacher will know this and will stop teaching him," Tan explains.

In common with most other teachers of traditional Chinese martial arts, Master Tan places much emphasis on form practice. This he sees as being the training ground where solid basic skills are developed. He also points out, as he teaches applications, that each move is applied against the vulnerable and weak points of an opponent's body. Chinese martial arts, as he understands them, are not a matter of simply flailing with your fists any old how. Rather, the opponent is to be set up so that specific targets may be struck.

Form practice alone is not enough, however, as sometimes the targets are disguised so that what is a shoulder strike in form is, in application, actually a strike to a vulnerable point on the chest.

"You must remember," Master Tan warned, "that form practice is dead. It is fixed. Every move has its precise requirements in order for it not only to be technically correct but also good to look at. Applications, on the other hand, are open to interpretation. If you have an agile mind you can work out the possibilities and ramifications of every move."

So saying, Master Tan directed me to attack him with a punch. Knowing by now that with him it had to be a real, committed attack, I lunged at his head. Parrying with his back hand Master Tan stepped in and caught me with a single "phoenix eye" strike under the ribs. Although it was pulled, the pain was sharp.

"Now again," he ordered and I complied. This time he stayed further back and executed the same parry against my wrist while striking me with the same technique in the same place. There was, however, more space between us the second time.

"These are just two variations of the same technique at close range and then at long range," he explained. "The variations are endless and it is up to you to practice and make them real for yourself."

I nodded. This was a common theme for Master Tan.

"But you must never forget to train one or two techniques so that they work really well for you and so that they are fast and powerful. These have to be trained on a sandbag and against static and moving targets. One or two moves is enough—that, and guts of course!"

It is on the subject of the realities of fighting that Tan Swoh Theng becomes the most eloquent: "Many students of martial arts fail to realize that there are people in this world who have never had a single lesson and yet they are very brave and love to fight, so every chance they get they do so. Even after two or three years of training, if you meet one of these people you will most likely be beaten. Gong fu alone is not enough; courage and strength are both vitally important factors!"

Tan Swoh Theng's whole approach to sparring is to practice in exactly the manner that you would wish to actually apply the techniques. So when he finds himself faced-off against an opponent, his only aim is to finish the encounter as quickly as possible. As soon as the opponent's attack is neutralized, or even in the process of doing so, Tan steps in and destroys his hapless enemy. This approach is a reflection of his background in five ancestor boxing and indeed is typical of the approach favored by the majority of southern style practitioners. Since most of the Chinese in Malaysia originated from the south of China it is not surprising that such an approach has become an integral part of their taijiquan.

• • •

Lee Bei Lei, although no longer practices the taiji form, is still able to demonstrate brutally effective applications of every move in the form. Underlying every technique is the momentum and power generated by constant forward movement so that every attack attempted by the opponent is returned to him faster and harder.

As part of my research, and feeling that something more was needed than the usual interview crouched over my tape recorder, I decided that I would ask Master Lee to explain the applications of the form movements and see where his explanations would lead. This turned out to be the right approach.

Early one morning I was picked up by one of my *shixiong*, a Mr. Lin who owned a local garage but was a taiji fanatic. He drove me the 10 miles or so out of Batu Pahat and into a small *kampong* area surrounded by rubber and palm-oil plantations. The low single-story wooden house standing in the center of a yard of cleanly-swept dust, still bearing brush marks, was typical of Chinese *kampong* dwellings. As we approached, Mr. Lin blew his horn and Master Lim Sou Yuan, whose house it was, emerged clad in shorts and singlet, his tree-trunk like legs bearing testimony to years of taijiquan practice.

Inside the large and cool living room was a collection of taiji exponents, all gathered to glean as much information as they could from Master Lee. Since he comes from a small village in the north of Malaysia and only visits the south about once every two months, Master Lee's visits are always treasured occasions; opportunities to revise, research, and learn new things. This time he was staying in his *shidi's*, Master Lim's, house.

Having finished greeting Masters Lee, Lim and Zhou Mu Tu and the four or so *shixiong* also gathered there, I began to unpack and prepare my paraphernalia: note-books, cassette recorder, camera, and video camera. Master Lee stood and watched by the door, a smoldering cigarette in one hand while the other thoughtfully rubbed the stubble of his crew-cut. Dressed like the others in shorts and singlet, he was a huge man amongst a group of big men, few of whom weighed in at less than 200 pounds.

"Ready," he grunted in his hoarse voice. I nodded and explained what I wanted to do. Basically, I was asking him to demonstrate every move of the form with its application. Master Zhou Mu Tu was chosen as his victim—excuse me, partner.

Starting with *chi shi,* a defense against a hold or bear hug, ending in a finger jab to the eyes, and working through the other moves of the form, Master Zhou was flung from pillar to post. At one point, when a possible application of "cloud hands" as a throw was demonstrated, Master Zhou flew through the open door and landed with an unceremonious and audible thump on the ground outside. On the receiving end of one of Master Lee's pushes Zhou smashed into the wooden wall, causing the windows to rattle and Mrs. Lim to come out of the kitchen to see what havoc was being wrought by her husband's playmates.

Every so often, chuckling as if surprised by his own strength, Master Lee would growl "sorry, sorry" and pull Zhou Mu Tu up or away from whatever inanimate object he had just struck.

At one point, however, Master Lee got stuck, for, due to his lack of form practice, he couldn't remember what "embrace tiger, return to mountain" was. It wasn't that he couldn't remember the application, he couldn't actually recall the move itself. Eventually, and with much prompting from the sidelines, he executed a parry which he then changed into a headlock at which point he commenced pummeling the immobilized head of poor old Master Zhou.

As I had hoped, this practice provoked an outpouring of information from Master Lee so that during such intervals Master Zhou was able to attempt to regain his composure.

In common with all the other teachers I had trained with Master Lee emphasizes the importance of forward motion—never allowing the opponent a moment to regain their balance, either physically or mentally. When he performs "brush knee twist step," the attacking hand is used to jab at the eyes, rather than the slap to the face, as favored by the majority of taiji exponents.

In "cloud hands," Master Lee uses his upper arm to control the opponent while his other hand attacks the groin; preferring this method to the more common control and throw usually demonstrated as an application of this move.

On one point Lee was adamant: a knowledge of these methods was worthless without diligent and extensive practice of those basic exercises which develop gongfu. Of these he has a wide range.

To develop finger power Master Lee manipulates a solid iron ball the size of a shot, occasionally throwing it in the air and catching it; at other times exerting pressure on it with his fingers one at a time.

Follow-stepping also plays a vital part in his training method, with students being expected to move up and down the training area executing the hand movements "ward-off," "roll-back," "press," and "push." At first this seems quite an easy task, but at the same time all the principles of the art must be adhered to, so that the head is held up, the spine erect, the waist flexible, and the hips sunk. Similarly, the exponent must avoid being double-weighted as he moves forward. All of this places a great strain on the legs and in the process develops the kind of spring power that Master Lee feels a prerequisite for the successful application of taijiquan.

On occasion he allows his students to spar, but like many of the teachers in Malaysia his idea of sparring is that the more skillful or powerful exponent beats up his less-able partner. Little or no attempt is made to limit the power of blows and to watch it is a brutal performance.

In Malaysia, opinions as to the validity of Master Lee's approach to taiji are divided. A newspaper report in August of 1992 described him as Malaysia's Zhang San Feng; that being the name of the legendary founder of the art. Others, however, are highly critical of his attitude to form training. Such criticism, however, is seldom openly voiced as Master Lee's invariable answer to critics is a challenge. Certainly, even his own students admit that he has little knowledge of the theory of the art and yet he is able to put it into practice where, for him, it counts: in the arena of personal physical combat.

Having both pushed hands and "sparred" with Master Lee I would have to say that his pushing is clear, clean, and un-telegraphed and his fighting methods differ little from those of other practitioners of Cheng Man Ching taijiquan. It seems to me that what he does is truly taijiquan. In judging him, it must also be remembered that he is a product of his time and cultural background, coming as he does from a tradition of "putting your money where your mouth is." He is more concerned with what works than how it works. He and his classmates, between them, have spread the teachings of Yue Shu Ting and Lu Tong Bao throughout Malaysia and have convinced the hardheaded descendants of southern Chinese immigrants that the northern Chinese art of taijiquan with its fanciful philosophy and intellectual trappings is in fact a functional and effective art. For that alone he deserves recognition and gratitude.

• • •

As I have mentioned before, Master Koh Ah Tee holds the position of taiji instructor at the Royal Selangor Golf Club. How he got the job is a testimony to his ability to put the art to practical use. Having heard that they were looking for a teacher he applied for the job and was duly called for an interview. Since the interview was to be conducted in English, which Master Koh cannot speak, he brought one of his classmates to interpret. The interview was held in the small poolside office of the recreation manager and was conducted by the manager, Tony Lim, and the pool manager, Steve Tang, both of whom were educated in English-medium schools. Both of these gentlemen are over six feet tall and with the hard bodies of exercise enthusiasts. In addition, Tony Lim holds a fourth *dan* black belt in taekwondo, while Steve Tang is a third *dan* in Shito-ryu karate.

The interview went the usual way with questions being asked about Master Koh's training background and teaching experience, all of which he answered to their satisfaction. Then came the crunch, as both of these exponents of external arts were extremely skeptical about taiji's effectiveness as a martial art. Furthermore, they indicated that they would not be willing to give the job to someone who was less than competent in all aspects of the art. It is worth explaining here that the membership of the golf club is made up of Kuala Lumpur's most successful businessmen, government members, and Malaysian royalty. This means that their expectations are high and whatever they do they want only the best. Thus, for them to study taiji it has to be with a world-class teacher.

The two managers expressed their doubts to Mr. Yang, the translator, but rather than translating he simply asked them to put Master Koh to the test. Unaware of what was going on Master Koh saw the two large gentlemen get up from behind the desk and, presuming that the interview was at an end, he too got up. Tony Lim launched a head height roundhouse kick at Master Koh. Seeing the kick coming he stepped to the side and pushed Lim's chest, sending him sprawling to the ground. Meanwhile, Steve Tang was intent on punching Master Koh in the head. Using "lift hands," Master Koh intercepted the punch and, with a seemingly casual turn of his waist, sent Steve Tang crashing into the wall. The whole encounter took only a few seconds. Mr. Yang beamed down at the two erstwhile attackers both of whom were struggling to get their breath back.

"What's going on?," asked the bemused Master Koh.

"You've got the job, I think!" Mr. Yang told him with a smile. It was true, he had.

Koh Ah Tee is renowned for his internal strength which, as a teenager, he frequently demonstrated at shows and competitions around the country. A typical demonstration would start with five or six burly classmates bringing on a log the size of a sawn-off telephone pole. This they would then proceed to ram full-force into his abdomen. At the same time Master Lau, who was supervising the proceedings, would smash a heavy wooden chair across Koh's back. As if this weren't enough, members of the audience would then be invited up to kick and punch the relaxed and often smiling Koh.

Now Master Koh uses his skill to convince troublemakers that there is little point in challenging him.

One evening after I had been staying at Master Koh's house for a few days R-and-R, we set off for his class at one of the city's Chinese Primary schools. As usual the KL traffic was appalling and we had left a good hour in advance. As we crawled along the highway into the center of the city Master Koh talked about the unique philosophy and methodology of taijiquan.

"Taiji boxing is the opposite of external methods of martial art," he said. "Where the external martial artist seeks more speed and power, we look instead for stillness and as little muscular strength as possible. It is easy in taiji training to get side-tracked into practicing particular methods for improving pushing hands or self-defense skills, but the essence of the art lies in simplicity. Taiji is simple: no secrets, no tricks, just *song*. It is human nature, however, to always want more, to accumulate; instead, taiji demands of us that we give up all the things we have accumulated and just trust in relaxation. Taijiquan looks like nothing; the strength is all kept inside just like steel wrapped in cotton. Furthermore, you mustn't have an attacking mind. Rather, you must just wait for what your opponent wants to do. This is why the taiji exponent moves slowly like a snake—but what happens when a snake is provoked, then and only then it moves with blinding speed. In fact, the taiji practitioner pays attention only to himself, constantly asking himself even when under attack if he is truly relaxed and centered."

By this time we were pulling in at the gates of the school and even with our early start there was already a large crowd of students milling around. The school itself was a large three-story building with a canteen area set in the basement which was open to the air at the sides. The first floor, which was reached by means of a broad flight of stairs, was also open to the air and served as a playground and assembly area. On the walls around the stairwells at the center of this area were notices exhorting the children to respect their teacher and always brush their teeth as well as advertisements for the school's taekwondo club. So much for the rich cultural heritage of China's indigenous martial arts!

The class started in the usual way with warm-ups followed by an extended period of standing post training—sufficient to soak my T-shirt and leave an unsightly stain around the crutch of my training trousers.

Then it was time for form practice. Once that was over and as everyone stood around drinking water I noticed Master Koh in what seemed to be rather heated conversation with two students from the beginner's group. I sidled over toward them, intent on eavesdropping.

"Yes, but I don't see what good slow form practice is against fast attacks," one of them was saying.

The other one chipped in, "When I did hongquan the teacher always stressed that we must move as fast as possible!"

Master Koh did not look as if he particularly cared about his students hongquan experiences. He merely smiled at them and said quietly, "In taiji we have to start with the soft and the slow. Relaxation: that's what we're after. Just relax and don't worry."

This was not convincing them, but catching sight of my not-so-subtle appearance in the vicinity Master Koh ambled over to me and led me off out of earshot of the two grumblers.

"This has been coming for the past few weeks," he explained. "I know that really they just want to test my gongfu, but I don't want to frighten off any of the other people in the class. Why don't you do me a favor and ask me some questions about *neigong*. Do it in a minute before the class starts again."

I nodded. This was going to be fun.

A couple of minutes later I did as he had asked. Making sure that my question was delivered in a loud voice. The grumblers looked up and joined the rest of the class in gathering around us. In fact, they pushed their way to the front.

"*Neigong* is an essential part of taijiquan," Master Koh announced. "It means you can stay relaxed even under the fiercest attack. Nigel, hit me as hard as you can."

I duly complied. The class was awed by the sound of my fist thudding into the Master's relaxed belly.

"No, no, that wasn't quite right." His eyes alighted, as if by chance, on grumbler number one. "Why don't you have a go and try to hit with a bit more force than Nigel. You've got an external martial arts background, haven't you?"

Victim number one nodded, took up a low stance and at a nod from Master Koh let rip with a mighty punch accompanied with a sharply audible exhale.

"Harder." I could tell Master Koh was holding back a smile.

Again a mighty punch and then another and another and another until it was obvious that each successive punch was hurting the poor attacker's wrist and fist more and more. In the end he could not continue; instead, he stood clutching his injured hand and shaking his head in troubled disbelief.

"What about you?" This to grumbler number two, but he was wiser than his friend and declined.

After that the fun was over and we returned to our practice but, surprisingly enough, that was the last night of training for the two troublemakers. I guess they felt that hongquan was a safer bet!

In the car on the way back from the class Master Koh told me that he had only had occasion to use his art for real once. That was only a few years after he had started taiji and he got in an altercation with a man on the street who threw a wild punch at him. Master Koh slipped the punch and stepped in punching his opponent in the stomach. The man promptly dropped to his knees, turned very pale, and then threw up. When he had finished vomiting he burst into tears. Master Koh confided to me that the whole incident had frightened the life out of him as Koh himself did not know the extent of his own ability.

Chapter Six

Baguazhang in China

hina in 1984 was beginning to really open its doors to foreigners again. Despite this, there were periodic campaigns against "spiritual pollution" or "cultural contamination." What this meant in practical terms was that although I continued my job as a teacher as usual, outside of class time none of the students would come to see me or any of the other three Western teachers at the college. It also became far more dangerous for any of the teachers I was training with to be seen with a foreigner on a regular basis. For this reason, and also because my time there was short, I tried to train with as many different teachers as I could and to learn as many different things as was possible. The Gao family, however, never seemed to care how often I trained with them. This was, I think, due to the fact that they were already so out of favor they just didn't care anymore.

Anyway, at the same time that I was training with them I was also learning bagua from two other teachers. One of these, Master Wong Tong, was in his mid-40s and a prominent student of the then chairman of the Beijing Baguazhang Association, Master Li Zi Ming. I had observed Master Wong's class at the prestigious Beijing University and on finding out that he held a regular class in a park just down the road from where I lived, I got a Chinese friend of mine to act as an intermediary and approach him about joining.

The author with the late baguazhang Master Li Zi Ming after winning a gold medal in competition.

It was Autumn and already the government-run classes had packed up for the Winter. The park in the mornings was left for the diehards. Master Wong's group were certainly that. The majority of them were students from the university who wanted to get extra practice. Many of them would turn up as early as 5:00 A.M., and commence their circle walking training. In the area of the park where they met the dusty ground under the trees bore deep circular grooves where each student had worn away their own path practicing the ground-scraping, mud-threading steps which are basic to the style. After all the details of when I was to train and for how long had been sorted out, Master Wong told me that he expected me to arrive and train every day at 5:00 A.M., like his other students. For the first hour I was to practice circle walking.

This struck me as strange, for Wong never turned up until 6:00 at the earliest—but I needed the basic training anyway.

After a while I began to notice a pattern. On the days that I arrived later or didn't do much circle walking, Wong would not teach me anything new. Obviously the other students had been told to keep an eye on me and they were informing him about my training prior to his arrival. Although the forms they practiced had the same names as those taught by the Gaos, they were performed in a different manner.

As the bitterly cold Beijing Winter set in, training continued. As the cold gradually necessitated the wearing of more and more layers of clothing, so did my resemblance to the Michelin man grow.

One morning Master Wong called over two of his students to perform the 64 hands form. This form consists of eight straight line forms containing eight moves each, hence the name. Contained within these forms are all the offensive and defensive moves that are later used in the circle forms. Both the Gao family and Master Wong taught this as basic, but I had earlier agreed with Master Wong that I wanted to concentrate on the *laobazhang* form (old eight palms), a core circling form. Now he wanted me to see the way that their 64 hands was practiced. There were differences, although I could identify many of the individual moves. In the Wong version the stances were much longer and lower and the techniques were executed at a longer range.

Then the students demonstrated something that I hadn't seen before: the two-person version of 64 hands. Now it was possible to see how the techniques worked at close range; many of them involving joint locks and limb breaks. When the students had finished they were sent off to train on their own again and we returned to the *laobazhang* form.

• • •

Although it was bitterly cold, training in the winter had an atmosphere all its own. In England I had always loved training in the snow, and the fact that this was China added an extra dimension to my enjoyment. It was not easy to turn out of a warm bed and a central heated flat when it was still dark outside and frost or a light powdering of snow lay on the ground. Getting dressed in long johns, two T-shirts, and then a heavy track suit, gloves, scarf, two pairs of socks, and thick, cotton shoes, it was time to go.

Out in front of the apartment building I fumble with the keys to the lock of my trusty Flying Pigeon brand bicycle. At the front gate of the hotel a large sign in English orders cyclists to dismount. It had become a point of honor amongst the foreign experts to ignore this sign, so I speed up and shoot past the armed police who guard the hotel. Their purpose: to keep the locals out of our little ghetto of cultural contamination.

Then I am turning right and speeding down the wide double lane road. On either side the skeletally bare trees stand like sentries. It is only a 10 minute ride to the park. By now I am immune to the stares of the locals as I park my bike among the several hundred already lined up in regimented rows outside the front entrance to the park. As I pay the parking attendant, a loud shout from the Central Gymnasium across the road causes me to startle. I look around. The armed police unit stationed there are doing their early morning martial arts training, drilling in what looks like a Shaolin form.

Every so often a particularly explosive move is accompanied by a loud shout. Sometimes I stay to watch them. Not today.

Once through the ornate gate and in the park proper I turn left. There is no grass in the park, sometimes I think there is no grass left in the whole of Beijing. Instead, there is the hard earth which in spring is turned to dust, in summer when the annual rains fall, to a muddy quagmire, and now, just iron hard earth. On my right is the children's playground where four or five old grannies hang from the climbing frame by their out-stretched arms. Their tiny bound feet hang a foot or so off the ground and they chirp to each other like strange, exotic birds. I'm so busy looking at them that I nearly bump into another old lady who is steamrolling down the path in front of me waving her arms in unison from left to right and back again. I dodge out of the way of this strange sight; she is practicing a kind of walking *qigong*.

Now the path veers around to the right and slopes downhill toward the lakeside, but I don't follow it. Instead, I turn off onto the hard-packed earth and head toward a small grove of winter-bare trees. Several of my classmates are already there. In a bright turquoise track suit Xiao Li, a 20 year old Beijing University student, gracefully twines and twirls herself around in a demanding circle form she has been working on for some months. She is entering an inter-university wushu competition to be held at the People's University in the spring, and everyday she works on the same routine.

Around two of the trees other students are practicing their circle walking. Going over to the tree I have "adopted," I jump up and down on the spot in an attempt to warm up. But it is not so much warming up as putting off the start of my training. Circling the tree, endeavoring to keep my back straight, my backside tucked in, and also to keep my feet sliding smoothly along the ground, I go round and round the tree.

At first I keep my hands at waist height, palms pushing down, in the first of the eight postures designed to develop and strengthen the body in preparation for the twisting, turning movements of the forms. Then, one-by-one, I run through the other seven moves of the sequence, ending up in the characteristic, circle-walking posture: inside arm outstretched toward the tree while the other hand is held underneath the elbow of the inside arm. Both palms are held facing the tree which is the center of the circle, the focus of my world. The constant adjustment of the body, checking that there is the right amount of tension in each body part is exhausting, and underneath my many layers I am soaked in sweat.

An hour spent in this manner passes surprisingly fast and there is Master Wong, flat workers cap perched on his head, his body slim and erect, his only concessions to the biting cold the scarf he wears tightly wrapped around his neck and the white woolen gloves. Otherwise, he wears the same blue Mao suit that he has worn every day that I have trained with him.

He looks with a critical eye at Xiao Li for a few minutes then comes over to my tree. I pretend to be immersed in my circling.

"Hmmm." I take that sound to be a sign that there are no obvious mistakes in what I am doing. He tells me to stop and asks to see the first few moves of the *laobazhang* form which he has been teaching me. This time he is not so happy. It seems that each move contains errors that need to be corrected and then practiced over and over again. There will be no new movements today. But now I am beyond caring. I am both cold and hot and my mind's eye is rapidly filling with steam from the piping hot bath which I intend to have when I get back to my flat.

Then the lesson is over and it is time to get back on the Flying Pigeon and head for the central-heating.

• • •

Master Gao Zi Ying is a native of Heilongjiang in North China, many hundreds of miles removed from the origins of many of the teachers I was later to train with in Malaysia. But he shares with them an attitude, and that is the attitude of the fighter.

The first time I met Master Gao he was 79 years old, about five-feet-four, and with a body which might best be described as "stocky." In fact, he was shaped like a barrel. I was taken to meet him by one of my students named Huang Fei Long, "Flying Dragon" Huang. A native of Guangdong Province, Huang was only four-feet-eight and all the girls in his university class called him "Little Boy" behind his back. He and I shared the same passion for Chinese martial arts and ever since he came to study in Beijing he had been studying with Master Gao.

From the university to the Gao's house was a good 20 minutes by bicycle through the dusty north-western suburbs of Beijing.

Xiao Huang, as I called him, was dwarfed by his old and rather rusty Flying Pigeon bike. His brush-cut hair, which resisted all efforts of the comb to produce order, stuck up in tufts as he raced ahead of me and I desperately peddled to keep up. Since I had never been to a private house in China before, I was not sure what to expect. In fact, such was the degree of segregation between foreigners living and working in China and the locals, that I knew people who had been in China for 10 years and never seen the inside of a Chinese house.

As we took our lives in our hands and raced across a major crossroads, Xiao Huang turned to face me and shouted, "We are here, we are here."

My heart was in my mouth as he narrowly missed riding into the back of a lorry. Then he was swerving out to the right, his little arm flapping. Eyes squeezed almost shut with fear I followed him across the stream of oncoming traffic and into the narrow entrance of a small lane. Xiao Huang screeched to a halt and jumped down from the heights of his saddle.

Now we were in the *hutongs,* that maze of small alleyways that twist and turn between traditional, single-story houses, all surrounded by high, gray walls which surround their central courtyards. In old Beijing, it was said, even people who had lived in the *hutongs* all their lives, could end up hopelessly lost after dark.

Since the foundation of the People's Republic, what had once been the homes of single families had been broken up so that now several families would live around one courtyard, with five or six people occupying one room. Such meager accommodation, of course, was reserved for those who had no clout in the new society; people whose background classified them as "class enemies" or "bourgeois influences." Master Gao fell into the category of the undesirable because, prior to the revolution, his family had been wealthy. Indeed, his father, Gao Wen Ching, had hired leading martial artists to train himself and his son.

We turned left, then right, then left again. Already I was disorientated, but Xiao Huang seemed to know where he was going. Then we stopped in front of a large, if slightly worse-for-wear archway. Stepping high over the lintel and maneuvering our bikes after us, we entered a courtyard.

Like the lane outside, the ground was hard-packed earth with a coating of the ubiquitous Beijing dust that supposedly blows down into the city from the Gobi desert.

Slightly offset from the center of the courtyard was a building which I discovered later was used as a communal kitchen by the five families which occupied this courtyard. Master Gao and his wife occupied a one room building about the size of a single garage.

Xiao Huang parked his bike against a pile of coal bricks which were neatly stacked against one of the rooms in anticipation of the winter that was now only a few months away. Then a short, stocky man dressed in blue, baggy trousers and a tattered gray woolen jumper appeared at the door of the same building. "Master Gao," Xiao Huang called and introduced us as we were ushered into his "house."

At one end of the room, dominating the whole area, was a large double bed, covered with a colorful quilt. It was on the edge of this that Master Gao perched while Xiao Huang and I sat on folding chairs at a table which stood in the middle of the rest of the floor space.

As Xiao Huang talked to the master I looked around. In one corner, next to a cheap-looking, glass-fronted wooden cabinet, stood a color TV. Behind it was a cluster of long weapons: spears, halberds, and staffs. These were the "real thing."

On the wall directly opposite where I was sitting was a photo in faded sepia of a young man, bare-chested, flexing his muscles and gazing fiercely into the distance.

"How old are you?" Master Gao's gruff voice cut into my reverie. I replied and he smiled, revealing one gold tooth at the center of his grin.

"I was the same age as you when that photo was taken." Quickly calculating, I worked out that the photo on the wall must have been taken in 1938, in what must have been a very different world. The picture was flanked by two pairs of bagua's short weapons: deer-horn knives and judge's pens. This place was like a cross between a museum and an armory.

While I was scrutinizing the rooms fittings, a bent, old woman, gray hair done up in a bun, had come in and placed a teapot and several cups on the table. Xiao Huang introduced me to the master's wife.

Over tea Xiao Huang told Master Gao something of my training background, informing him that my main motivation for being in China was to learn real Chinese wushu. This met with a nod of approval.

"The master would like to see you do some karate," Xiao Huang announced enthusiastically.

I wasn't sure whether this was at his urging or Master Gao's, but I had been prepared for this request so I stood up and went through a somewhat abbreviated version of the *naihanchi kata*—this being the only one that space permitted.

When I had finished, breathless not so much from the demands of the *kata* as from my desire to impress, I looked over at Master Gao. His face was impassive and it felt as if his eyes were burning into me. He held my gaze momentarily and then his whole face crumpled into a wrinkled smile, his narrow eyes disappearing into the folds of his face. His large hands clapped loudly three or four times as Xiao Huang also grinned delightedly—this meeting he had orchestrated was obviously proving to be a success. Then the smile was gone again from Master Gao's face and he barked something at Xiao Huang, who also stopped smiling and went to the door where he held a hurried and hushed conversation with the master's wife. Coming back in, Xiao said, "The master's son is coming."

After a few minutes of uncomfortable silence, a tall, thin man dressed in a dark blue track suit came in. After greeting his father he proffered me a hand and smilingly introduced himself as Gao Ji Wu.

Master Gao Ji Wu performs a standing pole meditation posture.

Gao Ji Wu was in his early 40s and had an open, smiling face. His father wanted him to demonstrate a form called 64 palms, which, as Xiao Huang explained, was one of the first things that Master Gao taught to his students. In fact, as a young man of 18, when he first started teaching, this was the only routine Master Gao taught.

Gao Ji Wu's movements were as clean and precise as his appearance as he went up and down the small room performing a series of linear movements. The emphasis was on open hand strikes, low kicks, and continuous twirling and twisting of the arms, changing from one technique to the next. There was a definite flow to his movements with none of the sharp focus I had been used to in karate.

The 64 palms consists of eight sets of eight movements which may either be linked together or practiced individually. It is said that within this form are contained all of the major techniques of the art and as such it serves as an encyclopedia of applications.

Xiao Huang now looked so happy that I thought he would burst. When he got the chance Xiao whispered to me that the master had agreed to teach me and that this would be the form I would learn first, together with the circling internal strength routine.

Once his son's performance was over, Master Gao got up and showed me the first move, which consists of a downward parry with one hand while the other jabs with the fingers at the opponent's throat or eyes. Commanding me to punch him, Gao proceeded to demonstrate how such a technique could be used against attacks from every possible direction. As he skillfully checked and countered, his eyes seemed to glitter like a cobra seeking its prey and everywhere his fingers touched my body it hurt, even though his blows were controlled.

As I was later to learn, his son could also effectively demonstrate each and every application, but there was not the same degree of pain involved. With Gao Ji Wu, it was always a matter of performance, of demonstration; with Master Gao, it was as if he were doing it for real.

On that afternoon I was handled as if I were an infant by a man over 50 years my senior, and there was absolutely nothing I could do about it.

At first Master Gao taught me very slowly, showing me only one move per lesson before having me perform it hundreds of times, up and down the length of his "house." As I then became more used to the body movement of bagua, he added on new movements and gave me auxiliary exercises to practice under the watchful eyes of Gao Ji Wu.

Gao Ji Wu also lived in the *hutongs,* only a two minutes walk from his father's home. Although the total area of his home was about the same as that of Master Gao's, his was divided by a wall into a living room and a bedroom. In the small area directly outside the front and only door was a thick wooden post protruding about a foot above the ground. This was for practicing low kicks and sweeps which had to be executed in such a way that the foot scraped across the ground until it was released to spring up into the opponent's ankle, shin, or kneecap.

Another delightful exercise designed to build up forearm strength was to hold both arms outstretched while holding a piece of broomstick handle with a rope tied on, to which a brick was attached at the other end. The brick then had to be wound up and slowly let down as many times as possible. Such was my lack of ability at this that other students would come to watch and laugh when they knew I was due to practice this.

Slowly, however, I became more proficient and started to practice applications with my classmates as well as being introduced to the Gao's version of pushing hands. This was basically single-hand pushing hands but with the front leg being pulled back and raised every time you were defending. The idea was not so much to develop sensitivity but rather to toughen the skin of the wrists so that any contact with an opponent could be used to create friction, thus causing distracting pain and enabling you to deliver a more devastating attack.

In this practice I enjoyed an advantage insofar as the hair on my arms caused my partner more pain than he would usually have felt, and so I was able to avenge myself on those classmates who laughed at my struggles with the brick.

The best in the class, however, was a man in his 30s, who us younger students called Lao Lian. Lao hardly ever smiled but nevertheless seemed, in a grim-faced way, to enjoy inflicting pain on his training partners. Most of the time he practiced on his own. Lao's favorite form was 64 palms, but the way he did it was not the same as we had been taught. When Lao Lian trained his movements were staccato and somewhat abbreviated; in fact, he made the form look quite ugly.

When I asked Gao Ji Wu why this was he just smiled and evaded the question. It was not until I had been training for quite some time that I found out why his practice was different.

With the arrival of spring we changed the location of our practice. Previously Master Gao had taught on a small side street outside a cinema, but as the weather got better we moved to an open area surrounded by large clusters of boulders on the edge of a public park. Here class was held on Tuesday and Thursday evenings. On Mondays and Wednesdays a master of meihuaquan used the same spot.

Then someone, whether it was the master or his students I don't know, decided that they would also like to practice there on Tuesdays and Thursdays. So one Tuesday evening we arrived at the usual time to find the meihuaquan people already there on "our" training ground, practicing their high kicks and long, deep stances.

Gao Ji Wu, who was taking the class that evening, hurried forward and demanded to speak to the teacher. A lengthy conversation ensued while the two groups of students glared at each other. In the end, Teacher Gao returned to where we were standing and with a nod of his head indicated that we should go.

With the rest of the students dispersed, Teacher Gao told me to go with him to his father's house. When we got there I was placed to one side with a cup of tea while father and son engaged in a discussion that at times became quite heated. Then they were interrupted by the arrival of Lao Lian.

"Master," he greeted Gao Zi Ying. "Elder Brother," this to Gao Ji Wu, "Some of the young ones are getting angry and talking about coming back tomorrow with swords and spears," he said.

Master Gao's face darkened and he roared out a response, his thick Heilongjiang accent making it almost impossible to understand the words, although his displeasure was clear.

"I agree, we have no choice," Gao Ji Wu said, "Lian, you sort it out."

Lian left the house after saying the appropriate good-byes, a purposeful look on his face.

Later when we were at Gao Ji Wu's house having a supper of noodle soup I asked Teacher Gao what Lao Lian was going to do. "Oh, Lao Lian is very good at sorting out problems," was his enigmatic reply.

The following Thursday we were back training in the usual place with neither sight nor sound of the Plum Blossom boxers. To find out exactly what had happened I had to ask Xiao Huang, who was talking excitedly with some of our other classmates.

"Lao Lian went to test the gongfu of the meihuaquan teacher. Lao Lian is very good at fighting, so now the problem is solved." He beamed at me and it suddenly all made sense.

Lao Lian was the group's fighter, that was why his forms looked different; he was practicing for one reason and one reason alone. Later on when I had more experience of the world of Chinese martial arts I found out that it was common practice for each school to have one or two "bruisers" who, while they would never win any prizes for the aesthetic beauty of their forms, loved to "mix it up," and they would represent the school when the occasion demanded it.

• • •

During the winter of 1984–85 I decided to enlist the aid of one of my baguazhang *shixiong*, Xiao Cao, to improve my standard as I felt I was making little progress.

Xiao Cao was a native of Shanghai who had studied bagua from his teens and when he came to Beijing to University he took the opportunity to continue his training with some of the best masters in China. At that time in his mid-20s and working in an insurance firm, he agreed to come around and train with me several times a week.

We would meet to practice in the central gardens around which the whole hotel complex was arranged. There in the shadow of the large rock garden we worked through three circling forms: *laobazhang, lianhuanzhang,* and *youshenzhang.*

Xiao Cao broke down each move, explaining not only the application but also how each body part contributed to produce a power that stemmed from the whole body. His particular forte was the spiraling energy by which the bagua exponent ensures that any incoming force is met with a circular reaction.

Xiao was never completely comfortable being in the presence of a foreigner twice his size, and this manifested itself in a nervous belching occurring at intervals of approximately 30 seconds.

One move that Xiao Cao was especially fond of occurred in the *lianhuanzhang* (chain palm) form where the practitioner leaps into the air delivering a front kick and then lands with the kicking leg extended while the back leg is bent in a squatting position. At the same time the hands deliver two palm strikes: one to the opponent's head and one to the body.

When Xiao Cao performed this move his body would fly high into the air and then land in an impossibly low crouch, one leg and one arm extended. The only sound was that of his soft belching.

Even when it snowed we would continue with our practice, circling each other, sometimes for up to an hour, breath frosting on the freezing air. As I saw him start to change I would have to follow, wherever possible using the same changing movements that he did.

My memories of that winter in Beijing were of two wraiths in the snow, one of them gently burping.

Chapter Seven

A Sense of Place

he Chinese have long recognized the way in which the place you practice influences your training almost as much as what kind of training you do. Chinese poetry records "sword dances" in sunny glades. The fact that two of the great centers for Chinese boxing—Shaolin and Wudang—are both situated in remote rural areas tends to reinforce this.

One of the great pleasures I get out of my training is the feeling that I am carrying on a tradition centuries old, so that by performing a particular routine I am able in some essential way to join with all those exponents of the past. This feeling is heightened when actually training in the East.

Chinese martial art traditions hold that some locations are better than others because the *qi* there is better. Under trees and by water are both good spots for gaining the benefits of positive *qi*, particularly in the early morning or evening; and many training groups try to find a regular practice spot which meets these requirements.

Batu Pahat, the small town on the western coast of the southern Malaysian state of Johor, is a place where I have spent a great deal of time training.

Originally, the main "industry" in this area was sex and the town was known as "Little Paris," and was within convenient striking distance of Singapore. When I first started visiting Batu Pahat the town was riddled with brothels, night clubs, hostess bars, and hotels which rented rooms by the hour. All that has changed now for there have been a series of government clean-up campaigns and an infusion of genuine industrial projects into the area. It is now one of the fastest growing urban centers in Johor state, with new buildings, factories, and housing estates springing up left, right, and center.

A few miles inland from the Straits of Malacca and situated on the banks of the Batu Pahat river, the town is flanked on the other side by a chain of several hills that seem to spring up from the jungle. Approaching the town from any direction, the first indication that you are near is the sight of these hills looming like sentries in ever-vigilant watch over the sprawling streets below them.

One of these hills on the western outskirts of the town was a favorite training spot for Master Wu Chiang Hsing. I say was because now developers have moved in and built right up to the foot of the hill, thus preventing the access we had previously enjoyed.

Time was, however, that we would meet at the foot of the hill before dawn, and hands clasped over the *dantian*, knees bent in a semi-crouch, we would walk in the fashion known as the "heart-calming skill method" toward the hill. This method, in which the feet are kept on parallel tracks and the hips and waist relaxed, is a training method for centering relaxation and the development of root. With Master Wu and the hill added it also became a test of stamina and agility. For, setting a cracking pace, Master Wu would storm up the path to the jungle at the base of the hill. Then, hardly slowing down to acknowledge the gradually increasing incline, he would pick his way up the narrow path. To one side of him was jungle and the other the steep slope to the bottom of the hill. The fact that we kept our hands clasped in front of us so that they were not available for balance, and that it was still barely light, made the whole exercise more than a little perilous. At last we would reach the point where the path stopped about two thirds of the way up, and we would stop and rest. In this small clearing with jungle encroaching on three sides and a sheer drop of several hundred feet on the remaining open side, was situated a small Chinese shrine to which enthusiastic worshippers would come to pray for lucky numbers for the lottery.

Usually by the time we had reached this clearing the first red tendrils of dawn would be threading their way across the sky. Most days the air at that time and height was cool, and so after a brief rest it was refreshing to slowly weave through the movements of the solo form without ending up drenched in sweat.

Occasionally a cool breeze wafts in from the sea; the only sound is that of the birds singing high in the trees. The scent of incense from the shrine lends the practice an air of sanctity. There is something paradoxical about practicing this art that is so centered on the internal while in external surroundings that command attention because of their beauty. So it is that from time to time I find my attention drifting away from the form to the town now clearly laid out below. High buildings like the Carnival Hotel and one or two banks are clearly identifiable. The early morning light glints off the serpentine meandering of the river while the green carpet of jungle, which stretches as far as the eye can see, spouts thin streams of smoke from the fires of rubber plantation workers.

Such calm surroundings are conducive to good taiji and the form is imbued with a feeling of peace and tranquillity which is sometimes difficult to find in the humdrum, everyday world. It is also easier to feel in tune with the environment and to begin to perceive how taijiquan is a reflection of universal rhythms. After a while I also found that I could reproduce the tranquil state of mind I enjoyed while practicing in such places by imagining myself in a similar area even when practicing at home or in surroundings less relaxing.

• • •

While training in both Singapore and Malaysia I seem to have spent an inordinate amount of time on the concrete playground areas of community centers and schools. Such training always takes place in the evening under the harsh glare of floodlights around which in droves swarm all sorts of insect life. In Singapore such training is usually at local community centers; the open area surrounded by thousands of twinkling lights from the windows of high-rise blocks of flats, which are home to the majority of Singaporeans.

Such training in the strange pools of light and shadow caused by the floodlights, accompanied by the encroaching and choking night heat, always has about it an air of the surreal. I always seem to feel more drained and tired after such a training session than I do after sessions held in training halls.

One time Feng and I were learning sword sparring from Master Tan Ching Ngee and had accompanied him to one of his classes. Around 50 students were already in lines warming up, when we turned into the car park in Master Tan's battered old Nissan. The assistant instructor who was leading the class came over to meet us as we approached. I had known him for a number of years and we exchanged pleasantries before we were cut short by Master Tan motioning Feng and myself over to a pile of wooden straightswords. When we were suitably armed Master Tan sent us over into a distant corner of the playground. We had already learnt the *wu xing xiang ke* (five element complementary form), which is an exercise somewhat similar to solo *da lu*, but with a sword. The movements were designed to allow the exponent to practice a combination of swift and agile footwork and basic handling of the weapon.

While Master Tan led the class through the solo form, Feng and I fumbled our way through the movements, slowly becoming more fluent as we warmed up and found a pace and rhythm that were suitable. I thought we were doing quite well. The sweat was pouring off me, but it was a warm, comfortable feeling. I didn't even mind the blank stares of passers-by on the other side of the chain-link fence, which separated the school from the housing estate, at whose center we were.

Then Master Tan came over and it was obvious that our performance was not up to scratch. With an impatient frown he took up an attention position in front of us and directed us to follow his count. One, two, three, four, five. Over and over again with the pace picking up slowly but steadily until we were running through the whole sequence far faster than Feng and I had been doing it on our own.

The lights of the tower blocks overlooking us seemed to be flashing and whirling past and my grip on the wooden hilt of the sword was slippery and unsure. Somewhere along the way I gave up trying to conform to taiji principles. Instead, I just gave myself up to the ride.

It increasingly felt as if the hot air was sticking in my throat so that breathing became more and more difficult and the wooden sword which before had seemed lighter than the metal one I was used to practicing with now felt so heavy that if we continued much longer I was sure I would drop it.

At last Master Tan began to slow down the pace until finally we ended up once again in the attention position from which we had started. Now that we had stopped I was afflicted with a parching thirst, but that I would just have to bear.

"When you're doing this kind of solo practice always start off slow to ensure that you are relaxed, but then you can speed up until at an advanced stage you alternate the pace and the rhythm," Master Tan explained. "This training is to ensure that you have a firm grasp of the basics and that your footwork is quick and agile," he went on.

All it seemed to ensure for me in the heat of Singapore was that I was near dehydration and in a state of utter exhaustion.

"Carry on at your own pace," Master Tan said, and returned to the rest of the class.

• • •

Several hundred miles further north in Kuala Lumpur, I have also spent a considerable amount of time on school playgrounds or basketball courts. One of the largest of Master Koh Ah Tee's classes is held at the Number Two Independent Chinese High School. This enormous, well-equipped institution is situated in one of the city suburbs and surrounded by housing estates; these, however, are unlike Singapore's in that they are composed mainly of single and double-story houses, many of which are detached.

In this particular class there are an average of 60 students who, when arranged in rows, completely fill the concrete training area. A typical training session starts with waist-turning warm-ups followed by a variety of different standing-post exercises which ensure that by the time you actually start doing the form your legs have turned to jelly.

When these preliminaries are finished the students divide into two groups: one of beginners and one comprised of those who have finished the form.

At these sessions I would always try to take advantage of the dark and hide myself at the back of whichever group I was training with. On occasion, attempting to brush up on some of the basics I would join the beginner's group, only to be spotted by Master Koh and banished to join the others. This group would start their training by running through the form two or three times at such a slow pace that my already painful leg muscles would be shaking and cramping by the time we had finished.

136

"Having trained fairly extensively in both internal and external arts, I find it interesting that this training with Master Koh's class is more strenuous and exhausting than any of the external training I have done."

And all the time Master Koh would be going from student to student, repeating the same advice: "Relax. Remember that in taijiquan there are no arms."

Of course part of the paradoxical nature of taijiquan may be found in the fact that the harder you try to relax the more difficult and painful the practice becomes. In trying to sink my hips, relax my shoulders, and loosen my waist it felt as if my legs would give way at any moment and I would just crumple to the floor.

After this particular form marathon the next stage was practice of individual movements. These we would perform moving from one side of the training area to the other. "Brush knee, twist step" was followed by "step back, repulse monkey," followed by "cloud hands," then finally "diagonal flying to the left and right."

The final stage was pushing hands, commencing with solo training of the *si zheng tui* ("ward-off, roll-back, press, and push"). This, Master Koh tells his students, is vitally important for training *ting jing* and teaching the exponent to respond to what his partner does rather than initiate.

The effect of such training sessions was to strengthen the legs. Often I would swear that I could feel the concrete burning the soles of my feet—such was the pressure placed on them.

There is no experience quite like training in the heat of a tropical night. The air seems thick and wet so that it can almost be tasted as it is gulped down the parched throat. Eventually, a combination of exhaustion, dehydration, and the shadows cast by the lights causes the surroundings to float and blur before your eyes—a sure sign that it is time for rest and fluids.

At this point in the class the students would congregate in small groups, chatting about their training or in some cases just having a gossip. The braver ones would come over to talk with me while the advanced and keener students would get out their swords and start practicing the *jian* form.

Master Koh's students practice the straightsword at a much faster pace than I am used to and keeping up with them is not easy. When I asked Master Koh why he taught the form this way he replied that with *jian* it is important for each move to flow into the next and for there to be no pause or disconnection between the movements.

"*Jian* teaches agility and flexibility while retaining and even extending your *ting jing*. How is your *ting jing* extended? Instead of using the body or the hands to sense with you now have to listen with the end of the sword which, of course, is much harder."

Then, quite abruptly, the class would be over and students without ceremony would just leave. One minute they are milling around and the next they are gone.

Having trained fairly extensively in both internal and external arts, I find it interesting that this training with Master Koh's class is more strenuous and exhausting than any of the external training I have done. The constant strain on the legs and the paradoxical "struggle" to remain relaxed cause one to lose pounds in sweat while also enjoying the contented feeling which accompanies physical exhaustion resulting from a pleasant activity.

• • •

In 1985 I visited the Shaolin Temple, on Song mountain in Henan province, China. Although at that time I was primarily practicing the internal martial arts I still felt that this was something like a pilgrimage. There is a famous Chinese saying that all the Chinese martial arts under heaven come from Shaolin. In fact, only a month before on my birthday, Xiao Huang had given me a plaque inscribed with this very saying.

Ever since I had first read *Moving Zen* and dreamed about going to Japan, the fates had been guiding me step-by-step to this point; that was my feeling.

After the nine hour train ride to Zhengzhou it was another four hour bus ride up into the mountains to the famed temple itself. On this journey I saw firsthand the attitude toward Buddhist monks engendered by the communist regime. At one stop a monk tried to get on the bus but was ejected roughly by the driver and conductor. He sat dazed in the dust as the bus left the small village without him.

At the time I visited, Shaolin was not the big foreign tourist attraction that it is now. The Shaolin training center had not been set up nor had the teams of bogus monks been sent out around the world to peddle their dollar-earning wares.

When the bus dropped us off it was at the bottom of a track flanked on either side by small stalls selling food and souvenirs. These were tacky and tawdry goods which the Chinese tourists, attracted by the recent success of the film *The Shaolin Temple*, loved to buy.

I set off, backpack on my shoulder, up the road. At last the ground leveled out and there was a clearing surrounded by the very pine trees which lent the temple its name. On the right were the temple gates with the famous sign which had been featured in so many films. Here, too, there was no escape from the souvenir stalls, and it was only with very careful camera angling that I managed to get another visitor to take a photo of me at the gate. The first steps into the temple were not a disappointment, although much of the rest of it was. To the left and right of me and standing a full 15 feet high the two temple guardians with fierce, scowling faces and brightly colored robes. It was here that I saw what was, for China at that time, a rare sight: an old lady, maybe in her 80s, kneeling down to pray. A crowd of Chinese tourists pausing from their efforts in gawking at me were now staring intently at her.

I escaped from the crowd and went on in. Much of the temple had still not been rebuilt since the last time it was burnt down in the 1920s by some rampaging warlord. The enterprising folks from the China Travel Service had set up a stall where for a few *yuan* you could dress up as a Shaolin monk and have your photo taken. I regret to say that I did not seize that opportunity. Instead, I went to look at the famous mural which depicts monks, both dark and light skinned, practicing martial arts. This was worth seeing, as were the depressions in the floor of one of the halls which according to legend were made by successive generations of monks practicing their techniques. I have since seen various fanciful attempts to try to decide exactly which movements would have caused these evenly spaced depressions in the stone floor.

As I stood there I tried to summon some kind of sense of awe; after all, here I was at the source. But as with so many of China's historic sights, I felt no real sense of history. Whether this is because so much effort in China's recent past has gone into denying and twisting that very history. I don't know. The only place where I really felt the tread of thousands of feet and the pulse of the lifeblood of the centuries was at the Great Wall, but that is such a feat of man over nature that one cannot help but feel wonder.

Having seen all there was to see in the temple I wandered down the main steps and outside and down the small path that led to the field of stupas, each one commemorating a former Abbot. Here it was easier to imagine that one was in Ancient China for this place had been featured in so many films as a backdrop for desperate fights and miraculous escapes as monks fled the evil invaders, perhaps casting one backlong glance at the burning temple before they set off to spread the martial arts of Shaolin throughout China.

More than a decade later I saw the "Shaolin monks" demonstrate in Malaysia. I was sitting with Masters Wu Chiang Hsing and Liang He Ching. As the monks cavorted through their gymnastic modern wushu forms and then performed various pieces of non-sense with swords, motorbikes, and even a Proton Saga saloon car, both of my companions voiced their disgust, pointing out that there was nothing the so-called monks did that local Chinese martial artists couldn't have, and indeed hadn't done better. One thing they definitely could have done better: when the monks came on at the beginning of the show, resplendent in their orange robes, they sat down supposedly in meditation, but not one of them had the straight back of the practitioner of Ch'an (Zen), and Shaolin is where Chan came from! Da Mo (Bodhidarma) spun quietly in his grave!

But back in 1985, standing looking at the green and brown of the hills as they paled away to the horizon, I still knew nothing of the future encounters I was going to have with the true descendants of Shaolin.

• • •

A year later and back in China again, this time not to work but to represent Britain, my teammates and I were on a mission to show our Chinese hosts that not only could we do wushu but that we knew how to have a very good time indeed.

As a team the eight of us had been together for the five months since the selections and had already suffered marathon training sessions at the hands of our coaches. We had also traveled around the United Kingdom giving demonstrations as well as having visited Germany. In short, we knew each other very well. Kim Han, the British Chinese team coach, had made me team captain as he felt because I was a school teacher I would be responsible. Bad mistake! In my case, responsibility ended the minute I finished work and I introduced my teammates to the delight of water pistol fights and never-ending practical jokes. Just because we stripped him to his underpants in the bar of the Tianjin International Hotel, Little Monkey, as one of the team was known, dismantled the furniture in my room and put it in the bathroom as well as filling my and my roommates beds with shaving foam.

The normally staid and respectable corridors of this colonial-style building echoed to our screams as we chased each other down the corridors, water pistols in hand. Not wishing to be left out, some of the hotel floor attendants also armed themselves and the war became more widespread.

There was, however, just a week before the competition. Still training to be done, in the evening we would travel by bus to the large arena, where the competition was to be held, to go through our paces. In the early mornings we were expected to do our own training and so the three of us who had become so inseparable that we were dubbed the three musketeers would be found in the extensive gardens of the hotel. Present at the competition were a number of China's leading masters, including Li Tianji and Sha Guozheng. The latter, famous for his bagua and xingyi, could be seen every morning running at a slow pace around the grounds executing the *paoquan* movement from xingyi. This exercise was said to be good for the heart.

We also considered our training to be good for our hearts. First we would start off with a desultory trot around the grounds, Little Monkey in the lead closely followed by Dave, the "Northern Man," and puffing along behind them, me, the "Flying Elephant."

This was only the prelude to the main event, however, for at 7:00 A.M. on the dot we would hurry to the rear of the hotel and amongst the quiet and beauty of the well-kept gardens behind a shrub just big enough for the three of us, we would engage in some spirited *qigong*. For us, the *qigong* consisted of deep breathing, but for the seven female members of the Japanese team who exercised just in front of our place of concealment, it was a matter of rhythmically tensing, contracting, and trembling their whole bodies; in particular their well-rounded, beautifully formed, pear-shaped hindquarters.

That for me was *Tianjin:* trembling Japanese bottoms in the early morning light.

Chapter Eight

Weapons Training

ince the Chinese martial arts in general were developed from battlefield techniques, the training in and usage of a variety of weapons is considered important.

Traditionally, there were 18 weapons which a candidate for the Imperial martial arts examinations would be expected to have gained proficiency in. These were divided into three groups: long weapons, short weapons, and flexible weapons. Saber and straightsword were considered to be short, while staff, halberd, and spear were categorized as long. Such weapons as the nine section steel whip and the rope dart were termed flexible.

Coming from karate where I had no experience with weapons, having previously only swung around a home-made pair of nunchakus, inflicting serious injury on the furniture and less serious but still painful injury on myself, I found weapons training initially very awkward.

The first weapon I studied was the one that is commonly regarded as being one of the most difficult: the *taiji jian.*

This was introduced to me by Coach Peng after I had learnt the 48-step composite taiji form from him. The *jian* form he taught was the 32-step, a simplified version of the traditional Yang style *jian.* While he was studying to be a teacher at Beijing Normal University, this was one of the forms he had specialized in and consequently he had repeated it thousands of times. In order to make this training easier he had had his sword especially ground down so that it was two thirds of the size of a standard *jian,* thus making it lighter and much easier to handle. This mini sword became the focus of much envy among his classmates and he was offered large sums of money to part with hit. This he refused to do.

The author practicing with the taiji sword.

Three times a week Coach Peng would turn up outside my apartment on his Flying Pigeon bike and un-strap his mini sword from its place on the crossbar and then we would begin.

The *jian* is regarded as being one of the most difficult weapons to master because it requires sensitive handling and agile footwork. Unlike the Japanese *katana,* the present day *jian* is comparatively fragile and whenever possible contact with the opponent's blade is avoided altogether. When absolutely essential the third of the blade nearest the handle—where the metal is thickest and most blunt—is used for parrying. The skilled swordsman seeks to use the end third of the blade—which is the sharpest—to cut the opponent's wrist or arm, thus rendering him harmless.

Throughout its history the *jian* has been associated with high rank, being carried as a symbol of authority by Imperial officials. It has also served as a magical tool in the shamanistic practices of Chinese folk religion. Thus, the *jian* is regarded as being far more than just a weapon.

In taiji *jian* the same principles are used as in empty hand taiji. The whole body is used in every movement and a clear distinction is made between the substantial and insubstantial parts of the body. Furthermore, the exponent learns to blend with the attacker's movements so that ultimately the enemy defeats himself.

But I was not to learn this for quite some years.

At first with Coach Peng I struggled with the problems of keeping my movements taiji-like while holding a length of steel in my hand. It took several months before I began at last to feel reasonably comfortable. The grip required of the exponent of taiji *jian* is very similar to that demanded of the Chinese calligrapher. The handle of the sword is held firmly but sensitively and a slight space is left between hilt and palm. The aim is to have control of the sword, but in such a way that the practitioner's awareness is always held on the very end of the sword. In Chinese this is described as "extending the *qi* to the end of the blade."

Despite the challenge, I kept at it and once I knew the whole form I endeavored to practice it at least 30 times a day. We would meet at the center of the Friendship Hotel complex in an area that was cemented over. It was prevented from looking like a car park by the fact that flower beds and grassed areas were laid out in a symmetrical pattern around the edges and in the middle. At one end of the area, which was flanked on three sides by evergreen trees, was a rock garden complete with hillock and grottoes. While, facing it across the square was the magnificent theater building with its green tiled and upsweeping Chinese-style roof. Unfortunately, this building was not open as it had been damaged by fire and was still in a state of poor repair.

We would practice on a wide path between two flower beds, our bicycles parked to one side. In the winter, the snow fell on us as we glided through the motions. There was something truly magical about practicing the graceful and seemingly seamless movements of taiji sword with a thin frosting of snow crunching underfoot. The vastness of the North China sky hanging over the surrounding snow-kissed trees also added to the atmosphere.

In the summer, we were both soaked until we looked as if we'd been swimming. Coach Peng had endless patience, although much of it might have been inspired by looking forward to the two or three bottles of beer that we always drank at the end of each session.

The movements of Peng's swordplay were very precise since he had been trained in the "by-the-numbers" tradition of the university sports coach. Each posture was explained not only in terms of possible application but also of visual attention, mental concentration, and "spirit."

Peng's main teacher had been the daughter of Li Tianji, one of the committee of taiji experts responsible for creating the 24-step taiji form in 1955. It was Li also who had helped devise the 32-step *jian* form that Peng was teaching me.

Having trained in the modern tradition, Peng was a stickler for precision, insisting that every move be correct and the foundation he laid was to stand me in good stead in later years.

Indeed, it was not until 1988 that I learnt the traditional *jian* form associated with the Yang family that was later modified by Cheng Man Ching. This I was taught by Master Tan Ching Ngee.

The major differences between the Yang style version of the form and that taught by Cheng lies in the emphasis on agility and flow; both of which were more important to Cheng than the actual precise application of each technique. In addition, Cheng saw *jian* as a means of training the *qi* and through doing so, developing greater *ting jing*. This, as I have mentioned earlier, is the process of extending the *qi* to the end of the sword, which in plainer terms means always being aware of the end of the sword, the sharpest and therefore the most dangerous part. This awareness may only be achieved if the practitioner is relaxed and the sword-wielding hand kept firm but flexible.

Great flexibility, too, is required in the wrist of the right hand. The left hand also plays a part with the first two fingers extended while the thumb is wrapped over the last two which are bent. This sword hand configuration, as well as holding magic symbolism as a means of channeling *qi,* also serves to counterbalance the sword hand and remind the exponent of the delicate nature of the weapon he is using.

What further characterizes Cheng Man Ching's practice of *jian* is the sword-sparring where two practitioners maintain contact between the blades of their swords while moving around freely, attempting to maneuver each other into a position where their partner will find himself in a position vulnerable to a cut. It is important that the exercise does not degenerate into two people just attempting to hit each other with swords. After all, in the best tradition of Cheng's taiji, the exponent should not be trying to do anything to his opponent; rather, the opponent should cause it to happen to himself.

The clearest way to understand sword-sparring is to see it as but an extension of moving-step pushing hands, wherein the aim is to develop sensitivity. In sword work, because you are using inanimate objects your *ting jing* has, if anything, to be keener.

I learnt sword-sparring in the best way: by actually doing it with experts. Both Master Tan Ching Ngee and Master Lau Kim Hong spent a great deal of time showing me how the *ting jing* developed in pushing hands practice may then be extended to be used with the sword. When I was too hard, gripping the sword too firmly, or exerting too much pressure against the master's blade, I would learn the hard way that this was wrong as the tip of his sword flashed past my face or thudded meatily into my ribs.

Master Tan relies on the speed of his footwork to weave intricate patterns around his opponent, who, in turn, is forced to move faster and faster until, inevitably, he stiffens and resists, which provides the needed opening so that he finds himself neatly skewered on the end of the master's sword.

• • •

Master Lau, however, is more sedate and measured in his approach, preferring to gently stick to your blade and just follow until impatience or carelessness allows him an opening.

At the first Johor State Taijiquan Championships I had had the dubious fortune to be Master Tan's partner in a demonstration of sword-sparring. Now here I was doing it again, but this time at a charity event in front of an invited audience, and again at Johor Baru's prestigious Number One Chinese High School. The event had been going on for several hours and the crowd was hot and restless. The fact that the large school hall was inadequately ventilated and filled with fans made the atmosphere not only tense but extremely uncomfortable.

As we marched out into the center of the floor I could feel my palm already sweaty on the polished red oak handle of my sword. The audience was almost quiet in anticipation of a performance which pitted an "angmolan" (literally, red-haired person) against a Chinese. For a Chinese audience to be quiet is no mean feat and it did not make me feel any better.

Master Tan Ching Ngee performing the taiji spear.

We turned to face each other, stepped back to ensure that we were at a safe distance to start with, and bowed to each other. Then it began. I initiated as we had previously agreed and stepped in making a chopping attack to Master Tan's throat. He intercepted and stepping in deeply turned my blade over so that his sword had an open path to my mid-section. This put me completely on the defensive and I stumbled backward as fast as I safely could, at the same time attempting to keep contact with his blade, but without making my touch so heavy that he could use my force against me.

Somehow I managed to evade and then I was moving forward, my sword darting toward Master Tan's seemingly unprotected legs. No stumbling retreat for him. He hopped and skipped backwards and in the process turned my sword over and suddenly the tables were turned. He was moving forward and his sword was flashing up high against my face. With a thwacking sound the wooden blade hit me on the neck. Although the sound of impact might not have been audible to the audience their response, a loud collective intake of breath, filled the hall. This was like a more painful re-run of our last such public encounter.

The convention in sticking swords is that after loss of contact between the blades, or one of the partners being hit, that the two should separate to a safe distance and either finish or restart the encounter.

We both stepped back. I could feel my neck burning red where he had hit it. I moved forward to attack again, making a thrusting attack at Master Tan's chest. His interception turned into an attack on my wrist and then we were locked into one of the basic training patterns for sword sparring. This one is known as "stirring" and consists of executing a circling action, mainly using the wrist and causing the point of your sword to revolve around the blade of your partner's sword. The ultimate aim being to cut his wrist either on the top or the bottom. Exponents of *jian* practice this move both with a partner, moving up and down and solo, a doorknob being a favorite aiming point during practice.

As Master Tan moved forward, I retreated in short, shuffling follow-steps, all the time trying to keep my blade both circling and threatening his wrist. Moving backward, whether in an empty-handed or armed encounter, is always discouraged for the taiji exponent, as an opponent can always move faster forward than you can backwards. The trick is to try to sidestep or turn the opponent's attack in some way before you lose control. Master Tan was far too skilled to allow me to do this so my only option was to attempt an attack myself, but first I had to ensure my own safety by engaging his blade and leading it away. Stopping my circling motion halfway through, I pushed my blade in against his, at the same time moving forward and pressing down on his blade.

My target was his abdomen, which I hoped to cut in the action described as "washing," which would be executed as I moved past him and toward his rear on a diagonal line. I had a feeling from the start that it was a move doomed to failure, but I had no choice. The first I knew of my failure was when I felt the cold wood of his sword sliding across my stomach. What he had done was use against me exactly the move I was hoping to use on him.

The crowd applauded as we separated, sword points and extended fingers of the left hand facing each other. Then we stepped back, bowed to each other and then to the audience.

• • •

Before he opened his now highly successful medical clinic in Singapore, Tan Ching Ngee spent over a year in Taiwan. His original motive for going there was to start a business, but when this failed he made his living by teaching taiji. In particular he taught *jian*. During his sojourn there I spent some time with him learning more about the *jian*. In order to facilitate the learning of this complex weapon by beginners Master Tan had developed a short solo form, which contained all of the 13 sword methods as well as giving vital practice in the six different grips used when holding the weapon.

Twice a week, on Tuesday and Thursday evenings, Master Tan held a class in the lobby of a large office building owned by one of his students. The class was small with no more than 12 people in attendance, but all of them were long-term disciples of the art and eager to learn more about the straightsword.

On the night in question it was dark and raining and John and I shook out our umbrellas as we entered the lobby and exchanged greeting with the other students. Master Tan had not yet arrived, so we warmed up and then started practicing follow-stepping and "stirring" up and down the marble floor.

Then in an explosion of raindrops and a shaking of the bright yellow rain gear that he was wearing, Master Tan arrived. Quickly we lined up—speed is always of the essence in Master Tan's classes. Facing him, we executed a standing bow and then went through a series of stretching exercises, all of which used our wooden swords as a kind of prop. Then it was time for follow-stepping. After we had become used to the fast forward and backward movements we changed to diagonal moves and constant changes of direction.

Partner work came next and John and I faced off, red-faced and panting from the exertion. Perhaps we had spent a little too much time recently in the bars and karaoke joints. We grinned at each other; we must both have had the same thought. Then it was up and down, first stirring, then cutting diagonally while your partner tried desperately to parry. Following that with swords sticking we took turns in overturning our partner's blade, putting ourselves in position to counterattack with a chopping action to the neck. In this way we trained all of the thirteen sword moves.

Now it was time for the five element solo form, again executed at a cracking pace. Finally we came to the *piece de resistance:* the 13 sword method form. This we started off more slowly as some of the students had only just completed it but as we went on the pace picked up.

At last Master Tan signaled us to stop, and we gathered around him as he explained: "In *jian* the arm and the body move together so that the very end of the sword, the tail, moves and has life. In *jian*, as in the solo form, *song* is of vital importance. It is something that you should have inside you that can be brought out at any time, even and especially in times of stress. A lot of people talk about *song* but real *song* is hard to get, although you can kid yourself that you are *song*. Real *song* is when you use it and it is not soft but rather is agile, so that all your joints are extremely flexible—the quality of bamboo!"

With a wave of his hand, Master Tan indicated that we should rest.

"When you've had a rest choose a partner for sword-sparring."

We rested.

• • •

From Master Liang He Qing I learnt a variety of both northern and southern weapons, including spear, broadsword, staff, sword, short stick, and walking stick.

One of Master Liang's favorite forms is the hongquan staff form called Yang Wulang bagua staff. The story goes that Huang Fei Hong learnt the form from Yang Wulang, who came from north China. The form had been a family treasure for generations and was originally a spear form. Master Liang's grandmaster, Lam Sai Wing, had added his own six-and-a-half point pole techniques to the form, which he had originally learnt from Huang Fei Hong.

The form itself is designed for what is called the single-headed pole. This is a pole which is tapered at one end; this end being the primary striking tool. It is usually over seven feet long and made of a heavy hardwood. Through training with the pole one's empty hand *jing* is developed as one constantly aims to get all the power to the end of the weapon.

Amongst students of Huang Fei Hong's lineage, this form is regarded as something of a treasure. On a number of occasions Master Liang's elder brothers in Kuala Lumpur have warned him not to teach the form too freely.

Included in Yang Wulang bagua pole is a full range of techniques from using the tip of the pole in precision strikes to huge sweeping motions designed to clear the immediate area of attackers.

Master Liang's teacher, Song Sao Bo, was famous for his skill with the staff and as a result during the Japanese occupation he was challenged by a Japanese officer skilled in the use of the sword. So severely did Master Song trounce the challenger that he was forced to go into hiding to escape retribution from other Japanese.

When I learnt this form, I did so together with a visiting student from England. We were forced to get up very early in the morning or train at locations away from prying eyes, because, for a number of years, various martial arts enthusiasts in the town had asked Master Liang to teach them this form and he had always put them off with one excuse or another. We were very honored that he had decided to teach us. That he had done so reflected the strength of his character and his strongly-held belief that the Chinese martial arts should be for all who were interested. In the past this had meant teaching them to all Chinese, irrespective to which dialect group they belonged, but as time passed this also extended to teaching foreigners.

Just a few weeks earlier Master Liang had been warned off teaching too much to the foreigner. His reply to this, however, was that if the Chinese were interested in learning they would come and learn from him. In the meantime if a foreigner was enthusiastic enough to dedicate himself to learning Chinese martial arts he would teach him. As he often said, "Our skin may be a different color but our blood is the same red."

Before learning the form itself we were taught a simple series of basic movements which included two blocking actions and a thrusting strike. Repeated in all four directions, this exercise teaches basic weapon handling and introduces the student to the way in which force is directed to the tip of the weapon.

Another method for developing the necessary power involves repeatedly lifting the staff up so that it is held across the chest, parallel to the ground, and then both hands push the staff down, attempting to make the end of the weapon shake. When lifting up, in what is actually a blocking action, the same shaking effect is sought. The downward push is a strike. A skilled staff wielder is supposed to have such a level of power that a strike on the opponent's weapon will at best smash it and at the least cause him to drop it.

Such basic exercises are meant to be practiced thousands of times on a daily basis. One by-product of such training is that it develops a *jing* that may also be expressed empty-handed.

In order to shake the end of the weapon, the whole body must be relaxed so that no tension impedes the release of force; such an absence of tension also enables power to be emitted from the hands and feet when the exponent is unarmed.

In addition to practicing the form students are also expected to practice auxiliary exercises to improve their accuracy. One such exercise includes spreading beans on the

Master Liang He Qing performs 5 Tigers spear.

floor and then smashing them with the tip of the staff. Another requires that the exponent repeatedly strikes at a sheet of paper which is hanging in the air.

In order to develop more power the student can make use of a heavier pole while still paying attention to extending *jing* to the tip of the weapon.

Pin-point precision with the staff makes the weapon extremely dangerous and, as Master Liang is quick to remind his students, the staff is not for playing around with. As a cautionary tale he recounts how two of his *shixiong* were practicing staff applications when one of them didn't move fast enough to avoid a blow and the tip of his partner's staff took out his eye.

One unique characteristic of the way the staff is handled in Wu Lang bagua pole is that the front hand is held with the index finger extended along the staff, pointing in the opponent's direction. This method of handling facilitates the turning, screwing movements which when correctly initiated from the waist produce more power. Critics aver that such a method of holding the weapon makes the index finger vulnerable to strikes from the opponent's staff, but as Master Liang notes it takes only a fraction of a second to remove the hand or place it under the staff in such a way that it is protected.

Throughout most of the form the left hand is held at the butt end of the staff with the right hand forward—the conventional method for holding the staff. However, during the movements of the six-and-a-half point pole added by Lam Sai Wing, the left hand is placed at the front. Thus, the exponent learns how to wield the weapon on both sides.

About an inch of the butt is left to extend beyond the back hand. This is done so that it may be used to strike the opponent or apply *chin-na* counters should the hand be seized.

Master Song was very careful about who exactly he taught the form to, insisting that students should have trained with him for a minimum of three years before he would even consider teaching them.

The form consists of 72 movements and as such serves as an efficient kind of cardiovascular conditioning. Kicking and jumping techniques also feature so that the total effect is to train the exponent's whole body. Tactically, the form teaches the exponent to change blocks and parries into crushing counters. The grip on the staff varies as the wielder moves to different ranges. Through repeated practice the weapon becomes an extension of the practitioner's hands.

The Chinese are aware of the way in which certain weapons suit particular people and this certainly proved to be the case with Miles, the young student visiting from England. The very first time he picked up the pole and swung it around his head it made a singing noise as it cut through the air. Try as I might, it was several months before I could make anything approaching the same noise. Now when Miles does the Wu Lang bagua pole he looks the spitting image of Master Liang and has acquired a real internal power which is evident in all the movements. He is truly a worthy student of Master Liang and carries on a proud tradition.

To return to Master Liang, he urges that the student should use the power of the whole body, which should then be augmented with a turning motion of the wrists so that even the smallest of motions is able to generate great power.

"The power of the staff comes from turning and rotation," Master Liang notes. "Without this rotation it is just a dead piece of wood."

Indeed, as Master Liang observes, the untrained man who picks up a staff is just depriving himself of his hands. But for the student trained in its use, the staff is truly a deadly weapon.

Master Liang's skill with the staff is of an extremely high level. After he had finished teaching me the Wu Lang bagua pole and I had learnt the applications to his satisfaction, we started on freestyle applications whereby I attacked and he defended and then we changed roles. No matter which role I played it invariably ended the same: with my staff knocked out of my hand and Master Liang's staff just millimeters away from some vital point.

"You must be extremely careful when using the staff," he said, "for the staff has no eyes. This means that it is extremely hard to control. When you are practicing empty-handed applications, if your partner moves into danger you can see it and control your actions. If you're using a staff, this is much harder to do as the end of the staff moves extremely fast and it is difficult to know how much force you are actually using as what feels like a small, soft movement, by the time it has reached the end of the staff, may well be extremely hard and fast."

One of his favorite moves consists of a number of strikes aimed alternately at each of the opponent's feet, all the time moving forward to put him on the defensive, and then finally aiming a strike at a point on the floor between his legs after which the staff is jerked sharply upwards, striking him in the groin.

As we practiced, Master Liang pointed out the similarities between staff work and taiji pushing hands.

"Once you make contact with the opponent's staff you must stick to it. If you take it off you give your opponent the opportunity to hit you. Once you are stuck to his staff, try to slide up the weapon to strike his hand but be careful because he will be trying to do the same thing to you."

One practice method known as staff-sticking involves the two exponents moving freely but attempting to ensure that their staffs remain connected and that they don't put themselves into a dangerous position.

A major criticism that Master Liang had of me during this exercise was that I used too much force; I was not relaxed enough. This was humiliating. I had spent the last two decades practicing taiji in an attempt not to use excessive force and I thought I had a grasp on relaxation.

For every move that I attempted, Master Liang had a counter and always in such a way that I was left fighting to regain my balance while he was in a strong stable stance.

"In reality," he said to me, "no encounter with a staff would last this long. One or two moves and it would be over. Against a real expert you have no chance to even hold up your staff, for with one blow it will be knocked to the floor, then you are finished. Even if you have a broadsword or a straightsword, honestly speaking, apart from in gongfu films you would stand no chance."

• • •

Tan Ching Ngee also taught staff-sticking, although in his case the weapons used—although poles—represented spears and were held with the right hand at the butt end. Before the student actually progressed to freestyle he first had to learn a two-person form which incorporated all the major techniques as well as giving practice in following a set pattern while sticking to your partner's weapon.

Master Tan's own staff experience was extensive. When he was in his early teens he spent three years with a Shaolin master named Huang Yi Mei. Huang was famous for his staffwork and he insisted that his young protégé should be able to break an opponent's staff with one blow. Once he had mastered this skill he was taught forms. Furthermore, with Chen Yu He, Master Tan learnt northern spear. All of this knowledge he synthesized into his sticking staff.

The author practicing "sticky" staff with Master Lau Kim Hong.

"Remember, in staffwork there are only a few moves; it is very simple but *ting jing* is the purpose of this training and as such you must rely on the skills you have acquired through practice of other areas of the taiji curriculum," Master Tan lectured, as I and my classmates took a rest under the harsh arc lights of the basketball court where we were practicing.

"When your staffs are in contact try to make no sound. If they are scraping together it means you are using too much force. Your footwork must be agile and nimble and you must use the waist to turn your opponent's weapon."

As we continued with the class Master Tan moved around offering advise and giving corrections where needed. He showed me how by gripping with equal amounts of force in both hands I actually hindered my ability to feel what the opponent was doing.

"This is taiji; that means that you must have *yin* and *yang* in the hands. If one hand is using force, the other must be relaxed. Also try to keep one arm, usually the back one, close in against your body so that when the waist moves everything moves."

Later on, when we were in the car driving back to his flat, Master Tan pointed out the similarities between this exercise and the sword-sparring.

"You must use a stance that is weighted 50/50," he glanced across at me and saw the look of shock on my face. This made him smile.

"This stance is called the *hun yuan bu*. *Hun yuan* is the state before taiji (it translates as primordial chaos). Differentiating substantial and insubstantial is for training. By being in the state before taiji you have the potential to move with blinding speed and use devastating power. You can respond instantly in any direction."

Interesting as this was, I found the most important lessons of the staff-sticking to be in the area of putting into practical effect the requirement of "giving up yourself to follow others." For it was only when my mind was quiet and my ego not involved to the extent that I was not concerned with having to hit my partner, that I could successfully stick to him no matter what he did.

As Master Koh is fond of saying, "taiji is very simple, but we human beings want the complex, and that is a hard desire to drop."

• • •

The weapons taught by Master Tan Swoh Theng are those of the five ancestor boxing system and, as such, are typically southern. The first weapon form I learnt from him was the double daggers. This form uses two double-edged knives, something like the famous World War II commando knife. They are held in an icepick grip—that is, with the blade protruding from the bottom of the clenched fist. While Western knife fighting experts point out that such a grip is inefficient as it does not allow for flexibility in terms of the type of cuts and thrusts delivered, as used in five ancestor boxing the fact that there are two knives more than makes up for this. Most of the strikes are delivered in long scything, sweeping actions with extended arms. And while the initial strike may well be blocked, the other arm's follow-through action stands a high chance of striking home. If, in turn, this arm is blocked then the other arm cuts through and so on. The double daggers may also be used against long weapons, with the nearest

The author's brother-in-law, Tan Ya Hak, practicing with the tiger fork of wuzuquan.

dagger being used to block and trap the weapon allowing the other dagger to strike.

Through practicing the double daggers, the wuzuquan stylist learns to operate at a longer range than in most of the empty-hand forms. Leaping techniques are included to enable him to get quickly in and out of range.

The weapons may also be hidden until the last moment by the simple expedient of lying them flat against the underside of each arm and then, with a flick of the wrist, bringing them into cutting or stabbing position.

After double daggers I learnt the plum blossom broadsword form. Unlike most southern Chinese systems, wuzuquan weapons usage does not include pretty movements or empty flourishes. Instead, each movement is purely functional. Southern broadsword relies on strong cutting and hacking actions with the strength of the whole body placed firmly behind each offensive and defensive motion.

Broadsword usage is characterized by the coiling action whereby the sword circles the head, blunt edge across the back. This action serves both as a defense against an attack from behind and to generate power for the next strike.

A figure-eight swinging action of the sword in front of the body is used to keep the opponent away until an opportunity presents itself to close in and deliver a finishing cut. The empty-hand is often used to intercept the opponent's attacking arm after you have stepped inside his attack, blocking it with your own sword.

154

Known as the "hundred day weapon" because of the number of days it took to train an exponent to a level of basic competence, the broadsword was a favored weapon of the Chinese foot soldier.

Master Tan insisted that a heavy weapon should be used and that all the techniques should be delivered with as much power as possible.

"The broadsword must convey the spirit of the tiger. You must be fierce, powerful, and overwhelming," he urged.

"Training with weapons develops the body and improves your strength, endurance, and agility," he went on to explain. "In all of the wuzuquan weapons forms you will notice that there is a characteristic side-stepping maneuver followed by an attack from the diagonal. This you could say is the secret of the art: when an attack comes in, side-step and attack from the diagonal."

And of course he was right, for the forms in all Chinese martial arts systems serve not only as catalogues of techniques but also as keys to explain how the techniques are meant to be applied both tactically and strategically.

• • •

Like his friend Liang He Qing, Master Lau Kim Hong has long been a staunch advocate of the use of the staff as a handy and truly functional weapon. His first lessons in its use came when he learnt white crane boxing from a teacher famed for his skill with the staff.

Although Master Lau soon gave up white crane, and eventually specialized in taijiquan, he never stopped practicing the staff.

In the late 1960s when racial tension in Malaysia was running high and many Chinese were afraid of being attacked by machete-wielding Malays, who are permitted to carry knives as a part of their national costume, Master Lau ran courses in staff fighting. In order to be able to teach people quickly and easily how to defend themselves, he had to encapsulate his knowledge into a simple system.

This system has stood the test of time and now over two decades later he is still teaching it. What Master Lau did was combine taiji's follow-stepping footwork and use of the waist with one thrusting attack, one overhead and one underneath strike, and five blocking actions that could also serve as strikes.

At first the student learns the thrusting attack and a simple downward movement of the end of the staff which could knock an opponent's weapon to the floor. These are practiced with both forward and backward follow-stepping. Then four more blocking moves are added, two on a high line to block attacks to the head or chest, two on the low line to block attacks to the legs and groin.

The student also learns a two-handed block to stop an overhead attack from hitting the head, and a lower block to stop an attack coming under and up at the groin. The two attacks are also practiced with the grip moving so that first one end of the staff is used then the other.

> **"Training with weapons develops the body and improves your strength, endurance, and agility."**

After the student has become familiar with these movements through practicing them in solo they can be applied with a partner. The attacker steps forward thrusting to the throat twice, and then on the lower line twice, and finally to the chest again. The defender steps back, parrying high to the outside and inside, low to the outside and inside, and, as the last thrust comes in, he knocks his partner's weapon down to the floor and starts his own thrusting sequence, as he, in turn, moves forward. In a variation of this same exercise the attacker strikes with a blow coming from the outside at the defender's head, then from the other side, then with a two-handed overhead strike, and finally with a blow coming up from underneath. The defender parries appropriately before changing roles and becoming the attacker.

Master Lau also includes actual striking training in his staff curriculum, whereby the students practice thrusts against a large tree stump which is placed upright in the middle of the training area. The students walk around this "target" hitting at different heights in response to shouted commands. This not only improves their accuracy and reaction-time, but also gives them the opportunity to feel and deal with the impact when the staff hits something other than air.

A number of Master Lau's students have had occasion to use their staff skills in self-defense when attacked by knife-wielding opponents. This is not to say that they carried six-foot poles with them wherever they went but that the same skills may be used with a shorter length of wood or even a piece of piping. By learning weapons skills the exponent gives himself another option should trouble arise.

Master Lau himself has had trouble involving the staff but this occurred, of all places, at his own training hall. He was teaching a class on the use of the weapon for self-defense, when out of the corner of his eye he noticed one student holding the staff as if he were about to attack. He was. He made a savage thrusting attack at Master Lau's mid-section but the master was able to step to the side and with a hard parry knock his would-be attacker's staff from his hands. Then in a follow-up move so fast that it seemed to be part of the parry, the end of his staff plunged into the student's stomach doubling him over so that he collapsed on the floor.

Another student, a friend of the man on the floor, angrily demanded to know why Master Lau had responded with so much force.

"I didn't," Lau replied. "If I had used a lot of force he would be dead. He tried to attack the teacher and he was not trying to control his force."

With that he instructed the two to leave his class. They didn't come back.

• • •

Another weapon that I learnt from Master Lau was the walking stick. This he learnt from Yang Ching Feng, a resident of Master Lau's hometown and who was also the taiji and northern Shaolin teacher of Master Liang He Qing. Master Yang was a graduate of the Xiamen Jing Wu school in China, but the walking stick didn't come from there. Where exactly he learnt it from I didn't find out until I met Master Liang.

It seemed that Master Yang knew a police inspector in a nearby town who had also trained extensively in Chinese martial arts. One of his specialties was the use of the walking stick and the short stick, which is the same length as the walking stick but without the hook at one end. Master Yang agreed to teach his policeman acquaintance the tiger and crane form of hongquan in exchange for the two stick forms.

Master Liang learnt both of these forms from Master Yang almost immediately because Master Yang had forgotten some of the tiger and crane form. Master Liang "helped" him to remember and in gratitude was given the two stick forms.

Suffice to say, Master Lau had modified the walking stick to accord with taiji principles and had renamed it the taiji walking stick. His logical mind and desire to systematically teach the weapon also led him to extrapolate a series of basic moves which the student practices first solo and then in application with a partner.

I learnt these from him in 1988 when I was staying at his Johor Baru training hall. While his *qigong* class cavorted around in the frenzied movements of "spontaneous *qigong*," I sweated over the 54 moves of the form.

As with all aspects of the taiji curriculum, I received the same basic advice: use your waist, relax, let the power come from the legs. It's surprising how such oft-heard and supposedly heeded advice is so swiftly forgotten when faced with the challenge of the new.

One nice aspect of this weapon is that both ends are used. At one point in the form the stick is grasped by the straight end, with both hands, and the hook is used to hook around the opponent's neck and then his ankle. The tip may be used for poking attacks and the length used for delivering stinging, lashing strikes. Believe me I know, for once, under the guise of testing out my *neigong* training, I got a martial arts brother to hit me repeatedly across the ribs, full power with one of the rattan walking sticks. The cuts healed quicker than the bruises and I guess I was lucky that none of my ribs were broken!

The Temple of Ten Thousand Lives is on a hill outside the town where I live. Like the majority of Chinese temples in Malaysia, it is dedicated to a wide range of deities and is run by one of the many "black societies" that are an all-pervading part of everyday life for the Chinese. At the front of the temple is a wide area overlooked by a landscaped mini-mountain, complete with flowing waterfalls and little pavilions. The temple has three floors, with most of the ground floor being dedicated to a large altar on which sits three life-sized Chinese deities. On either side of this altar stand racks of weapons which represent the warrior gods guarding the altar. The second floor contains a room used for meetings, while the top floor contains an altar dedicated to Ji Gong, the vagabond Buddha; a favorite god of the socially marginal and the dispossessed. Ji Gong dresses like a tramp and regularly breaks the Buddhist precepts; eating meat, drinking alcohol, and generally behaving in a disreputable fashion. Despite his appearance and superficial behavior, however, Ji Gong performs good deeds and helps the poor and weak on their way to enlightenment. In temples such as this, offerings of Guinness are placed on the altar—this stout also being associated with gangsters.

It was in this temple that Master Liang was teaching a group of Western students the straight short stick, companion to the curved one so beloved of Master Lau.

This form, consisting as it does of only 30 or so movements, is easy to teach and full of useful techniques.

We were assembled in the large covered area adjacent to the temple when Master Liang arrived, emerging from his Honda Accord, clutching a bag full of rattan sticks. He asked the students to gather around while he explained the background to the form and its basic usage.

The story concerning how Yang Ching Feng had learnt the form from a Police Inspector I already knew, but Master Liang filled in further details, explaining that the Inspector originally came from China's Shandong Province and this was where the two stick forms originated. It seems that this area of China was renowned for its cloth and itinerant cloth-sellers were common, traveling the countryside with large bundles of cloth held over their shoulders suspended from a stick. As times were lawless these peddlers developed methods of defending themselves using the sticks with which they carried their cloth. When attacked they simply dropped the bundle of cloth and used the stick as their weapon.

Master Liang explained that he was fond of this weapon not just because of its practicality but also because regular practice develops a kind of whippy *fa jing* which may equally be used empty-handed.

Calling me out to the front he next demonstrated the favored target areas when using the stick.

"Don't underestimate this weapon because it looks small and harmless," he warned with a smile. "All of the strikes are aimed at vital spots."

So saying he made his point by delivering a scything horizontal slash, which ended with the tip of the stick just a fraction of an inch from my temple. The next target for a similar strike was the neck. A crashing overhead blow stopped and hovered in the air over the top of my head, followed by a rising blow which took in my groin and then came to a stop under my chin. Then, in swift succession, the side of my neck, shoulder, elbow, and wrist were all the target of strikes which cut through the air with a cracking sound.

Having dealt with the upper body and torso, Master Liang next turned his attention to the legs, striking my hip, knee, and ankle in combination. The final strike was a downward blow to the foot.

"Pay attention to this technique," Master Liang urged. "Every time that you hit the stick on the floor, you are practicing this move." When I had first heard this it had suddenly made sense of a number of seemingly meaningless moves in the form, and it serves as a good illustration of the way in which every move in a form has some application.

For the next two days Master Liang led the students through the form, repeating each move again and again to ensure that both technique and application were firmly grasped.

When Master Liang was unable to be there it was my turn to take over. Rather than concentrating on technical aspects of each movement, Master Liang had advised me to

> **"Don't under-estimate this weapon because it looks small and harmless,"** he warned with a smile. **"All of the strikes are aimed at vital spots."**

lead the group in continuous practice. Many of the students were unused to this style of training and had to stop to rest so that only the stalwarts were left, panting and puffing behind me as we completed the form for the umpteenth time.

I could see that a rest was needed. Indicating that the students should take a break, I walked over to the table where a teapot and cups were placed for our refreshment. As usual, a group of the Temple's "regulars" were slumped and slouched on chairs around this table.

"Eh, Uncle!" We were about the same age but I took no offense at this common form of address. "You know you're the only one training out there!" The speaker was a mustached, dark-skinned Chinese clad in a singlet and a pair of shorts which had seen better and cleaner days.

"What do you mean?" I queried.

"Well, you're the only one who is sinking his hips and getting down in low stances. It's obvious to anyone who's watching."

A familiar voice joined in from behind me, Master Liang had returned.

"You're right; gongfu is in the legs, not in the mouth. Come on, let's try a few more times." And with that the class was called to order and the training continued.

Chapter Nine

Competitions and Demonstrations

he Western exponent of Chinese martial arts who finds himself living in Asia will often be invited to demonstrate at all sorts of functions. I regard such "ordeals" as the price to pay for all my teachers have taught me. For, very often, they arrange such demonstrations so as to gain face by showing off their foreign student. In a way this is a compliment, for were the student not up to scratch he would not be publicly exposed in this way.

One of the most memorable events I attended was the anniversary celebration of the Zhong Hua Wushu Association in Singapore. This association was originally founded in 1916 by Master Tan Swoh Theng's grandmaster, Master Gan De Yuan. Master Gan had been invited over from his native Yongchun County in Fujian Province to teach his art in Singapore. Now it is headed by his two surviving sons, Gan Oh Chiang and Gan Oh Hai. Master Tan's teacher, the middle son, died in a car crash and so now it is to his two surviving brothers that Master Tan goes when he needs advice or instruction.

The author with five ancestor boxing master Gan Oh Hai.

The occasion was memorable not so much for the dinner or demonstrations, although the lion and dragon dancing was impressive, but after five hours it started to lose its appeal somewhat. For me, however, the occasion was special because it was the first time I had had the opportunity to meet the older members of Master Tan's martial art family.

The journey down from Batu Pahat was fraught with the usual kind of frustrations one encounters when traveling in Malaysia. First we could only find a taxi driver to take us as far as Johor Baru. This meant we would have to look for another taxi to take us across the causeway to Singapore. Then when we did find a taxi, Master Tan decided that the quoted fare was too high. He strode off down the road with his attaché case in one hand and a look black as thunder on his face. The other member of our group, one of Master Tan's younger brothers who I called *shixu* (martial arts uncle) looked at me, smiled, shrugged, and we set off panting after him. In fact, it was me doing the panting, for as junior member of the group I had to carry all the luggage.

Leaving the taxi station behind us we followed in Master Tan's stormy wake. He seemed to be heading for the causeway—were we going to walk all the way there for the sake of a few dollars!?

Seemingly oblivious to the traffic, Master Tan plunged across a main road, parting traffic left and right like some Chinese Moses. Ahead of us was a coffee shop, its wide front opened out on to the pavement, where its clientele over-spilled. They were all young, male, and Chinese. Master Tan went in and shouted something in Hokkien. Straight-away he was surrounded by a crowd of patrons. Tension stiffened my spine and my eyes darted here and there looking for the first sight of a meat cleaver, but by my side my uncle did not seem perturbed and I took some comfort from that. Then Master Tan emerged from the middle of the crowd, a young, smartly-dressed man in tow. He was kited out with all the Chinese signs of wealth: gold Rolex on his wrist, gold Parker pen in his top pocket, and chunky gold ring inset with a huge piece of jade on one of his fingers. This, it turned out, was our driver. Master Tan had used his "connections" to acquire for us a cheaper passage across to Singapore.

We piled into his customized Proton Wira and we were off. Somewhere in the back of my mind was the nagging fear that passengers might not be all that our driver was carrying. It is not uncommon for unsuspecting travelers in Malaysia to be duped into carrying drugs, and the penalty for this is invariably death. I tried not to think about it, and then we were through immigration and customs. All around us instead of the friendly chaos of Malaysia was the sanitized perfection of the island Republic of Singapore.

Our destination was right in the heart of Chinatown, one of the few remaining parts of the city not yet torn down and replaced by sparkling constructions in concrete and steel. Not yet, anyway. In fact, the row of shophouses in which stood the family home of the Gan's and which also served as the headquarters for the Zhong Hua Wushu Association was due for demolition.

As we pulled through the narrow streets and Master Tan pointed out the Gan's house to me, I could see on the open area in front of the shophouses a huge open-sided marquee. At the far end of this was a stage in front of which were set literally hundreds of tables.

"That's it. That's where you'll be demonstrating," Master Tan pointed at the stage. "Don't make me lose face!"

Oh great, as if I needed any more pressure. While I was used to demonstrating taiji-quan, this would be the first occasion on which I performed wuzuquan before such a large crowd. What was perhaps even more disturbing was that a large proportion of the crowd would be people who actually practiced and knew something about five ancestor boxing.

Still, there was nothing I could do about it so I concentrated instead on enjoying the event.

As Master Tan and my new uncle walked in through the crumbling doorway I paused for a moment outside. The Zhong Hua Association had started here in 1916 and the faded sign above the door proclaiming that this was the headquarters looked as if it dated from that time. On either side of the door were two barred windows so encrusted with grime that nothing could be seen through them. As I walked in, directly in front of me was an altar to Guangong, the God of War, situated on top of a glass-fronted cabinet which contained a green-faced lion head. This lion is unique to Fujian province and unlike other lions is terrifying to look at. Protruding from its forehead are two knife blades and its hideously bared teeth are also knife blades. Whereas the normal lion head is three dimensional and hollow, allowing the performer to place his own head inside it, the green lion is actually flat and in fact doubles as a shield, being held by two arm straps which serve as handles when in use as a lion.

The lion is green as the Chinese word for green is a homophone for Qing, as in the Qing dynasty. In Fujian style green-faced lion dances, the performers actually fight the lion, thus symbolizing their resistance to the Qing dynasty, hence the horrible appearance of the lion. Instead of being a symbol of good fortune, as is the norm, the lion represents an occupying power against which the patriotic boxers must fight.

The green-faced lion's horrible appearance leads to it being regarded as having killer *qi* (*sha qi*) and is therefore seldom invited to perform on auspicious occasions, such as Chinese New Year or the opening of a new business. Instead, it is used as a fighting lion to demonstrate the strength of the system to all and sundry.

The lion head facing directly the front door, as it did, left the visitor with no chance of assuming this was an ordinary house. Such an impression would not have lasted beyond the visitor's first step through the door anyway. Immediately on the left were two racks of extremely vicious-looking weapons. These were not the floppy aluminum toys used in modern wushu competition, but were made of real iron—many of them lightly-speckled with rust; their handles made of heavy hardwood. Stacked everywhere else, behind the racks, against the walls, and seemingly in every available inch of floor space were conventional lion heads. Many of them appeared old and moth-eaten, with an eye missing here, half a tattered ear hanging off there.

We were met by a young man in his early 20s, smartly dressed, sharp eyes peering at us from behind metal-framed glasses. He spoke Hokkien to Master Tan and shook his hand. I understood enough to hear Master Tan call him brother. Then we were introduced. This was Master Tan's teacher's son—yet another uncle for me. I had heard about him; despite his youth he had already earned a reputation for himself both as a fighter and a businessman.

Later Master Tan was to tell me of one occasion when single-handedly this man had taken on a gang of 10 or more and such was his ferocity that he emerged the victor— talk about mild-mannered Clark Kent! He looked more like an insurance clerk than a martial artist. Once again I was reminded never to judge anyone or anything Chinese by appearances.

Uncle "Ah Hin" escorted us out of the house and up a small hill to the hotel where we were to stay. At the reception desk we were told that three rooms had already been booked for us. This was no good. Master Tan insisted that we three all be in the same room—the Chinese communal spirit at work. Later I was to be glad that he had so insisted.

We were told to rest for a couple of hours and then we would be taken out for a pre-dinner dinner before the event actually started.

My two roommates, after showering, lay straight down on their beds and went to sleep. A mixture of anticipation and over-tiredness kept sleep at bay for me and I spent the time lying on the bed, eyes closed but mind busy going over the forms I was to demonstrate later that evening.

The five ancestor boxing green faced lion head.

Ah Hin met us in the lobby at 6:30 P.M. sharp. Outside, it was growing dark and as we walked down the hill together toward the association headquarters, the marquee and the surrounding area was already a hive of activity. Students dressed in the association uniform were arranging the musical instruments for the lion and dragon dances, while a small army of cooks were sweating over their concoctions in the jury-rigged outdoor kitchen at the opposite end of the marquee from the stage.

The tables were already set for dinner and the stage now sported an impressive back cloth on which was painted a luminous sun, its bright rays shining over the foam-capped waves of a deep green sea.

We passed the scene of all this activity and turning the corner found ourselves on a quiet street. On the corner itself was an upmarket-looking restaurant. This was our destination. A table was already prepared for us with several other VIPs sitting there. These were long-term students of the Gan family who in some cases had traveled several hundred miles to be here.

The meal was good but the same factors that had prevented me from sleeping stopped me from doing more than just perfunctorily tasting the variety of dishes with which we were served.

Then swiftly, as all such Chinese meals ended, we were up and out in the street again.

Now it was dark and as we came insight of the Marquee our eyes were met with a blaze of light. The luminous backcloth was now spotlit and similar lighting illuminated the school's banners which were hung from every lamp post and balcony. Then the noise started: an explosion of drumming, heralding the arrival of one of the many lion and dragon dance teams which had been invited to perform. These teams from many different martial art schools were now arriving. Their lions and other paraphernalia, together with the performers, crammed into the back of rusty, broken-down old lorries. As these virtual antiques drove through the streets the musicians played their instruments to announce to the world that their lion was on the move. All of these lorries were now converging on this small street and the noise was incredible. Then someone switched on the PA system and started playing the theme tune from the Huang Fei Hong movies. In Malaysia and Singapore this music has become something of a Chinese anthem, representing the triumph of the Chinese over the forces of evil in general and foreign aggression in particular.

As we approached the marquee entrance Master Tan pointed out to me his martial arts uncles, the Gan Brothers. The older one was gray-haired, bespectacled, and slightly effeminate-looking, the younger one was the *yang* to his brother's *yin*. The top of his head was bald but at the side tufts of uncontrolled gray hair sprouted. Similar yet smaller tufts erupted from his ears and formed his bushy eyebrows. His mouth looked twisted down so that it permanently held the scowl that wuzuquan practitioners adopt when doing their forms.

The two of them stood in front of a long trestle table on which was placed the large piece of red paper, which was to be signed by all the guests and then kept as a memento of this auspicious occasion.

As we passed the table Master Tan introduced me to his uncles, a soft handshake from the elder, a firm squeeze and a growl from the younger, then we were meeting other dignitaries; the Chairman of the Singapore Wushu Association, such and such a government minister, the chief instructor of this and that martial art association. Lots of big face, lots of smiling faces.

We were ushered right up to the front; our usher was Ah Hin.

"You'll be alright. I've got a friend for you." Then he turned to Tan Swoh Theng and said in Hokkien, "We'll put the angmolan together." I understood that.

In fact, there was only one other white person in the place and I was sat down next to him. He was German and a visiting businessman whose Chinese counterpart had invited him to accompany him to watch the show. We exchanged pleasantries and then the food started to come. My mind was not really on small talk with the German and every so often I asked Master Tan, who was sitting to the other side of me, whether he knew when I was to do my bit. He nodded patiently and after the third time of asking disappeared off. When he returned it was with the news that I would be on in a few minutes.

That was enough to send me into paroxysms of anxiety. I hadn't even changed.

"Quick, go round the back and get into your costume," Master Tan encouraged me.

I nodded. But that was easier said than done, for by now the speeches had started and a crowd was gathered around the stage in front of us. I had to barge my way through, thus drawing even more attention to myself. Who was this large white man clutching a plastic bag and sweating profusely?

Eventually I got through and to the side of the stage, but this was not exactly empty either. All of the lion dance troupes were gathered here unpacking their equipment. I tried to find a dark corner to surreptitiously change into my performance costume. This attracted lots of stares so that by the time I had fought my way back through the crowd and to my place at the table I was thoroughly embarrassed. The drums started again. The speeches were over and the opening lion dance was beginning. My German companion had now noticed that I was wearing different clothes and he proceeded to inform me that he was a fourth *dan* in judo. He then asked me if I knew anything about this Chinese gongfu. I replied that I knew a little and then in the silence I heard my name called.

Master Tan patted my shoulder, "Don't make me lose face!" And I was up and on the stage.

I performed three empty-hand routines, remembering to move at a steady pace and to deliver the loudest, fiercest shouts that I could when the movement required it. Then it was over and I was bowing to the audience. The crowd erupted in noisy applause and there were shouts of *"hao, hao"* (good, good) from various corners of the marquee.

Master Tan had a broad grin on his face, which was still there and not lost. He let me pass to sit down and passed a full mug of beer into my hands.

"You forgot the downward punch in the second form," he reprimanded. I gulped my beer.

The next five hours passed in a frenzy of drumming, leaping lions, and swooping dragons. I didn't care, I'd done my bit.

At 1:00 A.M. the event finally ended. The German and his companions had left about three hours earlier, but still there was quite a sizable crowd streaming out of the marquee. As we got to the main exit we met the older Gan brother, Master Gan Oh Hai. He congratulated me on my performance and then announced that he was coming back with us to our hotel. Master Tan nudged me as if to say this is an opportunity.

• • •

Once we were in our room, the three of us perched on the end of our beds and Master Gan seated on a stool at the dressing table, the conversation inevitably turned to martial arts.

"You know Swoh Theng," he looked hard at Master Tan as he spoke, "for years people have criticized my style for being too soft. I don't use enough force, I'm not hard enough, all those things."

Master Tan indicated that he knew; he had told me about this as well.

The author receives a plaque from Master Gan Oh Chiang after a demonstration.

"Well look. I'm 72 and I'm still practicing. I've still got *jing* and am still agile!" So saying, he leapt to his feet and executed the jump ending in a squat which is characteristic of the five ancestor system.

I was impressed. I found that move as awkward as hell.

Master Gan then went on to explain that he had developed his own form by combining wuzuquan movements with *yin/yang* philosophy.

"Your movements must be soft and relaxed up to the point where you actually deliver your power. That is when you become hard, but only for a fraction of a second. As you punch, pay attention to tensing not the fist but the wrist. In this way you will develop real "inch power" so that even from a short distance you can punch devastatingly."

This I had heard before from Master Tan. What I found interesting was the fact that the old master felt that he had to justify his softness, for just recently I had translated some materials on the origins, philosophy, and theory of five ancestor boxing and I had been surprised at how close the theory was to that of taijiquan. Such expressions as using the soft to overcome the hard, using four ounces to deflect a thousand pounds, and differentiating the substantial from the insubstantial were all part of the art's theory. It seemed, however, that present day practitioners devoted too much time and attention to the hard aspects of the art.

Master Tan continued to question him, this time about the role of the five elements in wuzuquan. Once again the old man leapt to his feet and demonstrated the physical manifestation of each element. The one knuckle fist that may be used to cripple the opponent's limbs: metal; the straight punch delivered from short range to the opponent's ribs: wood; the open handed low parry: water; the strike with the back of the wrist: fire; and finally the descending strike also with the back of the wrists and fists: earth. He then proceeded to link them together in a form. Then he did a variation with different foot patterns, then finally another one. So that in all he had shown us three five element forms. Master Tan smiled at me. Staying in the same room had paid off!

But that was not all. Master Tan then carried on questioning the old man causing him to show us yet another form. So short are the five ancestor forms that if you are proficient in the basics, seeing such a performance once or twice is enough for you to have taken on board at least the basic sequence.

By the time Master Gan left to go home at 3:00 A.M., I had four new forms to play around with.

The next morning after a leisurely shower and feeling much refreshed, I followed Master Tan and "Uncle" down to the association headquarters. The younger Master Gan was in the back playing mahjong with a group of elderly women and he told us to sit ourselves down at the front. A large but immaculately made-up women in her mid-30s came to the front and lit some incense, praying to Guangong. She, I knew, was the younger of Gan Oh Chiang's two wives. Like many of his generation he had two wives. The first one having completed her duty of providing him with sons, the second was added to the household for recreation purposes! Or so Master Tan had told me with a smirk.

"Do you want some tea or coffee?" She asked, her prayers completed.

When we said yes, a minion was sent out on a rusty old bicycle to return a few minutes later with four Anchor beer bottles, two of which contained steaming hot coffee, two of tea. At that point the older Master Gan appeared. Grabbing a mug from the table he mixed together equal amounts of tea and coffee. This was the first time I had come across this particular mix, although I was used to the mixing of lager and stout, a concoction guaranteed to give explosive hangovers; perhaps this was the cure. I tried to keep the look of disgust off my face.

The conversation that ensued was all in Hokkien, and after a while I gave up all notion of attempting to follow what was being said. For the next hour and a half I sat and tried to doze with my eyes open, occasionally running through last night's material in my mind.

Finally Master Tan asked me if I wanted to go out for a walk. I declined and he smiled. I had obviously said the right thing. Indeed it was only a few minutes later that the old Master got up and announced his intention of teaching Master Tan the form that they had just been discussing. This routine was one that included movements from all of the five styles that made up the art and he seldom taught it. It was not for himself that Master Tan had asked, however, for after a few moves he complained that he couldn't possibly remember it all but that I had a very good brain; that was my cue. The time passed swiftly as my mind tried to cope with remembering the new moves while my body tried to do them.

When we got to the last few moves of the form things started to get really interesting, as young Master Gan came out from the back of the house and in a loud and angry voice had an argument with his older brother about exactly how the moves should be executed. In exasperation he took the middle of the floor and executed the three blocks and two punches accompanied with an absolutely terrifying shout that made all the hairs on the back of my neck stand up and even stopped the clicking of mahjong tiles in the back room.

"You have to project a terrifying spirit when you are doing these moves," he growled and then he was back to his mahjong.

As well as the forms I learned that weekend, the whole experience also reinforced for me an important point about the whole process of learning from the Chinese: namely, that patience pays off. Often I have noticed how other Western students, when spending time with Chinese teachers, often get bored and go off to do other things, thus missing some absolute nuggets of gold. Because very often I have had no choice but to hang around in the background, I have learned a lot.

• • •

In 1986, at the urging of Huang Jifu, with whom I was training at the time, I took part in the selections for the British Wushu Team. That year an international competition was to be held in Tianjin, China. Although Britain had taken part in competition in China the year before most of the team members had demonstrated traditional forms rather than those of the modern wushu variety. This year was to be different. The Chinese Wushu Federation had provided two coaches to train the team who were to take part in as many categories as possible.

The selections were a fairly nerve-wracking event with each participant, in turn, performing their routines in front of the selection panel. I performed the 48-step routine, legs shaking and stomach churning, and then it was done. Quite frankly, I didn't care whether I was selected or not, I was just glad that it was finished—competition had never really been my thing.

Later the same evening I received a phone call from Mr. Huang. I had been selected and not just to do taiji but also baguazhang. This was a surprise to me as I had not demonstrated baguazhang at the selections. It was, however, an example of how the

Chinese work when it comes to competition. A few days earlier at Mr. Huang's house, the two coaches, who had already been in the United Kingdom for a couple of weeks, asked me to show them some of the forms I had learned from the Gaos. That had been my real selection.

Then the training started—the eight of us who had been selected had been told quite plainly that we would have to commit ourselves to a period of intensive training over the summer months. Four nights a week we were expected to attend three hour training sessions, Monday was our night off, and the weekends belonged exclusively to our two Chinese coaches and their British counterpart, Kim Han.

These two coaches were as different as chalk and cheese. Coach Xiao was a north-erner, coach of the Hebei wushu team, and he specialized in a northern kicking system called cuojiao. Coach Qu, on the other hand, was a stockily built Cantonese who had been several-time winner of the nanquan (southern boxing) category in the All-China national championships. In addition, Qu was something of a film star, having played the lead role in a popular film called "King of Southern Boxing"—indeed this became his nickname in China.

To say I found the training strenuous is an understatement. For the sake of team spirit it was decided that all team members would undergo the same basic training. Now this was all very well, but I weighed in at 15 stones and was not built for leaping through the air or doing no-hand cartwheels. However, I had been appointed Team Captain. So I had no choice.

Watching me attempt to leap through the air, the British part of the coaching trio, Kim Han, christened me the "Flying Elephant." The name stuck.

At each session, after a short run and warm-up exercises, at least an hour was spent on stretching. It soon became apparent that both coaches had obviously trained as tor-turers before deciding on a career in wushu. Some of their stretching exercises involved two team members working on a third, each holding a particular body part and then using their strength to pull various limbs in different directions. As if this wasn't enough, from time to time one or other of the coaches would come along and leap on the struggling trio, adding their body weight to the equation.

After stretching, it was time for basics and we would parade up and down the hall punching, high-kicking, and leaping in unison through the air.

When it came time for practice of individual routines I spent most of my time with Coach Xiao, who worked on taiji and bagua with me. As well as these two events it had been decided that I would perform a chaquan routine. Chaquan is a style practiced by China's Moslems and contains many jumping kicks as well as low, long postures. I did not feel at all comfortable with this routine, but Coach Xiao pointed out that many teachers of this style had similar body shapes to mine.

This proved to be the least favorite part of my training; one section of the routine especially was the focus of my dislike. This came about halfway through the form and involved a series of gliding steps diagonally across the competition area, followed by a spinning jumping kick. I just could not get it right. Indeed, I don't think that I really wanted to get it right as it felt so "poncey," for want of a better word. My inability to do this move infuriated Coach Xiao, and on one occasion he stormed onto the mat and pulled me across the room alternately shouting and slapping me around the face. That was it; the team was on the verge of needing a new Captain and a replacement "Flying Elephant." I angrily shouted that while beating the team members might be appropriate in China it was not done in Britain. Kim Han stepped in and ruffled feathers were smoothed and the elephant was left to practice flying on his own for a while.

All of us in the team had moves which caused us particular difficulty and a great deal of time and effort was put into practicing them. This had the result that they tended to occupy our thoughts most of the time, even when asleep. On the 17 hour flight over to China, individual team members would fall asleep and then as their limbs twitched as they rehearsed the moves in their dreams. They would awaken startled.

Robert Zhang, who was taking part in the nanquan category, had one move which involved leaping high in the air and then landing in a crouch, right fist crashing into left palm accompanied by a loud shout.

I was sitting across the aisle from him on the flight and as he fell asleep not only did his fist smack against his palm but he also gave a muffled shout. Not so funny for him—as he jerked awake, eyes wide open and staring—but hilarious for the rest of us!

The intense training took its toll not only in terms of aches, pains, and minor injuries, but also in broken relationships. With all the effort and energy devoted to training there was little time for anything else.

We had just over a week in China to train and acclimatize before the competition actually began. During some of that time we stayed in dormitories at the Beijing Physical Education Institute. What was now a school for the study of all aspects of Physical Education had originally been started at the turn of the century as a martial art school where such notables as Wu Jian Chuan and Yang Cheng Fu had taught. While we were staying there I took the opportunity to go and visit Master Gao.

Then, several days before the competition, we were off to Tianjin, the coastal port where the competition was to be held.

The opening ceremony, the three days of competition, and the final awards ceremony all passed in a blur. The six-thousand strong crowd cheering when a member of the China team performed; the demonstrations by performers as young as six years old and masters in their seventies; the nerve-wracking anticipation before stepping out onto the mat to perform all passed.

After I had placed first in bagua—a category with so few entrants that it was to be dropped from future competitions—and fourth in taiji, I convinced the team coaches that I would only embarrass them with my chaquan and they finally agreed I would not have to perform.

The Chinese competitor from Hong Kong who placed second in bagua approached me, inviting me to come and visit his school in Hong Kong, but when I told Mr. Huang, who had come along as team interpreter, about this he was not happy. He explained that I had caused them to lose face and advised me that if I went there they would try to force me into a fight.

After the competition and the innumerable press interviews, we were back to Beijing for a week of rest and sightseeing. For me this meant a week's training with the Gaos and a chance to renew old friendships.

One morning the whole team accompanied me on an hour's bus ride across the city to a small park surrounded by blocks of workers' flats where we met Gao Zi Ying at one of his children's classes. We stood and watched as a squad of 10 children between the age of eight and 10, kicked and punched their way through a series of basic exercises. Then it was our turn to demonstrate our basics to the excited children. For many it would have been the first time they had actually met a foreigner in the flesh.

Then some of the teenagers performed, one after the other, a succession of stunning bagua forms. We followed with our own specialties, all of us feeling that our performance could not measure up to the superb standard of these young artists.

Afterwards the father of one of the young students, himself a bagua student of Gao Zi Ying, invited us up to his flat for breakfast—and what a breakfast!

Crammed around a makeshift table in what was the largest room in the house we ate course after course of beef, pork, mutton, and an assortment of vegetables and noodles. All of this was washed down with vast quantities of beer. As fast as our glasses were emptied they were filled again, so that by the time the feast was over and we staggered down the stairs and out toward the bus stop, we were all well on our way to inebriation.

On another day myself and two other team members, the Japanese team's fan club in fact, were taken by Gao Ji Wu to visit Li Zi Ming. At that time. although in his late 70s, Master Li was still the president of the Beijing Baguazhang Association.

When I lived in China I had been taken to visit him on several occasions and he had been kind enough to give me a signed copy of his book, as well as a painting he had done.

As we arrived at his *hutong* house I could see that nothing much had changed. A sign on the outside wall proclaimed that this was the headquarters of the Beijing Baguazhang Association and inside the neat courtyard was as I remembered it. It was a sign of Master Li's standing with the authorities that the whole of the courtyard house was occupied by him and his family.

Gao Ji Wu ushered us into the largest of the buildings which was a combination library/office. Here we found Master Li sitting at his desk working on some calligraphy.

"You'll have to shout," we were told by Gao Ji Wu. "His hearing's got much worse."

Gao introduced us and it was plain that Master Li did not remember me. When it came to introducing my teammate Dave Hawkins, "Northern Man," Master Li asked what art he practiced, but then he failed to hear Gao's reply of tanglangquan (praying mantis).

"Chaquan," he said, "Very good."

"No tanglangquan," this was a shout from Gao Ji Wu.

"Wudangquan, oh internal boxing like bagua," the old man smiled.

This went on for several minutes until Gao Ji Wu dropped into a characteristic mantis posture, swaying from the waist with his fingers held in the clawed grip that is the trademark of this style.

Deafness notwithstanding, he proved a kind host, handing out signed copies of his book, posing for photographs and finally giving me two pieces of his calligraphy which he wrote specially to honor my winning of the gold medal in the competition.

As well as these treasures to take away, all three of us have a treasured memory of an old man who devoted his life to martial arts and who generously gave us some of his time and attention.

• • •

After our time in Beijing was up we flew down to Guangzhou and from there took a bus to the Special Economic Zone of Shenzhen, just across the border from Hong Kong. At that time this area was as modern and developed as Hong Kong, but without the overcrowding. Surrounded by armed guards and barbed wire fences to keep the rest of Guangdong province from rushing in, it was the home of the favored, of sport and film stars, and of China's political elite who wanted a *pied a terre* close the Hong Kong's capitalist attractions.

We were to stay there for a week as guests of our coach Qu Jian Guo, who lived in a flat next door to Li Lian Jie (Jet Li, as he is known in the West, the star of countless action and martial arts movies).

While here, we visited the training hall where the Guangdong provincial wushu team trained, watching a youth team training session. Although their skill was spectacular, I found that I had little interest in this modern wushu—what really held my attention were the skills of the practitioners of traditional Chinese martial arts. After the communist takeover and the 10 chaotic years of the cultural revolution when the practice of martial arts was banned, such skills are now rarely found.

Qu Jian Guo had his own martial art training hall, which he took us to visit. Everywhere he went he was accompanied by four or five mean-looking "students," who, Huang later told me, were his bodyguards as he had some heavy secret society connections. This I found quite surprising as "officially" China had stamped out such activity. And while Chinese martial arts societies in Hong Kong, Singapore, and Malaysia were almost invariably connected with the triads, I did not expect this to be the case in China.

Once at his training hall the bodyguards dispersed and he took us over to the focal point, a full-sized boxing ring which stood in the center of the floor. He explained that it was here that he trained his fighters. Although a student of his had followed in his footsteps and won the national nanquan title on at least two occasions, it was plain that it was the future of his full-contact fighters that he really prized.

Like many other training halls that I visited where southern boxing was practiced, weight training featured highly on the training agenda. Also prominent were wooden dummies for conditioning limbs and practicing the combining of hand and foot techniques.

Nights in Shenzhen were spent dining out in various fancy restaurants followed by visits to the city's nightspots where we faced our greatest if least expected danger in the form of Master Qu's wife. A beautiful former gymnast who was now something of a film star, she displayed an unusual interest in dancing in a provocative and intimate manner with as many of the male team members as she could. One by one she picked us out while we on our part tried to politely keep our distance, particularly when her husband passed his not-too-interested glances in her direction.

And then, something of an anti-climax, it was back to England and the everyday world.

Chapter Ten

On Qigong

Master Koh Ah Tee takes a full-powered kick to the stomach

igong, which may be literally translated as "breath skill" but which more properly should be understood to be the training of vital energy, has been a part of the Chinese medical and exercise tradition for thousands of years. As well as being associated with the fields of medicine and physical fitness it is also found in connection with Buddhism, Daoism, and of course the practice of martial arts.

Exponents claim to be able to use their *qi* to cure illnesses, prolong life, and even to damage opponents; all of which serves to make *qigong* a field of study very attractive to a wide range of people. It also makes the art open to exploitation and misrepresentation.

While I have always found the stories very interesting and, even as a young and impressionable teenager had sat cross-legged with one hand over my ear in imitation of an exercise I had found in a book, on the whole I have remained skeptical about the superhuman powers promised to the *qigong* exponent.

In the majority of the systems of Chinese martial arts that I have studied, however, *qigong* in one form or another has played a part. As such, over the years I have learned quite a wide range of such methods.

In Cheng Man Ching taijiquan, as taught in Malaysia and Singapore, there exists a set of exercises for developing *neigong,* or internal strength, that many exponents believe to be absolutely vital to the development of effective martial skills. This particular form of *qigong* is, to the best of my knowledge, not found among the teachings of Cheng's students either in Taiwan or America, other than Chen Zi Chen, who as a youth helped Cheng with his internal strength training. Indeed, Song Zi Jian, one of Cheng's disciples in Taiwan, described in one of his books how Cheng went to Malaysia (then Malaya) in 1958 and taught a set of *qigong* exercises he had not taught before. Another version of this story tells how Chen Zi Chen taught Yue Shu Ting in return for a large sum of money.

This type of *qigong,* sometimes also known as "iron shirt *qigong,*" is not practiced solely for its martial benefits, as it is regarded as being something of a panacea as being good for improving male sexual performance!

While some teachers like to train their students to visualize the movement of *qi* around the body, often accompanied by specific breathing patterns, the majority of instructors I have trained with stress relaxing the mind and allowing the *qi* to flow naturally.

As Master Koh Ah Tee is fond of saying, "Taijiquan is a form of qigongquan, so if your form is correct and your body and mind are relaxed then the *qi* will flow naturally."

He also notes that those teachers of taiji who spend a great deal of time explaining where the *qi* is to go and what you should visualize often have little else to teach and are just trying to spin out the learning process. This I have found to be generally true.

In the realm of traditional Chinese medicine, practitioners identify a number of feelings associated with *qi* such as tingling, numbness, heat, swelling, and so on. Exponents of *qigong* are also told to be aware of these phenomena, but not to become fixated on them. Indeed, if aimed for as a goal they tend to become less rather than more accessible.

From the time that I first embarked on the study of taijiquan I had always been rather skeptical of this whole area of study, and it is only with the passing of years that I have noted the appearance of some of the phenomena associated with *qi* development in my own training.

It was while I was living in China that I had my first concrete experience of one of the manifestations of this inner energy, which is claimed to be the very stuff of life.

It was a Friday evening and myself and my two companions, one English, one American, had decided to go to a restaurant close to where we lived. In Beijing at that time there was a distinct shortage of eating places and that, coupled with the fact that they were open for only very restricted hours (usually only from 5:00 to 7:00 in the evenings), meant that you had to be prepared to grab any space you could find. Sharing a table was common.

This particular Summer's evening we had arrived early, just after 5:00, and so found a table quite easily. The restaurant was located at one corner of a large hotel complex which had been built by the Russians in the 1950s. Although the roofs featured upswept tiling and dragons in Chinese fashion, the gray cinder block walls and large spacy interior were of an architectural style which might be termed Soviet proletarian. The inside of the restaurant was vast with a ceiling that was more than 20 feet high.

After we had ordered from a disinterested waitress, we sat sipping flat beer from plastic beakers. As we did so the place began to fill up and it was not long before we were joined at our table by three young men dressed in the uniform of the People's Liberation Army. They nodded to us and, as our food came and we started eating, kept darting shy glances in our direction. Eventually they summoned up enough courage to prompt them to elect one of their number to strike up a conversation with us.

It turned out that they were bandsmen, and as members of an elite PLA band had even toured America. They then asked us what we were doing in China, and so the conversation continued. Upon finding out that I was interested in Chinese martial arts one of the trio exclaimed, as he pointed at one of his companions, that Xiao Hong had gongfu. My ears perked up. I had already seen members of the armed police unit, which served as a gate guard to the hotel complex where we lived, practicing martial arts before their early morning parades. What they practiced seemed to be a combination of changquan and *chin-na*. Maybe this musician/soldier would be able to show me some more.

But this was not to be, for the nature of his gongfu proved to be very different. It turned out that Xiao Hong was able to emit a kind of energy from his hands which was capable of curing headaches. This is known in Chinese as *waiqi* (outside *qi*), and much research has been conducted into the skills of the masters who are able to do this.

Xiao Hong said that he had been able to do this ever since he was a child and, in response to my question, had never undergone any kind of qigong training. This was all very well, but none of us had a headache so it would be difficult to directly experience his skill.

Seeing my look of skepticism, the soldier who had originally told us of his friend's talent said, "Look, put out your arm and feel."

Master Koh Ah Tee simultaneously takes a battering ram to the stomach and a chair broken over his back.

He grabbed my American friend's arm and with some more urging Xiao Hong was persuaded to run his open hand along it, palm down and about six inches above Doug's limb. I looked at Doug's face quizzically. He looked astonished.

"It's like electricity," he said. "I can definitely feel it!"

I put out my own arm and Xiao Hong made the same gesture. It was as Doug had said; like having a mild electrical charge run up and down your arm. At the same time all the hairs on my arm stood up.

Not wanting to be left out, the English woman with us allowed the soldier to do the same to her, but she felt absolutely nothing at all. Xiao Hong tried again but still no reaction.

Two out of three successes was obviously good enough for Xiao Hong's two companions, who beamed at him in congratulation and then insisted that we all toast each other in warm, soapy-tasting beer.

I have often thought back on this incident and wondered why both Doug and I plainly felt something while Denise didn't. It is true that both of us were training in martial arts at the time, so maybe we were somehow more sensitive to the body's energies or maybe we just wanted to believe in it more. I don't know.

Since that time other *qigong* teachers have sought to demonstrate the same emission of energy on me, but I can truthfully say none of them with as startling an effect as that PLA musician in a downtown Beijing restaurant.

In the People's Republic of China *qigong* has been the focus of much research, particularly as regards its healing benefits. Many new forms of *qigong* have been created or, as their founders often claim, "rediscovered" from ancient manuscripts. Some of these types of *qigong* have reportedly been responsible for the cure of patients suffering from such serious ailments as cancer, heart disease, and paralysis.

As a consequence of this there tends to be *qigong* fads. Usually their course runs something like this: a doctor or health worker "discovers" an ancient text and, after practicing the exercises contained therein, tries them out on his or her patients. Cures follow and then a famous personality, perhaps a pop singer or a movie star, is cured of some serious illness by this new, "old" method. The art becomes more popular and the founder starts an association. He or she then travels to teach Chinese communities outside China and an international association is founded. The art is taught free to the public and thousands flock to study it.

Of course like all fads it eventually wears off, numbers dwindle, the pop or movie star dies, and then along comes another form of *qigong* and the whole process starts all over again. This might sound overly cynical, but it is a relatively easy matter to look at the histories of some types of *qigong* that have become popular over the last few years and see if this is their story!

• • •

For as many years as he has been teaching taijiquan, Master Lau Kim Hong has also been studying and teaching various types of *qigong*. He is a firm believer in the therapeutic benefits of such training, and so whenever he has the opportunity he seeks out teachers in order to learn as much as possible.

One of the types of qigong he has learned and teaches is the so-called *ziran qigong* (natural *qigong*), generally known in English as "spontaneous *qigong*." Exponents of this style stand in a natural position, concentrating on their breathing until their body starts to move of its own accord. This is often manifested as a general shaking of the body, but then the practitioner might start performing movements representative of one of the animals of the "five animal play" system. The "five animal play" is a *qigong* exercise that is supposed to have originated over a thousand years ago, having been invented by the "father of Chinese medicine," Hua To. The exercise involves the performance of specific actions associated with the monkey, the bear, the deer, the crane, and the tiger. Exponents of spontaneous *qigong*, however, follow no set pattern but just move sometimes in imitation of these animals. Their movements, however, are not restricted to imitating animals; some may dance, reel drunkenly, or even perform martial arts routines.

Master Lau taught this art to a small group of students after his regular taijiquan class had finished. So it was that one exceptionally hot evening after two hours of taiji, which had left me sweaty and exhausted, I watched from the porch area of his house-come-training hall as four of his students unrolled a huge piece of carpet and covered the concrete courtyard where training took place. The climate of Malaysia is wonderful for martial artists, as there is no need to train indoors. The only thing that can prevent training is rain and to cover that contingency Master Lau had installed an awning which could be pulled out to cover the training area.

Most of the taiji students had gone home leaving five people—four men and one woman—to practice *qigong*. Master Lau sat on a plastic garden chair on the porch and watched the carpet laying. When it was finished the students spread out and stood, feet apart, facing in our direction. It was a still, close night, heavy with the sound of cicadas which seemed to chirp in a kind of throbbing rhythm.

The students had their arms down by their sides and their eyes were closed. Abruptly, Master Lau stood up and walked around from one to another, adjusting their stances by placing his hand on a shoulder, an arm, a waist, a leg, or just simply shaking them. Apparently satisfied, he stepped to one side, looked them over carefully one more time and then returned to his seat.

Slowly at first but then picking up speed, one by one they began to shake. After several minutes of this, two of the male students sat down cross-legged on the ground, while others began to move around. Now they were all moving in different directions, so it was hard to concentrate on them all at once. I decided instead to focus for a while on one of the seated students. By now he was rocking from side to side, the motions becoming stronger and stronger, until, with a shout, he threw his body to one side and rolled over and over. Master Lau was up and beside him very quickly and as he rolled to the edge of the carpet he gently rolled him back.

My attention shifted to one of the standing men who had started to make little meowing noises; gradually they increased in volume until they were a kind of growling roar. At the same time he shifted into a long, low stance and began to wave his arms, hands held in claws, through the air.

Master Lau, who had come to stand at my side leaving the prostrate students under the supervision of his assistant instructor, pointed to the growling man and said, "Tiger, he is performing the movements of the tiger." He went on to explain that in this kind of *qigong* the body regulated and healed its own energy system. Imbalances were automatically corrected and the manifestation of a particular animal represented the kind of energy needed by the exponent.

Now there was more action going on with another of the men standing on one leg and making the "hock, hock" noises of a crane. It made me think of the karate kid, and I had to stifle a giggle. I turned it into a question.

"Master Lau, have these students trained in tiger or crane boxing?" They did look remarkably like they were performing movements from these styles.

"No, never," came his definite answer. The average Chinese, however, is exposed to the movements of Chinese martial arts through the medium of film and television, so such martially correct movements without formal training should not be made the focus of too much emphasis.

But now something more remarkable was happening as the only woman in the group began what could only be described as ballet-dancing: jumping, twirling, and skipping across the carpet and in between the animal men and the rolling bodies. The sight was made even more bizarre by the fact that for most of the time she had her eyes closed. Her movement was so startlingly un-Chinese, being totally free-form and uninhibited that I looked at Master Lau to try to gauge his reaction. His face was impassive; this was obviously something he had seen before.

Master Lau's assistant, known affectionately by the students as "Old Yang," was rushing here and there on the carpet attempting to protect all of his charges at the same time.

Then, as if a switch had been pressed, the woman came to a stop, still up on her toes but now her body swayed from side to side.

The two men who were sitting and occasionally rolling continued in their own world, but the remaining two—the tiger and the crane—seemed somehow to be drawn to the would-be ballerina. They shuffled toward her like zombies from the film *Return of the Living Dead*. Then they started to touch her. To understand how shocking this was you have to realize that Chinese men and women, even those who are married, seldom touch in public. So for two men who were presumably not related to this woman, to be pawing her in the most public fashion, was an arresting sight.

Master Lau obviously felt that it required explanation. "In their trance their bodies' *qi* systems have detected an imbalance in her *qi* system and so they're giving her extra *qi*."

As a defense, I wasn't sure that it would stand up in court, but I nodded as if in dawning comprehension.

The fondling, for such it became, continued for several minutes with the crane and the tiger occasionally emitting grunts, presumably in conjunction with the release of *qi*, while the energetically-imbalanced ballet dancer gave little kittenish purrs from time to time.

Then all of the characters on the carpet seemed to wind down and Master Lau and Old Yang led them, one by one, back to their starting places where they stood as they had at the beginning, gently shaking to some internal rhythm which became slower and slower until they appeared to come out of their trances and, exhausted, stood rubbing their hands and faces. The practice was over.

Now, as I have said before, I am skeptical about the benefits of such training, particularly since, as many of my teachers have pointed out, they have no direct relevance to progress in the martial arts—which has always been my main area of interest. What it seemed to me with my jaded and cynical eye was that the woman was moving in an unrepressed and fully natural way without the inhibitions that everyday life in her culture placed her under. Her *qi* helpers, on the other hand, were getting cheap thrills, doing in their "trance" state what they could not have done otherwise, except in a place where the girls were paid for!

Master Lau, of course, differs in his opinion, feeling that spontaneous *qigong* not only corrects imbalances in the body's energy systems but also aids in the process of relaxation which is so important to the taiji exponent.

One of my students stayed with Master Lau for several months and during that time, as well as training in taiji, he also learned and practiced *ziran qigong*. When he returned to England he continued his practice for a while, discontinuing it when he found that it was doing little to improve his taiji skills.

• • •

The teaching and testing of *neigong* is an integral part of the taiji teacher's practice in Malaysia, and I have always taken every opportunity to extend my knowledge and understanding of this aspect of the art. So when a cousin of my wife's told me that he was learning *neigong* I jumped at the chance to be introduced to his teacher.

The class took place in a town about an hour's drive away from where I was living, and one Saturday evening just as darkness was falling my brother-in-law and I set off. The road to Kluang is narrow and winding and for most of the journey it cuts through a mixture of jungle and palm-oil plantations. As it quickly becomes completely dark and the road was comparatively empty it seemed almost as if we were on another, deserted planet.

Eventually, just as the air-conditioned atmosphere in the car was getting too cold, we crested a hill and there, spread out before us, was Kluang. I knew from daytime visits that surrounded on three sides by sharply-rising rocky hills covered with jungle vegetation, the town is similar to many other places in Malaysia. Rows of shophouses interspersed with the odd four or five story building, all crowded around the main street area, with housing estates clustered around the outskirts.

None of this was obvious in the darkness as all that could be seen were twinkling lights, some brightly colored, lending a festive air to the sight.

Following the instructions we had previously been given, we stopped at one of the four story buildings on the main street. It was the right place for, sure enough, Feng's cousin Ah Bing was waiting outside with several other people.

We were introduced to the group, which mostly consisted of Ah Bing's classmates. They seemed to be all middle-aged and looked like school teachers, which in fact most of them were.

With lots of polite gesturing and hanging back from the doorway we were ushered into the stairwell and up three flights of dusty, bare concrete stairs until we came to a doorway which bore the sign in Chinese "Kluang Qigong Research Association." The metal grill that covered the open door was pulled to one side and we entered a long empty room, as devoid of decoration as the stairway had been.

In the center of the room was a small man, barely five feet tall, who seemed to have one paralyzed arm. As we came in he was performing bagua circle walking, his disabled arm held tightly across his abdomen with the other extended into the middle of the circle.

Seeing us he stopped and came over where he was introduced to us by Ah Bing as Master Kang. It seemed that most of his students had been waiting for us downstairs, for there were only a couple of other people standing in "post" stances at the far end of the room. They were soon called over and after the initial ice-breaking was over it was time for demonstrations.

Two of the schoolteachers were called out and after taking off their glasses they began to take it in turns to enthusiastically hit each other on the chest, the arms, the stomach, and even the side of the neck.

Next, Master Kang asked if I would like to have a go, and the larger of the two educators smiled myopically at me as his teacher insisted that I could hit him anywhere on his abdomen with any kind of strike.

"Any kind of strike?" I queried.

The master nodded. I decided that the man was fair game so I gently placed my loosely-clenched fist on his solar-plexus and simultaneously sinking and contracting my muscles, delivered a taiji punch. This kind of punch directs all its force inwards, as little energy is lost at the initial contact because it is so soft. Very difficult to apply in a fighting situation, but as a demonstration "trick" it is quite impressive. As the fist travels such a small distance and the effects are often spectacular, with the "victim" either flying backwards or sinking to his knees, vomiting or any combination of the above.

In this case my target's *qigong* training must have stood him in good stead for he neither fell over nor threw up. He did, however, turn a nice shade of green and surreptitiously kneaded the spot where I had hit him.

Master Kang, meanwhile, became quite agitated.

"No, no. You can hit him any way you like, but not like that!" So saying he pushed target number one away and beckoned over another of his students.

Master Kang looked up at me as if to say, Where did you learn to do that? He should have known, as during the introductions he had been told that I had been studying the Chinese martial arts for some years.

This time to make sure that I delivered the "correct" kind of blow, he mimed a number of punches, chops, and open-handed techniques, indicating that any of these were permissible.

So for the next three or four minutes I chopped, punched, and hacked at the chosen student. In the end I had to stop because my wrist and hand were beginning to hurt. Throughout all this my punching bag stood relaxed and showed no visible signs of discomfort. It was impressive.

I asked Master Kang about the nature of their training and he replied that they practiced *qigong* breathing methods for about three months before they were able to withstand blows. I asked him whether they did any kind of conditioning such as beating the body and he replied with a definite no. Furthermore, at the end of three months each student had to take an examination before he could progress to the next level of training. This consisted of allowing senior students to strike freely at their abdomen.

"All of our training is natural and relaxed. Just look," so saying Master Kang walked over to where one of his students stood, back to the teacher, talking to two other men. Without warning Master Kang struck him forcefully in the center of his back. The student turned, not fast and with no trace of surprise or astonishment, and smiled at the master and myself.

"See, no preparation!"

I was even more impressed.

The demonstrations over we retired to a local coffee shop for a supper of noodles and strong, black Malaysian coffee. As we talked I learned more about Master Kang's background. He taught *qigong* and baguazhang, both of which he had learnt from his father. In fact, he told me his teachings were based on the Kang family's secret art. This all seemed a little far-fetched to me as he was a native of Fujian province, not an area renowned for its baguazhang.

Later on I was to find out that most local teachers believed him to be self-taught from books. If that was the case then his *qigong* certainly was impressive for the results could not be doubted. As to his bagua, well, from the little I saw, it tended toward the average. But, as we left Kluang, I felt that it had been an interesting evening and that his students, with their relaxed approach to both mental and physical training, had certainly achieved tangible results through their *qigong* study.

• • •

All of the "big three" internal arts—taiji, bagua, and xingyi—have their own *qigong* exercises, many of which involve holding static postures for varying periods of time.

When I first started learning xingyiquan in China my teacher insisted that I should master the standing post exercises before I could go on to learn anything else.

My teacher was a service attendant in the Friendship Hotel. Teacher An, as I called him, was in his early 30s and although he was probably about five-feet-six he carried himself very straight which made him look taller.

I had been introduced to him after I put the word around that I was looking for teachers. A colleague who lived in the block that Teacher An worked, told me that he taught wushu.

It turned out that Teacher An had practiced both Shaolin boxing and xingyiquan since he was a child. He had studied under a well-known master of Hebei style xingyi. Teacher An was willing to teach me. It was agreed that we would meet three nights a week outside the block where he worked and that he would teach me there while he was still on duty.

This particular block was in a section of the compound that housed not only for-eign teachers but also tourists.

An's workplace formed one side of a square of buildings a well-kept garden in the center bordered by pathways. At right angles from his block was the main dining room for this section, and, since my training time coincided with dinner time, there was a constant stream of tourists, mainly Japanese, passing by.

This would have been of no consequence were it not for the fact that Teacher An insisted that I practice on the path in sight of the window of his office. This office was on the ground floor, but you had to actually climb several steps up to it, so that he could look out to see whether I was practicing but I could not see in.

Wishing to train properly in the hope that he would teach me more I forced myself to continue training. In the first few weeks this meant doing one of the three basic standing-post exercises. The first two are executed with the feet together, knees touching and bent at an angle of about 45 degrees, while the back is held erect and the hands placed in front of the body. For the first minute or so you feel no great discomfort, but after that your thighs start to burn and in the early days your whole body starts to shake. At first you are tempted to cheat by straightening the legs just a little but then you find out that this only makes the pain worse when you return to the original position. With experience you learn that the slightest move of the body results in a subtle shift in weight from one leg to the other, which provides some measure of relief. Perhaps the most effective manner, however, of coping with the pain is to actually use your mind to explore the pain, to really feel it—this somehow seems to make it more tolerable until it subsides to a dull ache.

The purpose of this training is not only to strengthen the body but also the mind. Indeed dachengquan uses as its primary exercise standing post training, and exponents of this style are well-known for their fighting ability.

Teacher An started me off practicing holding each stance for five minutes at a time with my target being to hold each one for 15 minutes. So it was for the month or so that it took me to achieve this goal, my lessons with him consisted of me standing in the middle of the well-lit pathway, sweating copiously, while hordes of Japanese tourists trooped past me, smiling, bowing, and grunting, "Chinese taiji, Chinese taiji."

Teacher An, meanwhile, stayed in his office.

The stance training, however, provided a solid foundation when I moved on to practice other aspects of the art, for it lent a stability and power to my postures that they would not otherwise have had.

• • •

The *qigong* practice associated with baguazhang is not static but rather in line with much of the other training emphasized in the art. It is practiced while walking in circles. While the actual historical origins of bagua are unclear, it is generally considered that the first exponent to openly teach the art was Dong Hai Chuan, who lived during the Qing dynasty. Kang Ge Wu, a senior lecturer at the Beijing Physical Education Institute, focused on bagua as the topic of his Master's degree thesis. He concluded that the circle walking was most probably based on the meditative walking of Daoist priests.

Whatever the historical origins of the art, the first circling form learnt by the novice is usually designed to strengthen the body and develop postures that are strong in all directions. That this process is usually explained in Chinese as the development of different types of *qi* should not make it seem mysterious or mystical.

A number of my classmates had been sent to learn bagua *qigong* by doctors of traditional Chinese medicine. One little girl aged just eight, who had experienced breathing difficulties since birth, came along for therapeutic reasons. She attended every morning class throughout the year without fail. Even the coldest of winter mornings when the temperature was sometimes as low as negative 12 degrees Celsius, saw her wrapped up like a little round, woolen ball, stepping through the eight different moves of the internal strength form.

This form, however, provides more than just therapeutic benefits. One of my classmates who had been training for about a year and who in that time had only learned and practiced the first move of the *neigong* form, got in a dispute in a cinema over who had tickets for what seat. The argument swiftly grew heated until his antagonist took up an aggressive Shaolin-type fighting stance. My classmate panicked as the only thing he knew was the downward-pressing, double-handed first move and circle walking. But there was little time to worry for his opponent had thrown a kick. With no other option, he stepped around the kick and pressed down in the only move he knew with the result that the erstwhile kicker was thrown to the floor. After picking himself up he decided that he would give up, leaving the disputed seats to my classmate.

This story seems apocryphal in nature, containing as it does all the elements of a myriad of such legendary gongfu stories: the student who had only learned one move but who has practiced it patiently without knowing either how or whether it works; as well as the situation where he has no choice but to fall back on his art with results far beyond what he expected.

A similar story is told of Sun Lu Tang, one of the 20th century baguazhang greats, but whoever it happened to, or if it happened at all, it is a signpost in the form of myth which points us toward important training methods and their benefits.

• • •

After I had been training with the Gaos for about two years and had won the gold medal in the Tianjin competition, I found myself in a position to really get to the heart of baguazhang. This was because, as a result of the media coverage of my "victory," I was able to repeatedly mention and give credit to Master Gao Zi Ying as being the man who made it all possible. While this was undoubtedly true, and the correct thing for me to do, it also resulted in the Gao family acquiring a great deal of "face." Thus, when I returned to Beijing they were extremely happy to see me and very eager to teach me more. One day I took the bull by the horns and asked Master Gao what was the best way to learn how to use baguazhang for fighting. He smiled at me and took up a stance similar to the xingyi *san ti* basic stance, with 60 percent of his weight on the back leg and 40 percent on the front. Next, he raised his arms in the "tree-embracing posture" of standing post exercises, with both palms facing in as if he were embracing the trunk of a large tree.

"When you can stand like this for one hour, you will be able to use bagua as a fighting art," he said.

That was it right from the horse's mouth. To this day I have found that every teacher of authentic, traditional Chinese martial arts stresses the fundamental importance of standing *qigong*—the so-called "standing post" exercises.

• • •

From Master Liang He Qing I learned the traditional taiji *qigong* of the Yang family. It was in the home of one of his senior students that the fine-tuning took place. Each movement combined stretching, breathing, and visualizations so that mind, body, and internal energy were all exercised in coordination.

At one corner of the ample concrete courtyard stood a lamp post which in the evening, when we normally trained, was lit and attracted swarms of flying insect life.

The whole area was enclosed by a six foot wall, over which peeped the distinctive leaves of next door's banana tree.

At the front of the house next to where we trained was a lawn area surrounded with a variety of different palm trees. This was overlooked by the large French windows of the Malay-style wood-paneled living room. All in all a very pleasant place to train the body's energy system.

"The place you practice *qigong* in, or indeed any martial art," Master Liang explained, "is very important. If possible return to the same place every day. That way you will build up your own positive energy field and you will benefit from the good *qi* there. Similarly, when you have finished practicing do not leave the area straight away. Instead, after you have consciously sunk the *qi* to the *dantian,* you can walk around the training area and take in some of the good *qi* that your exercise has generated."

As we spaced ourselves out facing Master Liang he instructed us that before we started we should relax our minds so that we felt happy and comfortable.

"*Qi* flows easiest when the mind is relaxed. First of all let your eyes gaze out as far as they can; in fact, imagine that you can see all the way to the far, distant horizon. Then, slowly let your eyes focus back in until you are looking at a spot about an arm's length in front of you. This is in fact the distance an opponent would be away from you if we were doing martial arts. But for now just relax and let your attention move to the upper *dantian* (midway and slightly above the eyebrows and known in some spiritual disciplines as the third eye) and then down through the central *dantian* and into the lower *dantian*. To help you do this, swallow some saliva and with your imagination follow it as it sinks all the way down to the *dantian*."

Master Tan Swoh Theng demonstrates internal strength by keeping a spear from penetrating his throat.

Following Master Liang's advice, we each sunk into our own internal world as we proceeded to slowly and gently move through the qigong routine. There was no doubt that when you were finished you felt energized and for that alone it was worth doing.

Whilst earlier on in my martial arts career I had not seen much point in training *qigong*, preferring instead to concentrate on what I felt were the real fighting aspects of the arts, as I got more experienced and older I began to see the value of such gentle, restorative training methods. As a way to develop greater and more profound relaxation, *qigong* is invaluable; it also plays a vital role in increasing and enhancing the exponent's *ting jing*.

It is important, however, that you have the guidance of a teacher when practicing these exercises, for there are often very detailed requirements. When I first learned the taiji *neigong* exercises from Wu Chiang Hsing, he told me that when he learned from his teacher all the students were naked so that the teacher could check each aspect of their physical practice. He pointed out with a smile that this was when they were all male students and the sessions took place in his teacher's house in secret. At the time I was learning it there were two girls in the group of disciples training with Master Wu. What an interesting thought!

Perhaps the most profound form of *qigong* training, and one which every teacher I know wholeheartedly recommends, is seated meditation. This is what the Chinese simply refer to as quiet sitting. I am not going to say any more about this other than any student who wants to reach the highest levels of their chosen martial art must at some time sit down and confront the demons within. You might even find that this is, has been, or becomes the whole purpose of your training!

Chapter Eleven

Challenges

or many centuries, perhaps even from its earliest beginnings, the world of Chinese martial arts has been beset with intrigue, power struggles, and mighty conflicts between its members. In Malaysia where the art has always been approached in a pragmatic and functional manner, this has meant inter-school battles and wars as well as personal challenges.

Many of the larger-scale outbreaks of fighting have happened as the result of triad loyalties or disputes between dialect groups, while the personal challenges have usually been as the result of inter-style disagreements.

In the last 20 years or so with the establishment of a more stable political situation in the region and with the influence of China's "wushu as the people's sport" emphasis, there has been a decline in such fighting, but from time to time disputes are settled in the old way with a test of skill in the most concrete fashion possible.

One much-publicized affair that never actually came to blows was the dispute between martial art brothers Chen Zi Chen and Wu Guo Zhong. It was on the sidelines of this event that I became involved in another challenge, that ultimately was to prove equally as abortive as the main event.

When Wu Guo Zhong first came to Singapore Tan Ching Ngee did much to prepare for his visit and make it successful. He organized classes for him, accompanied him wherever he went, and generally did his best to promote him. All this was, of course, not totally altruistic; he hoped to learn as much as he could from this man who claimed to have received from Cheng Man Ching the true transmission, the refined and cultivated final product of Cheng's long years of practice.

Wu Guo Zhong, grateful for the assistance of Tan Ching Ngee, took him under his wing using him as an assistant instructor. However, as time went on, and for whatever reasons—competition, jealousy, or whatever—they fell out.

Seeing the publicity attached to the dispute between Wu and Chen, Master Tan decided to make his own contribution by going up to Kuala Lumpur where Wu was teaching at the time to challenge him. The purported reason for this challenge was that Wu, on a recent teaching trip to Indonesia, had not only criticized Master Tan but had suborned some of his students into switching loyalties and training with him instead.

The preparations for this challenge were painstaking. First, Master Tan amassed his "evidence," designed to prove the falsity of Wu Guo Zhong's claims to be the only one of Cheng's disciples to receive the real thing. Next, Tan arranged for one of my *shixiong,* Chen Yi Biao, to drive us up to KL; a clever move as Yi Biao had just brought a brand-new Mercedes—so we would be traveling in both comfort and style.

Yi Biao, in his capacity as Buddhist priest and *feng-shui* master, had a number of wealthy disciples who would serve as our host during our stay in the capital. Master Lau Kim Hong would also accompany us as he had his own score to settle with Wu.

So we set off, the journey passing in a comfortable air-conditioned hum. On arrival, our host, a young, English-educated Chinese called Ivan, treated us all to a hair wash and head massage at the hands of the beautiful young girls in his wife's beauty salon. This set the tone for the next five days.

Our efforts to locate Wu met with failure at every turn. He was not at his training hall and could not be found. In the meantime, we succumbed to the hospitality of our hosts. Every day at midday we would be picked up and whisked off to a plush restaurant for lunch, usually a lengthy affair which would last till mid-afternoon. Then we would go visiting, spending a few hours in the homes of one or other of Yi Biao's wealthy students, before returning to Ivan's house for an early evening siesta. Then at about seven we would be off for dinner; another extended feast usually involving much toasting and the consumption of copious amounts of whisky, brandy, and beer. Then the entertainment would really begin.

Yet another of Yi Biao's wealthy students was a millionaire who owned, among his other business concerns, a nightclub and karaoke bar. Every night of our stay from nine in the evening till four in the morning would be spent in the bar enjoying the company of the hostesses that he had booked for us. Not wishing to be regarded as stingy, he booked for us not one but two of these girls each. These Guest Relations Officers, as they are officially known, are there to dance, chat, and cuddle with their clients, but as our genial host pointed out there were some of them who were even more generous with their favors. He made sure that there were always several of these around!

Thus it was that one day blurred into the next, passing in an alcoholic haze. On the second day my hopes were raised when Master Tan asked me if I wanted to do some training. Of course, this was what I had hoped for. The training, however, turned out to be lessons in the cha cha. Master Tan, embarrassed by my refusal to dance with the GROs had determined that I should not disgrace him any more. So for several hours, with the help of a portable cassette player and Master Tan's own tape of non-stop cha cha music, we traipsed and tripped up and down the marble floors of Ivan's living room.

In order to encourage me and to inspire some enthusiasm, Master Tan expressed his opinion that the footwork of the cha cha was very helpful to the development of fighting skills. When I raised my eyebrows at this, he insisted on pointing out how it was just like the follow-stepping used in both taiji and xingyi.

That night I was able to demonstrate my new-found skills to Master Tan's approval and I only stood on my companion's toes once or twice; still she was quite lucky that she didn't receive a punch in the face or a kick in the shins as might have happened if I had forgotten whether I was dancing or fighting!

Every day some attempt was made to find out the whereabouts of the elusive Wu.

Then just when it got to the point where I thought my liver was going to give out, we received a phone call. A friend of Master Tan's assured us that Wu was now back at his training hall. The call came at 10:00 A.M., thus waking us up, for our new routine necessitated staying in bed till at least noon to recover from the previous night's excesses.

Before we left the house Master Tan took myself and Yi Biao aside and instructed us as to our role in the coming encounter. Not only were we to take as many photographs as possible but we were also to pay careful attention to the tactics and techniques used. He even went so far as to tell us what first move he hoped to use. If possible he would take Wu unawares by stepping in and using an upward hook hand, as in "single whip." His other preparations included swallowing two sticky, black balls of noxious-smelling Chinese medicine to prevent internal injury. He also surreptitiously slipped a cricket box (athletic cup) inside his trousers. This he did in the privacy of his room but

I happened to come in as he was doing it, and he turned away rather shamefacedly. For myself I thought it was quite a sensible move.

Then we bundled into Yi Biao's Merc for the 15 minute journey to Wu's training hall, which was located on a housing estate in the suburbs. The sign, hung high on the top floor of one of a row of shophouses, declared in Malay and Chinese that this was the headquarters of the Shenlong Taijiquan Association, Malaysia Branch.

As we walked up the narrow staircase leading to the third floor, Master Tan took off his watch—an expensive, bejewelled Rolex—and handed it to me. He then sent Yi Biao and me forward, saying that we should knock on the door first and when it was opened push straight in, cameras at the ready.

The door was opened by a tall, long-faced Chinese with a gormless expression made even more so by his mouth hanging open at the sight of a foreigner.

"Master Wu, a foreign guest," he called over his shoulder as he opened the door. He looked even more surprised as we barged past him before the door was fully open. However surprised the doorkeeper looked his expression could not match the flabbergasted look on the face of a half-dressed Wu Guo Zhong, who was stumbling sleepily out from a backroom. When he took in the fact that this was a large foreigner complete with a flash-popping camera in front of him, he fixed a half-hearted smile on his face and said in halting English, "Welcome, ah, welcome to my . . ." Then he saw Tan Ching Ngee behind me and the next moment the air was filled with Tan's bellowing roar as he stabbed his finger violently in Wu's direction and accused him of being a cheat and a liar who only wanted to steal his students.

Wu Guo Zhong had turned very pale and was visibly shaking as he tried to stammer out a rebuttal to these charges, but this only had the effect of making Master Tan shout louder.

"I don't know, I don't know. I'm sick. I've got shingles," Wu gasped. "Let's go into the back and discuss this."

Master Tan relented a little and went with Wu into the back room, the door of which he slammed explosively.

As the shouting from the inner room continued, Yi Biao and I looked around the training hall. In an alcove area to one side was a shrine dedicated to Cheng Man Ching, and I took several photos of this but my heart was not in it. The hapless doorman was standing, fixed eyes staring out of the window, while with one hand he nervously rubbed his head. Whatever happened inside that room he was in trouble, that was for sure.

Master Lau who had hung back by the main door now came forward and spoke quietly to him. I couldn't hear what was said but Master Lau's tone sounded conciliatory.

At last the shouting from the back room stopped and Tan Ching Ngee emerged, an angry look on his face.

"Let's go," he barked at Yi Biao and me. To Master Lau he gave a nod in the direction of the room, which seemed to say "your turn."

As we left by the same door which only a few minutes before we had barged our way in through, Master Tan said loudly, "He's sick. I'm not fighting a sick man. We'll wait for Master Lau in the car."

With these words of explanation we clattered down the concrete stairs. I gave him back the gold watch which had been burning a hole in my pocket and which he fastened back on his wrist as we stood around waiting for Lau Kim Hong.

When he finally came down and we drove off the car was filled with an angry silence, but I couldn't help but feel relief that my liver had been granted a reprieve for soon we would be leaving KL, back to the comparative peace of small-town Malaysia.

• • •

Master Lau Kim Hong emerged from perhaps his greatest taijiquan challenge with the title of Southern Malaysia's God of War. He was thus dubbed by the press after he took part in one of the notorious Southeast Asia Chinese Martial Arts Fighting Competitions.

He entered determined to prove to all that taijiquan was a viable fighting art. At that time he was in his 30s with a wife and young children and to cap it all a month before the competition he went down with some flu-like virus which try as he might he just could not shake off. His friends and family strongly urged him not to take part and he agreed but still went along to watch!

When his name was called, however, he entered the ring. Battering his way through to the semi-finals he faced an exponent of choy lay fut.

The bell rang and his opponent stormed forward with a swinging roundhouse punch. Master Lau calmly stepped in and punched him hard in the shoulder. There was a cracking noise and the man went down clutching his injured limb and groaning in pain. Medical assistance was called for but his opponent was not counted out. It was obvious that he was not going to be able to continue but no such judging decisions were being made. Deciding that he had proved his point and that the organizers were not being as fair as they should have been, Master Lau withdrew from the contest. Thus giving his opponent a crack at the victor's crown. But so severe was his injury that he could not participate in the finals and victory went, by default, to the winner of the other semi-final.

When questioned by reporters as to why he had withdrawn, the self-effacing Master Lau said that he had entered the competition to prove that a taijiquan exponent in his 30s could rely on the effectiveness of his art even when faced by younger, stronger opponents. This he had done!

The Chinese National Press in Malaysia, reporting on this event, splashed across the page the headline: "Guandi knocks his opponent off his horse and then spares his life!"

The article went on to praise this "quiet family man" who truly lived up to the taijiquan philosophy—no thousand pound sledgehammer for Master Lau, merely four ounces of grace, humility, and supreme skill.

And Master Lau's special training techniques for this challenge? When asked he smiled and said that they were really nothing special. Every day he practiced plenty of follow-stepping while executing "roll-back," "split," and "pull down," as well as one stamping, low kick, and, of course, numerous repetitions of the Cheng Man Ching taijiquan form.

• • •

In the time that I have been studying the Chinese martial arts in Southeast Asia I have become inadvertently involved in what might loosely be termed as challenges, or what might, more appropriately be termed "comparisons of gongfu." That this should happen is to a certain extent inevitable, for the foreigner is always a good way of testing whether Chinese martial arts are truly effective. Add to that the fact that I am far from being a small or even average sized foreigner, and you get the perfect combination for establishing reputations.

Only because such situations are part and parcel of the martial arts experience I have included them here; this is not because I am proud of them but rather because they illustrate the way in which study of the martial arts forces one to use the lens of very specific and physical encounters to focus on the wider issues concerned with being a fulfilled human being.

I have changed some names in order to spare some measure of embarrassment, although the greatest measure of shame must be said to be my own for getting involved in such situations.

In every martial art there are the gunslingers who go from school to school challenging people, sometimes in a spirit of inquiry and sometimes out of pure devilment. Taijiquan is no exception, and because of my build and my race I have been the target for more than a few of these characters.

On one occasion I was practicing at Wu Chiang Hsing's top floor training hall. It was mid-afternoon and strategically-placed around the room, a half-dozen or so fans were feebly attempting to do battle with the heat.

Master Wu and I were both dripping with sweat as we had spent the better part of the last hour or so "playing" push hands. This "playing" had involved both of us, at different times, hitting walls, pillars, and the floor. But never mind, we were both enjoying it.

Then three figures appeared at the far end of the hall; at that moment Master Wu had his back to them but I told him there was someone there and he turned; I couldn't resist the opportunity and I pushed him with all my might. With a flicking turn of his waist I was taken to the side and almost to my knees. I was only saved by his arm which caught me even as he started toward the unexpected guests at the door.

One of them Maser Wu knew because he called him by name; the other two were introduced to him as students of Wu style taiji who were interested in doing some pushing hands. The mutual friend was a man called Tey, who, like Master Wu, had studied with Lim Suo Wei. It was obvious that they were more interested in pushing hands with me than Master Wu, by the way that they kept eyeing me and asking questions about me, which of course I understood perfectly—but they weren't aware of that yet. The two of them were physical opposites; one was about five-feet-nine and quite well-built, while the other was five-feet-four or so and extremely skinny.

It was the smaller of the two who was the more aggressive, both in his questioning and in his general manner.

"Will he push with me?" The question was accompanied with a rude pointing finger in my direction.

I was getting fed up with this and I answered him directly: "Of course."

He looked suitably shocked, even though Master Wu had already explained that I spoke Chinese.

We stepped up to each other in the center of the pushing hands ring which was painted on the concrete floor. Joining hands, we started with a conventional double hands circling pattern. As soon as our arms touched I had a feeling that there was going to be trouble as I could feel coursing through his whole body a kind of tense, nervous energy that I knew would be directed at me. In fact, to begin with this nervous energy worked for me because he made all the effort while I just concentrated on sticking to him; his hand was my hand, his body was my body. But then he realized that he was not achieving much and his movements became more frantic and it was no longer so easy to keep up with him. Still I persevered, concentrating hard, too hard, for with a shift forward his right hand slipped inside mine, formed a hook and smashed up under my chin; the back of his hand causing my teeth to clamp firmly together. This in itself would not have been too bad were it not for the fact that in my concentration I had forgotten all the most basic things I had ever learnt, and my tongue was sticking out between my teeth at the moment of impact, instead of on the roof of my mouth where it should have been. Straightaway there was pain and then a salty taste in my mouth; I had bitten through my tongue.

While what he had done was wrong—for there was no doubt that his attack was deliberate—I should have known better, for correct tongue placement is one of the first lessons that a taiji beginner is taught.

I retired to the primitive washroom-come-toilet at the back of the training hall to inspect the damage, while my erstwhile opponent, after a show of concern, rejoined his companions who then took their leave of us.

My tongue had swollen up nicely and thick, dark-red blood oozed from a hole about a half an inch from the tip. Needless to say, chili, curry, and the host of delicious, spicy foods which Malaysia is famous for, were off the menu for the next few weeks. I have never forgotten to keep my tongue on the roof of the mouth ever since.

I still regularly see my little opponent and he always grins as he greets me, but so far he has refused a return match.

• • •

Over two decades after I first started kicking and punching in my bedroom I was in Kuala Lumpur, in Koh Ah Tee's house getting ready to go out for a class. The phone rang and surprisingly it was for me. The voice on the other end I recognized as being that of Master Zhen Ling Bo, a well-known Cheng stylist who had been active in teaching the art for over 20 years. Initially he had studied with Huang Hsing Hsian but had become discouraged when the master told him that he was going to take his real gongfu with him to his coffin! By that time he was already a senior instructor in

Huang's organization, and so this must have been a crushing blow for Huang was, in effect, saying that he had not taught the real thing to any of his students.

Looking for another teacher, Zhen found Wu Guo Zhong, who was then in Singapore. Zhen trained intensively with his new master until, riding on the wave of dissatisfaction with Wu's teachings, he, too, left and set up on his own.

I had met Zhen several times at Master Koh's house. They were, after all, martial art brothers through their connection with Wu, but their relationship went back further. Zhen was a friend of Lau Kim Hong's and, as such, the young Koh had been introduced to him early on in his taiji career.

On one occasion when Master Zhen had visited, with a great deal of urging from Koh we pushed hands. Master Zhen was competent, but I sensed an underlying need to prove his superiority over me. As this was in front of Master Koh's students I let him move me around a little and complimented him a lot on his skill.

But now here he was on the other end of the phone saying that he had a business proposition that he wanted to discuss with me; something about setting up an English Language school. The upshot was that he was in his car on the way over to Koh's house. Then there was a click. The call was finished.

I explained to Master Koh what Zhen had said and told him to go to the class without me, which he duly did.

A few minutes later Zhen arrived in his blue Volvo Estate, the car looking bigger because of his small body. He came into the house and we talked about the projected business deal. In fact, there was nothing really concrete and it quickly became apparent that this was just an excuse.

"Well then, do you fancy some pushing hands?" He queried as if the idea had just entered his head.

Now we were getting to the point.

Equally casually I agreed.

We went outside. I had already made up my mind that this time it would be for real. I would not humiliate him, but I wouldn't let him do what he wanted.

We started pushing and I neutralized his every push, sometimes gently moving him to one side or the other. His pushes became more frantic as he tried harder and harder.

Then he decided that he was getting nowhere because I was controlling his arm. I was. This was what all of my teachers had emphasized: stick to your opponent so that he can do nothing.

According to Master Zhen, however, this was not right.

"If you control me you are asking for a beating," he lectured.

And I had thought the actual expression was "if you separate you are asking for a beating." Not according to Master Zhen.

As we continued pushing Zhen continued trying to shake off my arm so that he could launch yet another savage frontal push. Again and again he said that I was asking for a beating.

I began to lose my calm and asked him to hit me if he felt that my controlling him made this easier. So he did. Blow after blow on my chest, my shoulders, my stomach, and finally a hook hand aimed at my chin. I had been here before. This was getting stupid—if he could hit me I could hit him back. So the next time he pushed in against me I let the resultant force flow out into a solid punch that landed with a thud on his chest. Instantly he leapt back, grimacing.

"No. I'm not going to do it if you're going to hit me. I was just showing your openings. You really hit me," he berated.

"I'm sorry, it was just a natural reaction," I explained. He could dish it out but he couldn't take it, I thought to myself

We carried on, but still he punctuated his pushing with comments about how I was using too much strength and was open for this or that attack. As he said this, my calm finally deserted me altogether and an old feeling returned that I thought I had left behind many years before. The red mist began to fall over my eyes and my conscious mind, its voice now quite small and distant, urged me to think of what would happen if Koh came back and found a corpse in his courtyard.

Too late, if this little so and so wanted a fight, then he'd get it. I was fed up with being the ignorant foreigner who knew nothing. His legs were in far too close to me and reaching down with one hand I grabbed his thigh from behind. The other hand was across his chest and I lifted him until his body was horizontal with the ground and about four feet above it. Then I let him go. He hit the concrete with a satisfying sound and in a flash the rational mind kicked back in again.

"Oh, I'm sorry. It was a reflex, you were too close. I must have been using a lot of force."

Master Zhen looked dazed and bemused, but he said nothing. For no more than two minutes more we continued pushing in silence. Master Zhen did not try to attack nor did he complain about my controlling hand. Then he noticed the blood. It was all over the front of my shirt but it had not come from me. In fact, when he hit the floor he had cut his arm and it was his claret that I sported. This was all the excuse he needed to go inside and have a rest.

My feeling after the event was not one of pride. I felt some shame—I had let myself down for I had thought that uncontrolled rage was a thing of the past. Not so. Master Zhen had been right about the weaknesses in my pushing hands, but he had not been honest with himself about his own abilities. He was unable to use his taiji skills to push me around. Even his punches had little effect and he was not prepared to receive what he dished out.

Master Koh, on hearing about what had happened, laughed with glee and told me that Zhen Ling Bo was famous for damaging his students who did not allow themselves to be pushed around by him.

I went away reflecting on how much more progress I needed to make to truly get to the heart of the martial arts and the peace they offered.

• • •

While living in Singapore, every Sunday morning I would go down to McRitchie Reservoir Park to push hands and exchange martial arts gossip with the group of aficionados who regularly met there. The place where we trained, under the shade of a large tree by the side of the still waters of the reservoir, was quiet and cool. On this particular Sunday the same bunch of "regulars" were there. They ranged in age from their early 20s to late 60s and had studied under a variety of masters, including Huang Hsing Hsian, Huang Jing Fu, Tan Ching Ngee, and others. Mr. Lim, one of the oldest in the group, was sitting on one of the park benches which surrounded the base of the tree, engaged in conversation with a figure that at first I didn't recognize. As I greeted him, the man stood up and I saw that it was Ah Luo, whom I had last met several years before when we had a brief pushing hands "exchange." At that time he had been introduced to me as, "the best pushing hands exponent in Singapore." This was followed by a whispered aside: "at least he says he is!" On that occasion his skills had proven to be nothing special, and after he had ended up in a hedge and I had apologized for my "roughness" we parted.

Now here he was again and eager for a rematch.

"We are only going to push softly, no *fa jing*, no tricky stuff!" This he said as he smiled down at me. At six-foot-four, he was in a position to do so.

I smiled, "Of course not, we'll just play." I replied.

Almost before the words were out of my mouth he launched a vicious and powerful push straight at me, which fortunately for me I was able to catch and neutralize. But this I realized was going to set the tone for the encounter. Undeterred by his first failure Ah Luo attacked again in a similar head-on manner several times. Seeing as I was not having much trouble with his tactics he decided to alter his approach.

"No *fa jing*, eh, just playing, and no cheating. This is not allowed."

So saying he grasped the flesh of my upper arms with both hands and pinched hard. I had determined at the start of this encounter to continue to work on *song*, which had been the focus of my study for the last few months. I had been really trying to maintain a state of centered calm no matter how hard or powerful the attacks.

Now was really the testing time. His fingers dug in deeper and deeper with an unrelenting pressure. I used all the mental tricks at my disposal to try to tolerate the pain; forcing my mind to focus on the *dantian,* and when the pain got too much to use that, the pain itself became the focus. All the time my torturer tried to shake me off balance.

"We're not allowed to do that," he panted at last and slackened off the grip of his talons. I had nothing to say, the pain had deprived me of the ability to speak. I was afraid that if I opened my mouth a scream would be all that came out! Instead, as his grip loosened, I stepped in and made my own move. Still, somewhere in the recesses of my mind that were not screaming with the burning pain of my lacerated arms was the thought that I should be training *song,* and so I just unbalanced Ah Luo.

This brought a verbal protest:

"No *fa jing,* we're just playing softly!" This guy was unbelievable! But no, I was determined *song* would prevail. Almost as this thought was going through my mind, Ah Luo's hand came up off my arm and his hand locked around my throat. Then he lurched forward so that the weight of his body was behind what had now become a palm thrust to my throat. I was barely able to neutralize the attack by the simple, if somewhat desperate, expedient of hunching up one shoulder and getting it under his attacking arm, taking some of the sting out of the thrust.

"Gentle, you said," I accused, and Ah Luo nodded his agreement. His face rapt with concentration as this time he brought up his elbow and rammed it in the general direction of my throat.

At this blatant and extremely dangerous disregard for the conventions of pushing hands, all thought of *song* went out of my mind. Instead of attempting to do the sensible thing and get out of the way, I moved forward into his attack so that, in effect, I blocked his elbow strike with my throat. Allowing the shock of the impact to travel down my body and be absorbed by my legs, I pushed my throat against his elbow. I was angry and consequently behaving in a stupid manner. Something had to give as the two of us locked against each other, all pretense of gentleness and softness gone. With a clicking sound something shifted in my throat and my head whipped to one side. Ah Luo's elbow continued on its path past my head and I was able to clumsily push him away.

"That's good, soft pushing hands," he stated, nodding his head and then taking a quick look around to see if he had an audience. He did; we did. I already knew that he was not the most popular figure because of his bullying tactics and this alone had drawn quite a crowd; many of them, I think, hoping to see him get his come-uppance.

The burning pain in my throat which got a lot worse every time I tried to swallow, had restored the practice of *song* as my number one priority and I had no interest in being the instrument of other people's vengeance. Nor was Ah Luo eager to carry on for he seemed to have vented his violence for the day and went off beside the reservoir to practice his form.

Shortly after that the session ended the various enthusiasts returned home for lunch or set off with friends for some other part of the island. I too returned home, but by now my throat was extremely painful and every time I swallowed I could feel a clicking sensation. Over the next week the pain gradually decreased, although swallowing food was not a pleasant experience. My feelings about the whole experience were ambivalent; on the one hand I had caused the problem myself by even getting into a contest of strength with a man known for his "cheap shots," and, furthermore, I had lost control, straying far from the *song* path; on the other hand, I had not retaliated as I knew I could have done. As far as possible I tried to mark the whole encounter down to experience, resolving in future to avoid such confrontations.

Unfortunately, that was not to be. On the Thursday after, I received a phone call at work from one of the Sunday "regulars" who also trained with my teacher, Lau Kim Hong. He had been in touch with Master Lau, he informed me, and had a message from him. I listened on with a sinking heart.

"Master said that being *song* is good, but don't cause him to lose face."

Message received and understood.

I sort of hoped that Ah Luo would not be there the following Sunday, but that's not the way life works. Here I was riding the horns of a dilemma: I wanted to be able to rise above the urge to seek swift and preferably violent revenge, but, my position as a disciple of Master Lau demanded that I act in a manner which would be seen to do him credit. In the latter case, I knew that this didn't mean showing my moral superiority by rising above the situation. While such a solution might seem perfectly acceptable in terms of self-cultivation, it would do little to convince Master Lau that I was worthy of continued tuition.

Still agonizing over what I should do, I pushed hands half-heatedly with several of my regular partners, but all the while I was conscious of Ah Luo over to one side holding court with a bunch of his cronies.

In the end it was he, not me, who made the first move and put an end to my worrying. I had just finished "playing" with Ah Hok, a gentleman in his 50s who had once studied baguazhang, which always made our pushing hands enjoyable as we circled each other looking for openings, each attempting to get behind the other or to execute a throw or lock.

"Nie Zhi," (the local pronunciation of my name which, pronounced in just the right way, comes out as "nipple" in Chinese—and that was how he said it). "Some gentle pushing, no *fa jing,* no cheating!" He offered.

The gall of the man! All of a sudden I was swallowing and still feeling the dull pain of last week's brutality.

"All right," and I joined hands with him.

"No *fa jing.*" So saying, I found his center of balance and in a smooth action knocked him backwards.

" No, gently!" His attempt to speak with authority came out a little high-pitched as he recovered his balance.

"That was gentle," I replied as we joined hands again. "You mean not like this." And this time I really let rip, sending him stumbling backwards. Only at the last moment was he able to regain his balance and avoid falling flat on his posterior in a most undignified fashion.

"That was using strength," he accused somewhat squeakily.

"No it wasn't," I assured him as we joined hands again, "But I could use some if you want."

He looked at me, his gaze less self-assured than it had been a few minutes before.

"Your front leg is in a very dangerous position," I warned. Indeed, he was very vulnerable to leg sweeps in his present stance.

He nodded and mumbled something so I repeated my warning. Never let me be accused of launching surprise attacks. I felt his hand coming up toward my throat so I swiftly took him off-balance and pushed him back a few paces. He hurried back at me both arms outstretched in front of him and there was a feeling of desperation in his touch.

"You mustn't cheat," his voice was now a definite squeal, but his faithful old right hand came up to my throat even before the words were out of his mouth. This time I was ready and I tucked my chin in allowing his strength to build up against me just enough so that I could be sure his weight was over his front leg. Using my right arm to push down while my left arm lifted up I swept away his supporting leg and as he fell stepped smartly backwards. Ah Luo measured his full length on the unforgiving paving stones and a muffled cheer went up from the spectators who had gathered to watch the rematch. He staggered, hands trembling to his feet and gave me a look of resentment:

"You cheated," he said.

"Oh, so it's OK for you to hit and elbow me in the throat and to pinch me?!" That said, I lifted up my T-shirt sleeves to show the still clearly visible purple and yellow marks from where he had grabbed me the previous week.

"It's OK for you to cheat, but not for me?!" I was annoyed and I could tell from the rumblings of agreement from the audience that I had majority opinion on my side.

"Just soft pushing hands," he mumbled, "Just soft pushing hands," as he limped away over to the bench where his towel and water bottle lay.

The only sequel to this story was that from that time on Ah Luo never asked to push hands with me again; indeed, he did all he could to avoid speaking to me. I did, however, notice that for several weeks afterwards he walked with a decided limp.

Once again I had lost control just when I was working on keeping a calm and placid mind and trying to deepen my understanding of *song*. In this case, however, I was seen by those who had watched the events as having been "in the right." Afterwards, I was told how Ah Luo had, on a previous occasion, knocked to the floor a man some 20 years his senior. Although not badly hurt, the older man had been shaken and was, from that time on, very reluctant to push hands with anyone.

• • •

There were many horror stories circulating about Western pushing hands exponents who had injured or bullied their Chinese counterparts and these made and continue to make it harder for those of us who visit the Far East in an attempt to improve our skills. As a rule of thumb, it is best on first pushing hands with a new partner to feel them out. If they are clearly soft and interested in exploring sensitivity, then this is the avenue you must follow. If, on the other hand, they are brutal and intent on destroying you, you must endeavor to defend yourself. In short, you have to have the ability to be softer than the softest and to take the hardest that the hard can give while still trying to stay softer than them. Above all, throughout the encounter you must remain sensitive to the issue of "saving face." It is easy to feel when you are superior to an opponent, and giving them an opportunity to feel that they gained something from your encounter endears you not only to them but to others who either watched or heard about it. In this way you will get a reputation as someone who is polite, and more and more opportunities for further practice will present themselves.

One lesson I have learnt is that, if one is pursuing study of the martial arts as a form of self-development then it is vitally important that you establish in your mind exactly why you are taking part in challenges, competitions or other such encounters, before you actually participate. If you feel that you are doing so to prove something to yourself, you must determine whether it is appropriate to do so in front of an audience. Will the presence of others affect your performance? And by this, I mean in terms of the way you will be tempted to act, not just how you will be able to act. In the first of the two incidents described above I acted out of ego; my anger arose from a sense of indignation that this man could treat me in this manner without getting a taste of his own medicine.

In the second incident my actions were definitely affected both by the audience and the invisible figure of my teacher who was there in my head insisting that I should not let him down.

Now you might wonder what has the point been of decades of martial arts training if this is the point and conclusion to which it brought me. But, in the words of Master Tan Ching Ngee, "Martial arts practice doesn't stop us being human." Indeed, my martial arts training has not stopped me from making mistakes, but it has given me a perspective, a point of view if you like, from which to examine those mistakes. It has also given me a moral framework, a blueprint, on which my life may be constructed. And, of course, both the messengers and the message, my teachers, have been there to provide role models and to share with me the benefit of their experience whenever they or I felt I needed it.

Chapter Twelve

The Journey Thus Far

Over the years my martial arts training has given me a tremendous amount of pleasure. I have been able to immerse myself in a different culture and have made many friends and have had many incredible experiences. As I write these words I am in my late-30s and still have at least another 20 years, as Chinese martial artists believe, before I reach my prime. While this is very heartening for me, as the more I learn the more I realize there is to be learned, what is even more exciting is the fact that I know of at least a dozen or more young students of the martial arts who are already incredibly skilled and who will truly be able to reach the highest levels. It is for them that I have written this book and one day I hope they will go on to write their own.

I have included in these pages many of the "secrets" that my teachers have so generously taught me. With careful reading the sincere student of the Chinese martial ways will be able to pick them out.

One of the most important things that this journey has done is to take me from the pursuit of the purely physical goals of the martial arts into a realm that might best be described as the spiritual. Increasingly, my physical training is now focused on disciplining and training the mind. But that's a story best left for another book.

For myself, the odyssey continues!

NOTES

Multi-Media/Unique Publications
BOOK LIST

Action Kubotan Keychain: An Aid in Self-defense • Kubota, Takayuki • 1100

Advanced Balisong Manual, The • Imada, Jeff • 5192

Advanced Iron Palm • Gray, Brian • 416

Aikido: Traditional and New Tomiki • Higashi, Nobuyoshi • 319

American Freestyle Karate • Anderson, Dan • 303

Art of Stretching and Kicking, The • Lew, James • 206

Balisong Manual, The • Imada, Jeff • 5191

Beyond Kicking • Frenette, Jean • 421

Bruce Lee's One and Three Inch Power Punch • Demile, James • 502

Bruce Lee: The Biography • Clouse, Robert • 144

Bruce Lee: The Untold Story • Editors of Inside Kung-Fu • 401

Chi Kung: Taoist Secrets of Fitness & Longevity • Yu, Wen-Mei • 240

Chinese Healing Arts • Berk, William • 222

Choy Li Fut • Wong, Doc-Fai • 217

Complete Black Belt Hyung W.T.F., The • Cho, Hee Il • 584

Complete Guide to Kung-Fu Fighting Styles, The • Hallander, Jane • 221

Complete Iron Palm • Gray, Brian • 415

Complete Martial Artist Vol. 1, The • Cho, Hee Il • 5101

Complete Martial Artist Vol. 2, The • Cho, Hee Il • 5102

Complete Master's Jumping Kick, The • Cho, Hee Il • 581

Complete Master's Kick, The • Cho, Hee Il • 580

Complete One and Three Step Sparring, The • Cho, Hee Il • 582

Complete Tae Geuk Hyung W.T.F., The • Cho, Hee Il • 583

Complete Tae Kwon Do Hyung Vol. 1, The • Cho, Hee Il • 530

Complete Tae Kwon Do Hyung Vol. 2, The • Cho, Hee Il • 531

Complete Tae Kwon Do Hyung Vol. 3, The • Cho, Hee Il • 532

Deadly Karate Blows • Adams, Brian • 312

Deceptive Hands of Wing Chun, The • Wong, Douglas • 201

Dynamic Strength • Wong, Harry • 209

Dynamic Stretching and Kicking • Wallace, Bill • 405

Effective Techniques of Unarmed Combat • Hui, Mizhou • 130

Effortless Combat Throws • Cartmell, Tim • 261

Nunchaku: The Complete Guide • Shiroma, Jiro • $12.95

Pangu Mystical Qigong • Wei, Ou Wen • 242

Practical Chin Na • Yuan, Zhao Da • 260

Science of Martial Arts Training, The • Staley, Charles I. • 445

Searching for the Way • Sutton, Nigel • 180

Secret History of the Sword, The • Amberger, J. Christoph • 150

Shaolin Chin Na • Yang, Jwing-Ming • 207

Shaolin Fighting Theories and Concepts • Wong, Douglas • 205

Shaolin Five Animals Kung-Fu • Wong, Doc-Fai • 218

Shaolin Long Fist Kung-Fu • Yang, Jwing-Ming • 208

Study of Form Mind Boxing • Tang, Sun Lu • 235

Tai Chi for Two: The Practice of Push Hands • Crompton, Paul • 568

Tai Chi Sensing Hands • Olson, Stuart A. • 287

Tai Chi Thirteen Sword: A Sword Master's Manual • Olson, Stuart A. • 285

Tai Chi Training in China: Masters, Teachers & Coaches • Thomas, Howard • 567

Taijutsu: Ninja Art of Unarmed Combat • Daniel, Charles • 125

Tang Soo Do: The Ultimate Guide to the Korean Martial Art • Lee, Kang Uk • 585

Traditional Ninja Weapons • Daniel, Charles • 108

Training and Fighting Skills • Urquidez, Benny • 402

Tomiki Aikido: Randori & Koryu No Kata • Loi, Lee Ah • 551

Total Quality Martial Arts • Hess, Christopher D. • 447

Ultimate Kick, The • Wallace, Bill • 406

Warrior Within: The Mental Approach of a Champion • Brewerton, Kevin • 450

Wing Chun Bil Jee • Cheung, William • 214

Wu Style of Tai Chi Chuan, The • Lee, Tinn Chan • 211

Xing Yi Nei Gong • Miller, Dan • 226

Yang Style Tai Chi Chuan • Yang, Jwing-Ming • 210

Yuen Kay-San Wing Chun Kuen • Ritchie, Rene • 275-1

MULTI-MEDIA/UNIQUE PUBLICATIONS

4201 W. Vanowen Place, Burbank, Calif. 91505

Please write or call for our latest catalog

(800) 332-3330